**THE LIBRARY OF
PHILOSOPHY AND THEOLOGY**
Edited by
JOHN MCINTYRE AND IAN T. RAMSEY

CHRIST THE CRISIS

Titles available

CHRISTIAN ETHICS AND CONTEMPORARY PHILOSOPHY, edited by Ian T. Ramsey

CREATIVE SYNTHESIS AND PHILOSOPHIC METHOD, by Charles Hartshorne

DO RELIGIOUS CLAIMS MAKE SENSE?, by Stuart C. Brown

FAITH AND UNDERSTANDING, by Rudolf Bultmann

FROM ROUSSEAU TO RITSCHL, by Karl Barth

JESUS – GOD AND MAN, by W. Pannenberg

KIERKEGAARD ON CHRIST AND CHRISTIAN COHERENCE, by Paul Sponheim

NORM AND CONTEXT IN CHRISTIAN ETHICS, edited by Paul Ramsey and Gene H. Outka

PRINCIPLES OF CHRISTIAN THEOLOGY, by John Macquarrie

SCHLEIERMACHER ON CHRIST AND RELIGION, by Richard R. Niebuhr

THE SYSTEM AND THE GOSPEL, A Critique of Paul Tillich, by Kenneth Hamilton

THEISM AND EMPIRICISM, by A. Boyce Gibson

THEOLOGY AND METAPHYSICS, by James Richmond

TOWARDS A THEOLOGY OF INVOLVEMENT, A Study of Ernst Troeltsch, by Benjamin A. Reist

CHRIST THE CRISIS

FRIEDRICH GOGARTEN

SCM PRESS LTD
BLOOMSBURY STREET LONDON

Translated by R. A. Wilson from the German
Jesus Christus Wende der Welt
J. C. B. Mohr (Paul Siebeck), Tübingen 1967

334 00174 9
FIRST PUBLISHED 1970
© SCM PRESS LTD 1970
PRINTED IN GREAT BRITAIN BY
WESTERN PRINTING SERVICES LTD
BRISTOL

CONTENTS

1	The Christology of Early Church Theology and the Christology of Luther	1
2	The Question of the Historical Jesus	7
3	The Question of the Historical Basis of the Kerygma	17
4	A New Quest of the Historical Jesus	23
5	The Task of Christology	44
6	The Christology of the New Testament	52
7	The Historical Basis of New Testament Christology	65
8	Faith in the Primitive Christian Kerygma	79
9	The Preaching of Jesus	95
10	The Preaching of Jesus and the Present World	117
11	Jesus's Preaching is without Authentication in the Present World	129
12	Jesus and History	140
13	Two Kinds of History	156
14	The World of Each Individual Man	177
15	The World of Jesus as an Individual	193

16	Jesus's Unity with the World	214
17	Jesus's Unity with God	235
18	Faith in Jesus and His Rule over the World	254
19	Postscript	281
	Index of Subjects	301
	Index of Authors	304
	Index of Scripture References	305

I

THE CHRISTOLOGY OF EARLY CHURCH THEOLOGY AND THE CHRISTOLOGY OF LUTHER

THE CENTRAL question of christology is that of the unity of God and man in Jesus Christ – who, in the words of St Paul at the beginning of the Epistle to the Romans, was born of the seed of David according to the flesh and designated Son of God in power according to the spirit of holiness by his resurrection from the dead (Rom. 1.3f.). For theology the most important problem raised by this question has always been the concern that both God and man should be thought of here in their true nature: true God and true man. This unity must be such that neither God nor man forfeits anything at all, the one of his deity and the other of his humanity. For, as Luther expressed it in a sermon: 'The manhood would be no use if the godhead were not in it. Yet again God will not and may not be found otherwise than through and in this manhood.'[1] Thus the God whose union with the man Jesus of Nazareth is at issue here is, according to Luther, to be found only in the manhood of this man, and nowhere else. Thus before one apprehends God, one must apprehend the man Christ. If one does so possess the man, then he will add to it Christ as God, through his power, that is, the power of his humanity.[2]

The christology which was worked out by the church fathers and defined by the great councils sought to resolve this basic problem with the aid of the doctrine of the two natures of Jesus Christ, his divine and his human nature. The real difficulty was how to think of the human nature of Christ as unimpaired. That this was not done successfully is most clearly shown in the fact that the theology of the early church was unable to predicate of Christ himself his abandonment by God on the cross, which is the most decisive revelation of the 'true manhood' of Christ. For example, Cyril, a theologian of this period for whom the maintenance of the true humanity of Christ was of particular importance, and for whom, according to Werner Elert, 'Christ's sufferings were not only bodily, but also affected his soul' and for whom it was 'inconceivable that by virtue of his deity the Logos may have been spared some of the sufferings associated with being incarnate', nevertheless says that the assertion 'that Christ was overcome on the cross with fear and sweat' would make it impossible to profess his godhead. He consequently argues that his statement that God had forsaken him must be understood in such a way that Christ spoke it 'not in his own name, but in the name of the whole nature' of humanity. For 'it was only they, and not he himself, who had fallen prey to corruption'.[3] Even Augustine shrank from applying to Christ the statement that God had forsaken him. For since Christ was God himself, he could not be forsaken by God. Consequently, it was said of his body, that is, the church. Thus it was the church that was forsaken by God in the death of Christ. But while it was Christ who spoke this word, 'it was not his own personal distress which caused it'.[4] Thus at this point, which is the ultimate revelation of Jesus's manhood, the christology of the early church was not able to conceive of the unity of man and God in Jesus Christ in such a way that it maintained the whole manhood of Christ. Even someone who, like Hilary of Poitiers, explicitly asserted that God was to be seen in the suffering Christ, only found it possible to do so by understanding his suffering as 'triumphal', as a suffering borne 'through freedom and power'. Of course, as Elert says, Hilary can find support for this statement 'in the portrait of Christ in the gospel'. But by the standard of this portrait, 'the triumph of the sufferings detracts from the profundity of suffering, and so from the reality of the suffering as a whole'.[5]

Though one may ask why the theology of the early church was not able to sustain the unity of God and man in such a way that Christ lost nothing of his humanity, one cannot say that it completely lost sight of the gospel picture of Christ. It is true, as Elert says, that

> in long sections of the polemic for and against the Chalcedonian definition one must often make a singular effort to recall that the argument is supposed to be about christology.

The Christology of Early Church Theology

If we did not have the portrait of Christ which is given us in the gospel, it would be very difficult to reconstruct it from the works of the sixth century.

But 'this is only one side of the matter ... while one often looks in vain for this portrait of Christ in the polemic writings, it can be rediscovered in the commentaries and homilies'.[6] The reason for this failure was to be sought elsewhere.

The saying of Luther quoted above shows us where it can be found. This reads: 'The manhood would be no use if the godhead were not in it. Yet again God will not and may not be found otherwise than through and in this manhood.' What Luther is saying here signifies neither more nor less than that one can only think aright of the unity of God and man in Jesus Christ when one begins with his manhood. Thus, for example, in the great series of lectures on Galatians in 1531, he says that apart from this man one ought not to know of any God, and that therefore one depends upon this humanity.[7] Consequently, as he already says in his lectures on Hebrews in 1517, one must give up human and metaphysical rules for the knowledge of God and exercise oneself in (the knowledge of) the manhood of Christ.[8] For it is insufficient and useless for anyone 'to know God in his righteousness, if he does not know him in the humiliation and shame of the cross'.[9] Thus one should not set out to contemplate the godhead in Christ and comprehend his grandeur, but rather one should pay attention to the flesh in which he lives.[10] Consequently, the right rule for the knowledge of Christ is: 'The deeper we can bring him into the flesh – but we are never able to do so enough – the better.'[11]

When one considers these statements by Luther, which are only a few examples from a great number, one can understand that he did not shrink from the most extreme and radical statement about the manhood of Jesus which is made in the New Testament, that he was forsaken by God on the cross. In fact he points out explicitly and reproachfully that 'from the very first the whole concern of reason has been to separate Jesus from sin and sinners, and to make him an example to be imitated, and therefore a judge'. Instead,

> we must link him with flesh and blood and recognize that as with flesh and blood, so he is intimately linked with sin, death

and all punishment. If I deny that he is a sinner, then I deny that he is crucified. It is no less absurd to say of him that he was forsaken by God, and killed by death, than that he is a sinner.[12]

It would be to misunderstand these statements if one failed to recognize that not only are they intended to refer to the humanity of Jesus, but also, by the very fact that they speak so resolutely about his manhood, they are intended to be statements about God, as God reveals himself in the very humanity of Jesus as the God who he is. This is what Luther means when he states in his first lectures on the Psalms: 'This is wholly and entirely the righteousness of God: to humble himself to the very depths', and when he goes on to add, 'the real reference here is to Christ, who through the greatest and most profound humiliation is the power and righteousness of God'.[13] To know this, however, one must know with the fourth psalm that

> God deals strangely with his Holy One. That is, he abandons him to every suffering, death and affliction, and at the same time saves him. And if he wholly forsakes him, it is then that he takes him unto himself in the highest degree. And if he damns him, then he wholly saves him. According to Isaiah 28 it is in this marvellous way that God carries out his purpose: while what he is doing is strange to his true nature, he is carrying out his true work. . . . Thus he saves through the foolishness of the cross, and most men are scandalized by it. In this way one can see how everywhere in the Bible we read of the suffering and the cross of Christ, so that we can say with Paul that we know nothing except Jesus Christ and him crucified.[14]

> It is in this way that God acted in his true work, which is the first and the original of all his works, that is in Christ, whom, when he wished to glorify him and set him up in his kingdom, he allowed, in the greatest contradiction to this, to die, to be destroyed and to descend into hell.[15]

When Luther in this way makes the humanity of Jesus the starting-point of theological thought – for it is this humanity, in its ultimate revelation, in its *humilitas*, which he means when he speaks of the *Christus crucifixus*, and will know of nothing else but this – he does so because he has realized that theology must return from metaphysical speculation and go back to scripture.[16] We must learn from scripture that man can have dealings with God only in the way in which God has turned to him in his act of revelation. It is not necessary, as traditional theology holds, to know God's existence and his being in itself, but to know his act of revelation, and this means the way in which he turns to man. Thus Luther says that God not only exists, but also acts.[17] For anyone who understands aright the scripture and what it says about God knows that 'the true works of God are those which he does in us'.[18] These are such works as God carried out in Christ as the original pattern of all his works. Thus Christ in his humanity, or more precisely in the strange double action, in itself so curiously contradictory, which God carried out in him, in this man, is the direct revelation of God. According to Luther, this revelation is different from that through Moses and the prophets, in so far as in the latter God speaks only indirectly. For in these cases only a man sent by God is speaking. Such a man is not the word of God in its own effective reality, but a mask, the word concealed in another language. But here, in Christ, God is speaking through himself. And because he speaks directly here, he speaks with full effectiveness.[19]

It must be recognized at once that the thought in Luther's christology is quite different from that in the christology of the early church. Roughly speaking, the latter proceeds from an idea of God derived from speculative philosophy, whereas the point of departure in Luther's christology is found in the man Jesus of Nazareth. The God of early church christology is the first person of the triune God, understood as the being of God in himself in a speculative doctrine of the Trinity. If one begins with this principle, Christ can be none other than the second person of this triune Godhead, that is, the *logos asarkos*, the eternal logos who has not yet taken on flesh, and who, as the Son, is co-equal and co-eternal in essence with the Father, the first person of the triune deity. In accordance with this, the *incarnatio*, the becoming man, can only be realized in so far as it is permitted by this equality of essence, worked out in speculative terms, of the second and the first persons of the Trinity. As we have already seen, with this point of departure it is impossible for the idea of the humanity of Christ to be thought out to its conclusion, in such a way that it forfeits none of its true human nature and is the humanity in which alone God can be found. But this in fact is the starting-point of Luther's christological thought. And the essential thing about Luther's christology, the point indeed which alone makes his thought christological, is that it asks not only about man, but also about God, whose unity with the man Jesus of Nazareth makes Jesus the Christ.

NOTES

1. *Weimar Ausgabe* (the Weimar Edition of Luther's works, Weimar 1883–, cited throughout as WA), 10 I.i, 208.
2. WA 5, 129.
3. *Der Ausgang der altkirchlichen Christologie*, 1957, p. 95.
4. Op. cit., p. 95.
5. Op. cit., p. 85.
6. Op. cit., p. 67.
7. WA 40 I, 77; tr. J. Pelikan, *Luther's Works*, Concordia Publishing House, and Fortress Press, Philadelphia, 1955–, Vol. 26, p. 29.
8. WA 57 H, 99; tr. James Atkinson, *Luther's Early Theological Works*, Library of Christian Classics, The Westminster Press, Philadelphia, and SCM Press, London, 1962, Vol. XVI, pp. 31f.
9. WA 1, 362; tr. Carl. W. Faulkner, *Luther's Works*, Vol. 31, p. 54.
10. WA 9, 440.
11. WA 34 I, 147.
12. WA 1, 434.
13. WA 3, 458.
14. WA 4, 87.
15. WA 56, 377; tr. Wilhelm Pauck, *Luther: Lectures on Romans*, Library of Christian Classics, Vol. XV, p. 242.
16. WA 9, 84.
17. WA 4, 262.
18. WA 3, 54.
19. WA 3, 347.

2
THE QUESTION OF THE HISTORICAL JESUS

IT IS NO exaggeration to say that at the present day the question of the historical Jesus has become one of the most important problems of theology, if not the most important of all. But this is not due, as one might suppose, to the influence of the new point of departure in Luther's christology. In the theology which followed Luther, up to the very recent past, this had virtually no effect. What Luther calls the manhood of Jesus, which should take precedence over all speculations concerning his godhead, before the might, majesty and wisdom of which the soul of man cannot endure,[1] is not all the same as the 'historical Jesus' which is the object of our present-day theology. The quest for this has a different origin. It came into being when the Enlightenment, and above all the rise of historical thought, made the theological dogma of the early church increasingly unintelligible and caused it to disintegrate. Since then, the methods used in the quest of the man Jesus of Nazareth have been the same as those of critical historical study.

Here the starting-point is found in the not inconsiderable differences between the figure of the incarnate God, as traditional christological dogma understands Jesus, and the Jesus of the New Testament, and of the synoptic gospels in particular. The intention is to divest the New Testament Jesus of all the lofty and sublime divine attributes which were heaped upon him, first by the faith of the earliest congregation, and then, with infinite and never satisfied subtlety and profundity, by the dogma of the early church theologians. The purpose of this is to return to the real historical human being which Jesus undoubtedly was according to the New Testament witnesses, and to arrive, with the help of these witnesses, at a historical portrayal of Jesus of Nazareth like that of a biography. The category in which it is therefore thought necessary to understand the historical and human form of this man is in virtually every case that of personality. And it is supposed that the historical reality of this man can be perceived in the religious effects which the personality of Jesus, arrived at in this way, exercised on many of his contemporaries, and which it can still exercise today upon those who believe that they can recognize him in this way. Faith in dogmatic formulae and in the divine attributes which have been applied to him since the days of primitive Christianity, are regarded as secondary to this reality. For they are all conceptions which enjoyed a greater or lesser currency in the religious movements of the Mediterranean world of that time, and which religious veneration applied to Jesus in order to make intelligible the nature of his powerful personality. The same is held to be true of belief in the various greatly differing doctrines of the atoning and redeeming power of the death of Christ, by which the Christians of that time explained to themselves the effects of this personality. This belief is now seen as the appropriate contemporary form in which a period which had not yet learned to think in historical terms would achieve in its own way such an understanding and experience; although of course the danger remained that the historical reality of the figure of Jesus would be obscured by these conceptions and dogmas.

In the period which Albert Schweitzer described as that 'from Reimarus to Wrede', that is, from the last third of the eighteenth century to the beginning of the twentieth century, numerous attempts, each different from the other, were made to present a historical and human reality of Jesus in the form of biographies, or, as they used to be called, 'lives', of Jesus. The intellectual assumptions of this theology of the historical Jesus can be very clearly seen in a lecture by Johannes Weiss on 'Jesus in the Faith of Primitive Christianity'.[2] Here Johannes Weiss puts forward the thesis that instead of disputing about the theological forms and conceptions in which the earliest Christians made the personality and effect of Jesus intelligible to themselves, one ought to 'study the religion which produced these formulae as an expression, in many respects very imperfect, of what moved their hearts'.[3] According to Johannes Weiss this religion is faith in the God who is 'not the God of merciless reckoning and condemnation, but the Father of his children, who desires nothing but complete devotion, love and adoration'. Accordingly, the significance of Jesus for the primitive Christian church and its faith was that he gave his disciples courage to have this faith. 'And the way he did this was not only by speaking about the loving Father in heaven, but also by demonstrating in his own person how securely and joyfully one can rest in his love.'[4] Thus according to Johannes Weiss, 'the faith of the earliest congregation rests upon the impression of the personality of Jesus; it captivated the disciples for ever'.[5]

Here the religious conceptions and formulae in which the New Testament seeks to understand the significance of Jesus, and which are certainly very strange and difficult for modern man to understand, are reduced to a 'joyful trust in God and the harmonious conjunction of a serious attitude to life and joy in existence', which, in the opinion of Johannes Weiss, is 'the innermost essence of Jesus', and which gave rise to these forms. It became, however, totally impossible to do this when the study of comparative religion, such as was carried out, for example, by Bousset, reached an understanding of the meaning of religion which was completely new but nevertheless much closer to the New Testament. It was now thought possible to show that the religion expressed in the christology of the New Testament was the '*kyrios* cult', through which

> the man Jesus of Nazareth is turned into the divine being Jesus Christ, the pre-existent Son of God, the cosmic figure who becomes man, brings revelation, is crucified, rises and as the exalted Christ rules at the right hand of God.

This is asserted of the God-man Jesus Christ, the figure who in the worship paid to him

> is present to the congregation, who works in it in miracles and signs, in inspired enthusiasm and heroic witness, who imparts his power in the sacraments and implants the divine nature into believers.

This is how Rudolf Bultmann describes the understanding of Jesus in terms of comparative religion.[6] Primitive Christian religion, seen in the framework of Hellenistic religious dogma, as is done by the study of comparative religion, is consequently a phenomenon of psychical life, it is a cult, and more precisely a cult of redemption against the background of a dualistic world-view; it is a mystery religion, which as such lives in the consciousness of being liberated from the darkness and misery, baseness and death that are found in corporeal and material existence, and of undergoing this liberation in psychical experiences, in the cult, in ecstasy and in union with the cultic deity, who contains within himself the powers of the world of light, and imparts them to those who participate in the mystery.[7]

Those who adopt this approach consequently believe that the christology which is found in the New Testament in Paul and John can be understood as the 'exposition of this cultic piety under the influence of the christology of the mysteries and other traditions'. In accordance with this theory, Christian faith is therefore

not really faith in Christ. . . . If any special object of faith is named, this can really only be God, which then means nothing other than the divine in general. . . . If Christ is named as the object of faith, then this strange duplication of the object of faith is really illegitimate, since Christ is in fact nothing other than the embodiment of the divine power, the symbol of the irruption of the divine world into the darkness.[8]

As a result of this understanding of primitive Christian religion as cultic piety, and of New Testament christology as the expression of this piety, 'the necessity is removed of understanding christology as the expression of a personal link with the historic Jesus'.[9] There was as a result no further concern with the personality of Jesus.

But, at the same time, this theory was faced with increasing difficulties when it was recognized that the New Testament writings were not, as had been supposed for about one hundred and fifty years, adequate historical sources for a biographical 'Life of Jesus'. Of particular importance here was the realization, which it became increasingly difficult to dispute, that these writings could be regarded for the most part as sources for the history of the primitive Christian church. This implied, moreover, that they were written with the intention of bearing witness to the faith of this church. With regard to the historical Jesus, this led to the realization that

> we learn anything of him only through the preaching of primitive Christianity and the church dogma associated with it, and we can no longer distinguish him precisely and in any way adequately from what is believed about him.

Once this is recognized, then the attempt which theology has been making for two hundred years 'to set the historical Jesus free from the chains of ecclesiastical dogma . . . is condemned to failure from the first'.[10]

This was roughly the situation at the end of the first world war. A result of the rise of 'dialectic' theology and the passionate concern it brought with it for genuinely theological, or if one will, dogmatic questions, the question of the historical Jesus with its associated problems was at once subordinated to that of the Christ 'of faith'. One might have supposed that the former question had been disposed of, just as it had not existed in previous periods. There was no immediate change in this situation. On the contrary, the impression was strengthened by Bultmann's book *Jesus*, and by the essays which he wrote on the theology of the New Testament.[11] The general thesis which these works put forward was that 'to speak theologically of Jesus Christ is to speak of him as he is visible to faith'.[12] It is consequently Bultmann's opinion that one may not

> go back behind the kerygma (the preaching based on the faith of the primitive Christian congregation), using it as a 'source' to construct a 'historical' Jesus with his 'messianic consciousness', his 'inner personality' or his 'heroism'.

In this way, it was alleged, one encountered only the 'Christ according to the flesh', 'who belongs to the past'. Not the historical Jesus, but Jesus Christ the crucified, is the Lord.[13] Not until the essay 'The New Testament and Mythology' was published in 1941 (later published in *Kerygma und Mythos*, edited by H. W. Bartsch, Hamburg, 1st ed. 1948; ET *Kerygma and Myth*, 1953, Vol. I), in which Bultmann developed his 'programme of demythologization', did he provoke the violent opposition that might have been expected. It is as a result of this that the question of the historical Jesus has once again become the subject of extremely heated debate.

Since this debate has been provoked by the theses advanced by Bultmann, and since its further course has in essence been determined by these theses, it is necessary, in order to understand it, first to recall what they were. It is of particular importance in this context to be clear about the two concepts of history expressed in German by the words *Historie* and *Geschichte*. Bultmann uses these two expressions in order to distinguish between the Jesus of factual and literal history (*Historie*) and the Christ of interpretative history (*Geschichte*). His distinction is so sharp that he can say – to quote what is perhaps his most pointed and scandalous statement:

> The Christ according to the flesh – and it is this which is the Jesus of *Historie* – has nothing to do with us. I do not know what the man Jesus looked like, and I do not want to know.[14]

In order to do justice to these utterances by Bultmann, and so to understand them in the sense in which they were meant, one must not overlook the fact that their meaning is derived from his opposition to the 'theology of the historical Jesus', and it is in the context of this opposition that they are meant to be understood. As we have seen, it is characteristic of this theology that the category in which it proposed to understand the historical reality of Jesus is that of the individual personality. Consequently, Bultmann speaks of the Jesus of *Historie* when he is thinking of Jesus understood as such an individual personality. He does, however, also use the expression *Geschichte* in the same way. He is doing this, for example, when he says:

> Neither St Paul nor St John mediate a historic encounter with the historic Jesus. Even if the synoptic gospels appear to do so, that is only when they are read in the light of the historical problems which have arisen since their day, not when they are read in their original sense.[15]

Jesus, understood in the sense of *Historie*, would fall into the realm of that which is the 'subject of direct experience in the world'. In Bultmann's terminology this expression means 'that which can be known in its immediate presence in the world, visible to everyone'.[16] It is the world and man itself, as he is understood 'on the basis of' the world – Paul would say according to the world or the flesh – and man does this as long as 'he does not allow himself to be crucified with Christ', and is consequently not 'crucified to the world', so that 'to him the world has not passed away nor he for the world'.[17]

In Bultmann's terminology the opposite to the Jesus of *Historie* is 'Jesus Christ who is preached'.[18] It is the latter, and not the former, who is the 'Lord' who is referred to and encountered in the kerygma, that is, in the preaching of the New Testament. Bultmann describes the Lord who is encountered here as an 'eschatological phenomenon'. He is 'eschatological' as the Saviour, 'through whom God delivers the world by passing judgement on it and giving the future as a gift to those who believe in him'.[19] That Jesus is in this sense the *Soter*, and is encountered by man as such, is the decisive factor for the New Testament kerygma, and therefore forms its essential message. For this reason, the kerygma is not concerned to provide an encounter with the historical Jesus. For 'for Jesus to be understood as an eschatological phenomenon all that is necessary is the proclamation of the fact of his coming. This happens quite clearly in John'.[20] Consequently, Bultmann argues that Paul, too, considers Jesus neither as a human personality – this would be Christ according to the flesh (II Cor. 5.16) – nor as a heavenly divine being.

> Although everything depends on the person of Jesus, this is so in the sense that his person and what happened to him are regarded as a unity: Christ is important as a historical (*Geschichte*) event, as the event which happened in the fullness of time, and which inaugurates the new aeon, and which gives the possibility of new life, a possibility apprehended in the ὑπακοὴ πίστεως (obedience of faith).[21]

Consequently, for Paul faith in Christ is 'subjection to that which God has done in Christ'.[22]

The objection has been made to these theses of Bultmann that – in the words of Paul Althaus – they make the New Testament kerygma the object of theology in the sense that the 'basis of the kerygma', as it is present 'in the figure and history of the historical Jesus, falls into the background and is disregarded as being of no significance for theology'.[23] To quote another formulation of this disagreement, Hermann Diem objects that according to Bultmann the faith by which the person who hears the kerygma decides that it is true, is 'not a decision to participate in the history of Jesus Christ who proclaims himself' (Diem has defined faith as such a participation), 'but a decision for the "historicity" of the hearer's own existential life'.[24] In the objections which both Althaus and Diem make against Bultmann, they have failed to take sufficient account of the fact that in Bultmann's work the place of what Althaus calls 'the figure and history' of the historical Jesus, and Diem calls 'the history of the Christ who proclaims himself', is taken by what Bultmann calls 'the historical events' or 'the fact that Jesus has come'. Whatever objections one may make to this formula which Bultmann uses, one has no right, as Diem does, to speak of this event as the '"mere" fact that Jesus has come'.[25] For Bultmann characterizes it quite clearly as an 'eschatological event'. But it remains true of this 'historical event' of Jesus's coming, that it 'inaugurates the new aeon', and that with it 'the possibility of new life' is given. Thus it is not the case, as Diem asserts, that in Bultmann's work 'there is a complete cleavage between the "historical fact" of Jesus and preaching about him'. But Diem and Althaus suppose that what is decisive for the kerygma is the 'historical Jesus', seen in the concrete picture of his life and personality. If this is so, then Bultmann's thesis that the 'fact that Jesus has come' is the only decisive factor, does indeed contain a cleavage between the historical fact and the preaching about him, and moreover

> the great enigma of New Testament theology, *how the preacher became what is preached*, and why the church does not proclaim only the ideas which are found in his preaching, but also, and in the first instance, proclaims him personally, and finally, why Paul and John are ignorant of the content of his preaching, remains unsolved.[26]

But if one understands that the fact that Jesus has come, which for Bultmann means no less than 'his person, not his personality, but its existence here and now, the event which it is, the task it imposes, and what it says to us' is the decisive element in the kerygma, then one can also understand that 'the preacher must become what is preached'.[27] It becomes possible to understand, furthermore, not only that 'Jesus, and indeed his cross and resurrection, or exaltation, possesses the meaning of an eschatological event, for Paul, and even more radically for John', but that the same is true of the primitive church. Admittedly, the latter did not work out, as Paul did, such an understanding of Jesus's person and history in explicit terms, but it 'nevertheless did implicitly understand him in this sense, by the fact that it understood itself as the eschatological congregation'.[28] If the fact that Jesus has come is understood in this sense as an eschatological event, then one can no longer say that faith in the kerygma that Jesus has come is merely a decision for the historicity of one's own existential life, but not for participation in the mystery of Jesus Christ who proclaims himself. It is, however, the case that the decision for what takes place in this eschatological event, that is, the making possible of new life, in the 'obedience of faith' in which the possibility is apprehended, brings with it a decision for the historicity of one's own existential life.

From what we have said it will have become clear that Bultmann's christological theses modify the basic assumptions of modern christology in two very important ways. The first concerns Jesus's preaching. Bultmann's view is that this 'is not new as far as its contents and ideas are concerned'. For in his view, its content is nothing more than pure Judaism, pure prophetic preaching. But the unheard of thing is for him to say it *now*, in the final decisive hour. 'Not *what* he proclaims, but *that* he proclaims it, is decisive'.[29] The other modification is the reduction of the history of Jesus to a *single* event, the fact *that* he has come, which 'inaugurates the new aeon' and 'gives the possibility of new life'. With these two modifications, everything that is historically concrete and visual is taken away from the history of Jesus, and as a result its historical reality is also made highly questionable. If the content of the kerygma is what is historically concrete, then these two theses seem also to have brought about the disappearance of the kerygma. It is these two theses which have provoked the most fierce resistance to Bultmann's theology. Let us now ask how those who oppose Bultmann understand the basis of the kerygma.

NOTES

1. *Weimar Ausgabe* (the Weimar Edition of Luther's works, Weimar 1883–), 1, 329.
2. Verhandlungen der XIII. Christlichen Studenten-Konferenz der Deutschen Schweiz, Aarau, 22–24 March 1909.
3. Op. cit., p. 1.
4. Op. cit., p. 16.
5. Op. cit., p. 7.
6. Rudolf Bultmann, 'Die Christologie des Neuen Testaments', in *Glauben und Verstehen* I, p. 253.
7. Op. cit., p. 256.
8. Op. cit., p. 256.
9. Op. cit., p. 254.
10. Ernst Käsemann, 'Das Problem des historischen Jesus', *Zeitschrift für Theologie und Kirche* 1954, p. 127.
11. 'Zur Frage der Christologie', 1927; 'Die Bedeutung des geschichtlichen Jesus für die Theologie des Paulus', 1929; 'Die Christologie des Neuen Testaments', 1933.
12. Bultmann, *Glauben und Verstehen* I, p. 92.
13. Op. cit., p. 208.
14. Op. cit., p. 101.
15. Bultmann, *Kerygma und Mythos*, ed. H. W. Bartsch, Hamburg, 1951, Vol. I, p. 148; tr. R. H. Fuller, *Kerygma and Myth*, SPCK, 1953, Vol. I, p. 112.
16. *Glauben und Verstehen* I, p. 185.
17. Op. cit., p. 207.
18. Op. cit., p. 208.
19. *Kerygma und Mythos* I, p. 148; tr. p. 117.
20. Ibid.
21. *Glauben und Verstehen* I, pp. 259f.
22. Op. cit., p. 260.
23. Althaus, *Das sogenannte Kerygma und der historische Jesus*, p. 10.
24. Diem, *Dogmatik*, p. 118.
25. Op. cit., p. 118; author's italics.
26. Bultmann, *Glauben und Verstehen* I, p. 266.
27. Ibid.
28. Bultmann, *Theologie des Neuen Testaments*, pp. 37f.; tr. Kendrick Grobel, *Theology of the New Testament*, SCM Press, London and Scribner's, New York, 1952–55, Vol. I p. 37.
29. *Glauben und Verstehen* I, p. 265.

3

THE QUESTION OF THE HISTORICAL BASIS OF THE KERYGMA

THE REDUCTION of the content of Jesus's coming and of his preaching to the mere fact of its occurrence particularly affects the synoptic gospels, which have usually been regarded as the real source not merely for Jesus's own preaching, but also for knowledge of the course of his life, or at least of his personality. One may say that opposition has been provoked against this modification from almost every theological party. And this is true not only of theologians who regard the whole structure of Bultmann's theology as more or less a failure, but also of those who describe themselves as his pupils, who carry out their work for the most part on the assumptions made by his theology, and who, as James M. Robinson remarks in a short account of the 'post-Bultmannian' quest of the historical Jesus, 'can in fact appeal to an undercurrent in Bultmann's writings which already moves in this direction'.[1]

The position set out by Paul Althaus in his work *Das sogenannte Kerygma und der historische Jesus* ('The so-called kerygma and the historical Jesus'), in 1958, can be regarded as an example of the view of those theologians who reject Bultmann's theology as a whole. Althaus does accept Bultmann's thesis that we only encounter Jesus Christ in the New Testament kerygma. This thesis had already been advanced by Martin Kähler in his work *Das sogenannte historische Jesus und der geschichtliche biblische Christus* ('The so-called historical Jesus and the Christ of biblical history'), and in Althaus's view one element in it is 'undoubtedly correct, and must never be abandoned, that is, the recognition that there never has been nor is any other gospel than the apostolic gospel *of* Jesus Christ'.[2] But Althaus goes on to limit this thesis by the argument that 'as surely as it is forbidden for theology and dogmatics to go back beyond the kerygma and the Jesus it presents', we have nevertheless to ask whether theology must not go back beyond the kerygma in another sense, that is, 'in search of its *relationship to the historical facts* which it recounts and to which it testifies'.³ Althaus gives two reasons for this. The first is that 'the language of primitive Christian christology is still largely mythological'. Because this is so, we cannot simply ignore the question whether the matter of which this language speaks may not also be a myth. But in Althaus's view, this means that we must inquire into the historical basis of the kerygma. Secondly, in addition to the 'wholly and completely kerygmatic apostolic writings', the New Testament also contains the gospels. Although 'the kerygma has certainly had a part in their formation', the gospels are distinguished from the apostolic writings by being accounts of the history of Jesus Christ. In them the church 'retold and preserved its memories of the words and history of Jesus, although they are of course embedded in the interpretation given them after Easter'.⁴ Althaus also distinguishes two relationships to historical fact, which correspond to these two reasons for inquiring into the historical basis of the kerygma, which although they are closely linked, must be distinguished for the sake of clarity, and which, in his view, must be sought in a study of the kerygma.

The first of these two relationships is intended to provide an answer to the suspicion that the theology of the New Testament is a myth. Thus, it is concerned with the question whether 'the history of Jesus Christ' really happened, or, to put the question more pointedly, whether Jesus really lived. The objection may still be made, however, that the New Testament christology could still very easily be mythical, even though historical proof existed that Jesus lived. It would not be the first time, and probably not the last time either, that a myth has formed around a historical figure. Whether or not the 'substance' of theology is a myth can only be shown from this 'substance' itself. Consequently, the second of these two relationships is that with 'the history as it really happened', and this must be sought in the kerygma, because the kerygma derives from it. The question is then that of the nature of this relationship. In other words, what are we seeking to know here? What is the 'substance' of this theology? This is the question which is really in dispute between Bultmann and Althaus. Both assert that the 'substance' of the kerygma is something historical. They disagree about the meaning of 'something historical'.

For Bultmann it is the eschatological event that Jesus has come. But Althaus disputes that this is 'genuinely historical'. To him, it is self-evident that this 'substance' is the concrete and individual personality of Jesus, which in his view is portrayed for us above all in the synoptic gospels.[5] If one could not regard the kerygma as 'filled with the living portrait of the Jesus of the gospels', it would be nothing more than 'a statement, a dogma', something so empty that it could not 'arouse any faith' in man. For 'the power of the gospel to convince us and give us faith' depends according to Althaus on 'the kerygma including in itself the gospels with their concrete portrayal of Jesus'.[6] It is in this figure of Jesus with its concrete and living features that Althaus sees the 'clear historical reality'.[7] It is consequently in this figure that the kerygma has 'its historical basis',[8] its 'origin and history as it really happened'.[9] It is inevitable that such a requirement regards the 'eschatological event' to which Bultmann reduces the history and life of Jesus as extremely colourless, if not completely intangible. For it is entirely lacking in what Althaus calls 'genuine history', or, a term which means exactly the same, 'clear historical reality'.[10] For Althaus everything depends upon this history being a 'genuinely historical event' in the sense of 'something factually historical',[11] which can be demonstrated with the aid of 'a historical investigation'.[12] What Althaus calls 'the genuine historicity of the history of Jesus Christ', to which the kerygma refers,[13] is 'history' in the sense of 'something factually historical'. This, however, is confirmed by the fact he repeats and emphatically affirms that 'God's action as such cannot be proved in what has happened in history. It is only recognized in faith.' Thus it is not the case that 'here historical evidence is being adduced for the character of the history of Jesus and the revelation and act of God, as though historical knowledge could here replace faith'.[14] For revelation, the presence of God in Jesus Christ is recognized only in faith. 'No compelling proof of it can be given from historical facts.'[15]

Thus Althaus distinguishes two ways of knowing Jesus. The one is historical knowledge about him, and the other is a knowledge which is only found in faith. He sees as the basis for this that

> preaching contains a double content in an inseparable unity: it is an account of something that has happened, which happened in our human history and of which the time and place can be determined; and secondly, both in the indicative and the cohortative senses, it is a testimony that the meaning of this event is both salvation and judgment.[16]

The knowledge that it happened in the first sense, as a matter of pure fact which the kerygma recounts, can only be achieved by historical means; the knowledge of the second, the action and revelation of God in this event, is accessible only to faith. Now, according to Althaus, that which can be shown by historical means to have happened as a matter of fact, and to be 'clear historical reality'[17] and 'a genuine historical happening',[18] is not merely the bare fact that in Palestine at the period of which the gospels speak a man lived called Jesus who came from Nazareth, was crucified under Pontius Pilate, and whom the church believes to have risen from the dead. According to Althaus, that which history is capable of knowing reliably about the history of Jesus, through its own methods, is in particular the concrete portrait of his individual personality, as it 'appears, undisguised and unmistakable, prior to every interpretation placed upon it by faith'.[19]

Consequently, it is wrong to refuse to ask how this historical knowledge of the history and portrait of Jesus, for which, as Althaus affirms, 'faith is not yet required', but which 'is independent of faith and can precede it',[20] is to be distinguished from the knowledge which Althaus repeatedly affirms is accessible only to faith. But it is difficult to take what Althaus says to mean anything other than that the concrete portrait of Jesus, in which 'the character of God is apprehended', and in whose 'spiritual countenance the countenance of God' looks upon us, and which, therefore, as something which can be shown historically to be a constituent part of the kerygma, gives it a power to 'convince us and bring us to faith',[21] is the historical element which is perceived by 'reason'. Thus it is reason which is the 'openness to reality', to which we owe the impression of the unimaginable reality of the figure and history of Jesus 'in its essential features'.[22]

Althaus does say that 'the revelation, the presence of God in Jesus Christ, is only known in faith', and that this faith 'is the miracle of the Holy Spirit'. But if it is the case that in the portrait of Jesus 'as it is visible, undisguised and unmistakable, before every interpretation on the part of faith', 'the character of God is apprehended', is this historical reality of Jesus ascertained by 'reason' anything other than 'the experience of God and salvation in the person of Jesus', as Althaus understands it?[23] And is what Althaus calls the faith brought about by the Holy Spirit anything other than this historical knowledge? Is he saying anything other than this himself, when he says: 'In the acceptance of the preaching of Jesus Christ' – this means in faith, as faith is understood here – 'a judgment of reason is also contained'? And must we then ask whether a christology which is built upon such a foundation of historical fact and reason, which Althaus regards as indispensable, can really be distinguished in essence from the '"Jesus-worship" of liberal theology'? Althaus considers as a 'necessary antithesis' to this 'the taking out of theology by Bultmann and others of the "assessment" of the "personality" of Jesus'.[24] But has Althaus not thereby shown, admittedly against his own will, that Bultmann's antithesis also holds good against his own, Althaus's, theology?

NOTES

1. James M. Robinson, *A New Quest of the Historical Jesus*, London, SCM Press, 1959, p. 19.
2. Althaus, op. cit., p. 12.
3. Op. cit., p. 13.
4. Op. cit., p. 14.
5. Cf. my book *Die Wirklichkeit des Glaubens*, pp. 114f.
6. Althaus, op. cit., p. 27.
7. p. 20.
8. p. 13.
9. p. 31.
10. pp. 18, 20.
11. p. 24.
12. p. 39.
13. p. 39.
14. p. 18.
15. p. 45.

16. p. 16.
17. p. 20.
18. p. 24.
19. p. 45.
20. p. 15.
21. p. 27.
22. p. 45f.
23. p. 45.
24. p. 20.

4

A NEW QUEST OF THE HISTORICAL JESUS

IN HIS work *A New Quest of the Historical Jesus*, James Robinson says that one might well expect as a result of this first post-war phase a 'period of Bultmannian scholasticism'. Instead we seem to be entering a new phase, characterized by a critical reappraisal of the Bultmannian position by his leading pupils – itself a rare tribute to the critical scholarship represented by Bultmann. This second phase of post-war German theology, he says, is led by outstanding pupils of Bultmann, is based upon a thorough appreciation of the achievements of Bultmann's brilliant career, and could not have taken place without these achievements. Yet it sees its task as that of carrying through a critical revision of Bultmann's position.[1]

One can perhaps best characterize the position taken up by Bultmann by the statement that it is 'not the historical Jesus, but Jesus Christ who is preached, who is the Lord'.[2] We have already seen that in the opinion of Althaus the thesis 'that theology must begin with the kerygma as the final accessible datum for faith in Christ, and must not go back beyond it' is 'undoubtedly correct, and must never be abandoned', in so far as this implies the recognition 'that there never has been nor is any other gospel than the apostolic gospel *of* Jesus Christ'.[3] But Althaus's understanding of this thesis is that although it is 'theologically and dogmatically' correct, it does not prevent one from going back beyond the kerygma in historical terms. But in his work this historical quest beyond the kerygma unobtrusively becomes no longer a purely historical quest, but a theological and historical quest. For in it he seeks the personality and life of Jesus as the real historical reality which Jesus has for faith. And since, as a result, in spite of all assurances to the contrary, he is unable to make a clear distinction between what is known historically and what can be known only in faith, in practice he goes back beyond the thesis which he himself has described as irrefutable, not only in historical terms but also in theological and dogmatic terms. Bultmann, on the other hand, understands this thesis in such a way as to make it impossible to go back beyond the kerygma not merely in theological and dogmatic terms, but also in theological and historical terms. He says that one may not use the kerygma as a 'source', to 'reconstruct a "historical Jesus" with his "messianic consciousness", his "inner personality" or his "heroism"'. For what one obtains in this way is only 'Christ according to the flesh, who belongs to the past'. We do not encounter Jesus Christ in historical knowledge of any kind whatsoever. This, because it is historical, can only concern the Jesus of the past. We encounter him 'nowhere other than in the kerygma'.[4]

The revision undertaken by Bultmann's pupils consists in negative terms of their refusal to share Bultmann's 'lack of interest in the earthly Jesus'. In positive terms, it means that they are convinced 'that they have to inquire into the significance of the historical Jesus for faith'.[5] But with the exception of the work of Günther Bornkamm, the quest of the 'historical Jesus' is not principally a quest, as in the case of Althaus, of the individual personality of Jesus, but seeks to find out what Jesus's own preaching was. For in Käsemann's view it is here that 'the specific characteristic of the earthly Jesus is to be sought', and on this basis that 'those of his acts which we know in other ways, and what happened to him, are to be understood'.[6] But in this inquiry into Jesus's preaching,

> under no circumstances may the distinction that came into being through the emphasis on the events of the passion and of Easter in the preaching of the church, be blurred. But this means that Christian preaching may not be understood as simply the continuation and reflection of the *ipsissima verba* of Jesus, however certain it is that the two are not merely parallel but unrelated. Thus everything depends upon defining anew, and better than before, the relationship of the message of Jesus to the proclamation of the crucified. But this will not be possible without first taking into account the real intention of

the preaching by the primitive church of the cross and the resurrection.

Of particular importance here is the recognition that in this preaching 'more is preached than mere brute facts', as is clearly shown by the message of Paul and John.[7]

These statements by Käsemann show that he poses the question of Jesus's preaching in two directions. He first looks for the difference between the teaching of Jesus and the later preaching of the Christian community, and then goes on to seek the link and connection between the two. As far as the difference between the two is concerned, the inquiry is of course extraordinarily difficult, because the historical study of the gospels has destroyed the belief that they represent reliable historical tradition concerning the earthly Jesus.

> We can no longer take for granted the general reliability of the synoptic tradition concerning Jesus. . . . [For] in the first instance this tradition presents the primitive Christian kerygma and describes individual words and acts of Jesus only as they are embedded in the latter.[8]

And this is the case, because the primitive Christian church, to which we owe the gospels, 'was concerned not with the reproduction of a remarkable event, but with the decision between belief and unbelief which it demanded'. Thus 'its own kerygma overlays and conceals the picture of the historical Jesus'. But this is the way in which the primitive Christian church 'bears witness to past history as living and present', and how it 'declares that Jesus is not merely a miracle worker, but the *kyrios*, by whom it knows that it is given grace and placed under an obligation. As a result it 'delivers the facts of the past from the possibility of being regarded as curiosities and miracles'.[9]

But the consequence of all this is that

> we do not encounter the historical Jesus in the New Testament, the only genuine document concerning him, as he was in himself, but as the Lord of a church which believes in him. . . . Everything else about him is completely excluded from view, so that we are no longer in a position to determine even with partial adequacy what he was like, his development, and the actual course of his life, but for the most part are groping

completely in the dark in this matter. The significance of this Jesus for faith became so strong that at the very earliest period it completely absorbed into itself the historical facts about him.[10]

As a result of this situation, the historian is faced 'with immeasurable difficulties, and on the whole with the impossibility of reconstructing' the history of Jesus.[11] Nevertheless, Käsemann does not think it right to admit 'that in view of this situation the last word must be one of resignation and scepticism, or must lead to a complete lack of interest in the historical Jesus'. There are still 'parts of the synoptic tradition which the historian has simply to recognize as authentic, if he is to remain a historian'.[12]

In Käsemann's view, the real problem of the quest of the historical Jesus ultimately lies in the fact that although 'the exalted Lord has absorbed the portrait of the historical Jesus completely into himself' the church 'nevertheless asserts the identity of the exalted and the earthly Jesus'. But a solution of the problem that is so posed, 'if it is to have any prospect of success, cannot proceed from the alleged brute facts of history, but only from the link and tension between the preaching of Jesus and that of his church'. Thus the formula at which Käsemann ultimately arrives is that 'the quest of the historical Jesus, carried out legitimately, is the question of the continuity of the gospel within the discontinuity of time and the changes in the kerygma'.[13] Consequently, the inquiry into the teaching of Jesus is concerned with the link and relationship between it and the preaching of the church. This question necessarily arises from the fact that however much the primitive church 'may have concealed the true historical facts about Jesus beneath its own preaching', it nevertheless maintains the identity of the earthly Jesus with the exalted Lord. It does so because it neither was able nor wished to distinguish from its own history the historical facts concerning Jesus, facts which it was experiencing in its faith as living history.[14] It thereby declared 'that it had no wish to replace history by a myth, or the Nazarene by a heavenly being'. This can be seen from the fact that

> in practice the very earliest church opposed an enthusiastic docetism as much as it did a historicizing doctrine of kenosis. It was obviously of the opinion that the earthly Jesus

could only be understood on the basis of Easter, and therefore in his status as Lord of the church, while on the other hand Easter could not adequately be understood except in relation to the earthly Christ.[15]

The result is that for the faith of the primitive Christian church, 'an inquiry directed to the historical Jesus alone' was impossible. Notwithstanding this, the gospels ascribed their kerygma, 'whatever its origin may have been, to this same earthly Jesus, and so unmistakably accorded to him an exceptional authority'.[16] This means that 'the historical facts about Jesus are a constituent factor in the faith of the primitive Christian church', because it regarded 'the earthly and the exalted Lord as identical'. This leads Käsemann to ask 'how far we must or can make our own the decision which this implies'. His answer is 'that we, too, cannot abandon the identity of the exalted and the earthly Lord without falling into docetism'. But we would then be faced with the same 'problem which our gospels settled and solved in their own way'.[17] There is of course the difference that we cannot avoid 'posing the question of the earthly Jesus . . . in spite of the risk inherent in this inquiry, when it is carried out in isolation, and in spite of the difficulty in finding an answer to it'.[18]

The direction in which Käsemann believes the answer to the question of the historical Jesus must be sought points towards what Bultmann terms the eschatological event or the 'fact that Jesus has come'. There is, however, a difference of some importance, and that is that Käsemann is convinced that on the basis of the New Testament concrete historical statements can be made about this event. It is clear from Käsemann's statements about the 'problem of the historical element in our gospel', that he does not mean this in the historicist and positivist sense which we encounter in Althaus's view of history. He means first of all, with respect to the knowledge and understanding of history in general, that

> historical facts are significant for the intelligent study of history only in so far as they pose questions and offer answers to our own present time, and therefore find interpreters who hear and propound their questions and answers to our own time.[19]

And therefore it is not

> the discovery of actual historical facts and the chain of causality which relates them ... but only their interpretation which makes clear to us what they have to say and the claim they make.

For if one limited oneself to transmitting the bare facts, one would be prevented by so doing from having a true understanding of past history. Only someone who accepts a new claim upon him through the interpretation of past history obtains historical continuity with it. Consequently,

> it is only in the choice between faith and unbelief that the history of the facts of Jesus, fixed as they are in their past form, can once again become living history.

This is also the reason why 'we only encounter these historical facts through the kerygma of the church'.[20] In addition it is the reason why the gospels, apart from Luke, who attempts to

> draw the life of Jesus into the categories of historicity ... were not interested in drawing together all the historical facts about Jesus, and in the reliability and faithfulness to reality of what they recounted. For them factual history is only the point of interception of eschatological events, and is taken into account only in so far as it is so; it is from those events that it receives its true life, not from within itself. In the extreme sense, this is true of Jesus himself in so far as he is the eschatological event in person. Naturally, his historical existence is taken for granted, and this appears in so far as he leads the course of an ordinary human life upon earth. But as soon as he speaks and acts, this human course becomes an unceasing chain of divine revelations and mighty acts, which render impossible any comparison with the course of any other human life, so that it can no longer be understood as such within the category of historicity.[21]

But the gospels do not regard what they tell of Jesus as something which can be understood from its historical setting, but as a unique event. This is made particularly clear by the fact that 'the gospels are concerned with the arbitrariness with which the eschatological event is associated with this Nazarene, with

Palestine as the scene in which it takes place, and with a concrete moment of time with its particular circumstances'.[22] They are concerned with this arbitrariness, because it is that which makes unmistakable the eschatological character of this event. That is, no basis can be found for it other than in the 'freedom of God who acts', and who reveals it as 'the possibility for our decision', for which it is the only foundation. Thus this arbitrariness brings about the *kairos*, which 'according to the situation is one of grace or of guilt. Primitive Christianity wrote gospels because it experienced the earthly history of Jesus in this way as a *kairos*.' For this reason it 'did not simply abandon the historical facts about Jesus, even after Easter'. For 'Easter did not simply repeat this experience but, on the contrary, confirmed it'.[23] The 'once' of the historical facts about the earthly Jesus before Easter became after Easter the 'once for all' of the lordship of the risen Christ.[24] In this way

> the gospel is linked with him who before and after Easter revealed himself to his disciples as the Lord, by placing them face to face with the God who was close to them, and thereby gave them the freedom and the responsibility of faith.[25]

By seeking the answer to the quest of the historical Jesus 'in the links and tension between the preaching of Jesus and that of his church', and by recognizing that 'the arbitrariness of history is true of Jesus above all', Käsemann can say that 'the problem of the historical Jesus is not our own invention, but the enigma which he himself poses to us'. And in the same way, Käsemann can continue: 'The historian may confirm that this enigma exists, but cannot resolve it'.[26]

While Käsemann remains, in his statements about the historical Jesus, within the limits of what is accessible to the historian, Günther Bornkamm does not seem to me to have escaped the danger of going beyond these limits. It is true that the title of the book in which he deals with this question[27] shows that he intends to give an account of what in his view can be known with such certainty about the historical Jesus. But he expressly states that he seeks to give 'a historical presentation of Jesus and his message'. Here he proceeds from the fact, generally acknowledged in present-day theology, that the sources which provide such knowledge, that is, the synoptic gospels in particular, 'are not merely historical sources which the historian, inquiring into Jesus Christ as a figure of the past, could use without examination and criticism'. For

> they ... unite to a remarkable degree both record of Jesus Christ and witness to him, testimony of the church's faith in him and narration of his history. Both should be continually distinguished in the understanding of the gospels and in each individual part of their tradition; on the other hand, both are so closely interwoven that it is often exceedingly hard to say where one ends and the other begins.[28]

Bornkamm is nevertheless convinced that historical and critical study cannot avoid an inquiry into the historical Jesus. This endeavour is also required by the gospels and their tradition, the reason being that it can hardly be disputed that they are interested in the earthly history of Jesus, 'different though this interest is from that of modern historical science'.[29] But it is the same Jesus who lived before Good Friday and Easter who is viewed by the gospels 'from the Easter aspect' (op. cit., p. 20; ET pp. 22f.).

> They bring before our eyes, in very different fashion from what is customary in chronicles and presentations of history, the historical person of Jesus, with the greatest vividness.

Thus

> what the Gospels report concerning the message, the deeds and the history of Jesus is still distinguished by an authenticity, a freshness and a distinctiveness not in any way effaced by the church's Easter faith. These features point us directly to the earthly figure of Jesus.[30]

And although the gospel sources do not make it possible 'to reproduce the course of his career in all its happenings and stages, in its inner and outer development', they nevertheless give a quite original account of 'the person and work of Jesus, in their unmistakable uniqueness and distinctiveness'.[31] Bornkamm's purpose is only to 'desist from rash combinations of biographical data, and use the greatest critical caution, in order to be able really to focus those facts' in the history of Jesus 'which are prior to any pious interpretation and manifest themselves as primary'.³² He does this by giving an exhaustive account of Jesus's own preaching, which takes up the greater part of his book.

By contrast not only with Bultmann's book *Jesus*, the sole content of which is Jesus's own preaching, but also with the approach of the other pupils of Bultmann to the quest for the historical Jesus, Bornkamm presents his account of Jesus's preaching against the background of a portrait of the personal characteristics of Jesus. But he uses his account of Jesus's preaching to make concrete the portrayal of Jesus's distinctive personality, which precedes it. It becomes clear that when Bornkamm describes the task he has undertaken in his book as 'to seek the history in the kerygma of the gospels, and in this history to seek the kerygma',³³ he is giving a prominent place in this history to the personality and individuality of Jesus, as they are portrayed in the kerygma. He regards this portrayal as the true context of the kerygma of the primitive Christian church. He scarcely mentions the fact that in the form in which this kerygma is transmitted in the Gospel of John and the New Testament epistles we find virtually nothing of the personality of Jesus, and its distinctive features, nor does he discuss what history may be sought in this kerygma. And no account is taken of the fact that, as Käsemann puts it, the quest of the historical Jesus in the proper sense 'is the question of the continuity of the gospel within the discontinuity of time and the changes in the kerygma'.

These seem to me to be the two real reasons why Bornkamm does not properly succeed in making a distinction between the kerygma and history, although he considers it necessary to do so, 'if only for the purpose of revealing more clearly their interconnection and interpenetration'.³⁴ He is right when he says that the distinction between the two is necessary for the sake of the connection between them. But on the other hand, because of this distinction, the distinctive characteristics of both the kerygma and the history must be sharply delineated. It is true that Bornkamm's book is praised by Althaus for clearly setting out the differences between the history and the kerygma by clearly distinguishing the two certainties which are proper to each: the 'rational certainty about the historical reality of the figure of Jesus' and the 'certainty of faith concerning the presence of God and his salvation in Jesus'.[35] But Bornkamm speaks of 'Jesus's astounding sovereignty in dealing with situations according to the kind of people he encounters'[36] and of which he quite rightly says: 'We are concerned here with a most characteristic trait in the historical Jesus, one which quite accurately is confirmed by the nature of his preaching'. And he not only says of this 'sovereignty of Jesus' that this is what the gospels call the 'authority' of Jesus, but goes beyond this to say: 'The word "authority" certainly contains already the mystery of Jesus's personality and influence, as understood by faith.'[37] He also adds that this mystery 'transcends the merely "historical" sphere'. Is not Bornkamm here regarding each of these two certainties, the historical certainty and that of faith, as being inherent in the other? He is doing exactly what we noticed in the case of Althaus: he equates something which is said to be directly accessible to historical knowledge with what is accessible to faith. In the case of Althaus, this was 'the human portrait of Jesus' as it can be known historically, but in which at the same time 'the character of God is apprehended': in Bornkamm's case it is the 'sovereignty' of Jesus, a reality which, as Bornkamm puts it, 'denotes a reality which appertains to the historical Jesus and is prior to any interpretation'.[38] Here as in Althaus there is a characteristic attempt to gloss over the difference between ascertained historical fact and faith, an attempt typical of the theology which produced the 'lives' of Jesus. The christology associated with it cannot be anything other than one of many modifications of the Jesus-worship of liberal theology. The reason, both in Althaus and Bornkamm, is that insufficient attention is paid to the nature of historical knowledge. Thus the problem of history, as it arises in the relationship between history and faith, is side-stepped.

Ernst Fuchs also believes that the question of the historical Jesus can only be answered by seeking to come to grips with his preaching. But he says that the 'attitude' of Jesus is the 'characteristic framework' of Jesus's preaching, within which alone it can be understood. It might well seem that he means by this the concrete portrait of the personality of Jesus, in which Althaus and Bornkamm seek to apprehend the historical Jesus, as in their view he is to be found in the gospel. But this is not what this expression means. If I understand Fuchs aright, he does not mean this attitude in itself, as it is rooted in the personality and points back to it. He is concerned with the claim expressed in Jesus's attitude to men, to manifest the will of God 'in such a way as if he stood himself in the place of God'. This attitude is 'neither that of a prophet nor of a teacher of wisdom, but the attitude of a person who dares to act in the place of God by – so we must add – drawing close to him sinners who, without him, would have to flee before God'. This attitude is so daring

> that he was executed outside the gates of the city of Jerusalem, which was far from being godless, because it was denied that he had the right as a human being without official authority to put himself in God's place, that is, to give immediate effect in his own attitude to God's will as a gracious will.[39]

But in Fuchs's view, Jesus's attitude is daring in a further sense, not only with regard to God, but also with regard to men. For he 'stakes everything, even his own existence' upon men and upon their paying attention to his 'attitude', especially as it is to be found in his preaching. 'Because he stakes everything on his disciples', he speaks 'in the style of the commandments'.[40]

If those who hear his word remain true to him,

> then, Jesus believes, his hour would have been for them the beginning of the kingdom of God. As eschatological preaching, Jesus's preaching is intended to be accepted in this way. The demand made in the present is tied to the future in so far as God's redeeming action is still anticipated in the future.

On the other hand, the future coming of the kingdom of God depends upon 'whether it has already come in the obedience of the disciples to Jesus's work'.[41] Thus Jesus's attitude demands a decision from his disciples. This 'is the purpose of the critical precision of his exposition of the law, with its emphasis on the indivisible will of God', as it is expressed in the unbreakable link between the commandment of the love of God and that of love for one's neighbour.

> Jesus's words centre upon the decision which they demand. But one must be aware that this demand is simply the echo of the decisions which Jesus himself has taken. We must

understand Jesus's attitude as likewise determined by a decision, and we can therefore work back from what he demands to what he himself did.[42]

The decision which Jesus made is that for the power of love. And 'he had to demand love, because he himself lived by its power'.[43] But 'love does not come from the *demand* for love, but love comes – from love', and consequently, 'Jesus's demand for love is directed at the *faith* of the disciples'. They

> had to believe not merely that God demands love in all things and desires it to be affirmed in all things, but also and above all, they had to believe in the *power* of love as the actual and saving decision concerning our existence.[44]

Fuchs is trying to provide the basis for a contribution to the answer to the question of the historical Jesus which seems to me to consist in the realization that it is not possible to pose this question aright 'without having in mind the christological problems, albeit with a consciously objective attitude and with a critical purpose', as Ebeling puts it in his essay 'The Question of the Historical Jesus and the Problem of Christology'.[45] Fuchs does this not only, however, with regard to our christological task, but also with regard to the theology of the New Testament. He draws attention to a danger which threatens when, as at the present day, we must recognize that 'the *historical* truth of the gospel must be emphasized against a view of the gospel which is fundamentally independent of (the historical) Jesus'. For a historical truth 'by contrast to a universally valid truth, is never repeated unchanged'. But

> Jesus's words and acts also belong to a historical situation in the 'here and now' of the past. If we sought to bring these words and deeds without more ado into the present day, we would do violence both to Jesus and to ourselves.

Nor can Jesus be understood by attempting 'to repeat not Jesus's words and acts, but Jesus's own being, his existence itself'. We are not concerned, however, with Jesus understood in this way in historical terms, but with the Jesus of the gospel.

> Our translation is *not* the repetition of the historical existence of Jesus, but the appropriation of the interpretation – already

A New Quest of the Historical Jesus

reduced to a written text – of the apostles and evangelists, that is, those who were the teachers of primitive Christianity. This does not exclude, but requires that we form for ourselves conceptions about the historical Jesus which are based upon the text.[46]

According to Fuchs, this 'translation', by which he means the knowledge of the reality of Jesus, signifies for us that we must

come to terms with the portrait of Jesus given by the apostles and evangelists, and regard as the vital decision the question whether in this encounter we become the church and remain the church, as was once the case when the first congregation gathered together on hearing the outward word of the apostles and evangelists.[47]

In an essay on 'The Relationship of the Primitive Christian Message to the Historical Jesus'[48] Bultmann himself has recently commented on this development in the quest of the historical Jesus. He characterizes it by saying that whereas the concern was previously for the affirmation of the difference between Jesus and the kerygma, that of the present day is 'the working out of the unity between the historical Jesus and the Christ of the kerygma'.[49] In his view recent attempts to answer the question of the historical Jesus are motivated by this concern. It is hoped through these attempts to get beyond the bare 'fact that Jesus has come', which he, Bultmann, asserts to be the real content of the kerygma, and to show that the continuity between the historical Jesus and the kerygma is in practice an equivalence. These attempts are made in two ways. First of all, 'by showing that the kerygma assumes not only the "bare fact" that the historical Jesus came, but also "what he was like and what he did", and requires these both to be intelligible answers'. Secondly, they seek to show 'that in the activity of Jesus, both in deed and word, the kerygma is already contained *in nuce*'.[50] Bultmann does not wholly reject the first of these attempts; but he believes that, because of the nature of the New Testament tradition, extraordinarily little can be deduced from it concerning the activity and change of Jesus, and certainly not enough to demonstrate that 'the historical continuity between Jesus and the kerygma is in practice an equivalence'.[51] He himself would not think of breaking down this historical continuity, but is of the opinion that it does not amount to an equivalence in practice between the 'substance of the activity of Jesus' and the 'content of the kerygma'.[52] Moreover, as far as the question of the 'credibility' of the kerygma is concerned, this question was quite foreign to the kerygma by its very nature.[53] With regard to the second attempt, to set out the unity between the historical Jesus and the preaching of the kerygma by demonstrating that in the deeds and words of Jesus the kerygma is contained *in nuce*, it seems at first as though Bultmann holds a more positive view of this. He says that it 'can be taken for granted, that *the preaching of Jesus was "kerygmatic" in character*'. It is true that his preaching was not 'christological preaching', not even if 'he had regarded himself as the Messiah and demanded faith in himself'.[54] But one 'can say that *the appearance of Jesus and his preaching implies a christology*, in so far as he demanded a decision about his person as the bearer of the word of God, the decision on which salvation or damnation depends'. Bultmann expresses this by saying that Jesus understood himself as an *'eschatological phenomenon'*,[55] But even this 'does not yet demonstrate the factual unity of the activity and preaching of Jesus with the kerygma'.[56]

Bultmann makes clear the difference which still remains by pointing to two different ways of interpreting the activity of Jesus, one of which 'remains within the framework of traditional historical and critical study', whereas the other 'seeks to understand history on the basis of an existential attitude to it'.[57] With the first kind of interpretation, one can indeed perceive 'the eschatological conscience of Jesus' as 'a historical phenomenon'. Yet to do so does not bring an 'eschatological understanding of one's own self'. But it is this which the kerygma seeks to give, 'for it claims to be of itself an eschatological event (II Cor. 5.18–20; John 5.24, etc.), giving a direct promise of death and life' (II Cor. 2.15f.).[58] But it is another matter when one does what, in Bultmann's view, has been done in the new quest of the historical Jesus, and chooses the second kind of interpretation, 'which is based upon a historical (that is, existential) encounter with history'. This is the encounter in which one 'remains open to the possibilities of self-understanding presented in history, as a possibility for one's own self-understanding', and in which, 'because it consists as it were in hearing, rather than in looking from a distance', history is 'addressed to us'.[59] In Bultmann's view, everything depends upon this latter kind of interpretation, which he terms existential, being carried out consistently. One must not slip back 'into an interpretation in terms of Jesus's actual historical psychology'. One would then be turning Jesus and his attitude into phenomena accessible to the 'objectivizing historian'.[60] If the existential interpretation is carried out consistently, it can 'demonstrate the identity of the activity of Jesus with the kerygma', and the latter can be understood in such a way that 'in it the demand for a decision made on the actions of Jesus which took place in the past, is repeated'.[61]

But if it is the case that with the help of this existential interpretation the historian can attain to an existential encounter with the history of Jesus, and so bring himself and his audience 'into the situation of a decision with regard to Jesus', in which 'the possibility of new existence' is revealed to him, what, Bultmann goes on to ask, can be the meaning of the apostolic kerygma of Christ? And why could 'the apostolic preaching not limit itself simply to *repeating* the preaching of Jesus, as other disciples repeated the teaching of their master?' What is the significance of the fact that the apostolic kerygma, as we find it in Paul and John, makes no attempt at all to repeat the preaching of Jesus? According to Bultmann, this brings us back to the old question, why Jesus the preacher had to become the Christ who is preached. And this question is now 'not a question of historical continuity, of the causalities within the historical process, but has become a question about inherent necessity'.[62] Bultmann believes that he can answer this question by pointing to the church, the basis of which is that 'the earliest congregation *understood the history of Jesus* (with increasing clarity) *as the decisive eschatological event*, which as such could never become simply a thing of the past, but remains *present*, and does so *in preaching*'. Thus 'the kerygma changed the "once" of the historical Jesus into a "once for all"'. The difference between the kerygma and the 'mere "repetition"' of the preaching of Jesus – either through the working over of the tradition by the synoptics, or by modern history writing' is consequently as follows. Modern history writing, of course, 'makes the past present by placing the hearer (or reader) face to face with a decision for (or against) a possibility of self-understanding revealed in preaching'. But the 'Christ kerygma demands belief in the Jesus made present in it, who does not only promise salvation like the historical Jesus, but has already brought it'.[63]

The answer which Bultmann gives to the question why Jesus the preacher had to become the Christ who is preached, seems to me to avoid the real significance of this question, if it is meant to be a question of the 'inner necessity' of this change. That is not really demonstrated by stating that the apostolic kerygma changed Jesus who promised salvation into Christ, who 'has already brought salvation'. What gave the kerygma the right to make this 'change'? And if it 'claims that in it Christ is present',[64] what is the basis of this claim? How can the word 'which comes to the hearer in the kerygma' and offers him the salvation that has been achieved, be the word of Jesus,[65] when he is only the one who promises salvation? What Bultmann ascribes to the word of the kerygma can only be asserted if Jesus who promises salvation is himself the salvation to come, and as such the Christ. Only if he is the Christ in this sense is it possible for the kerygma to find Christ 'in the words and deeds of the historical Jesus'.[66] But this would mean not only that, as Bultmann holds, the paradox 'life dwells in death', which became the reality of salvation in Christ, first became explicit in the kerygma.[67] It would mean even more: that it was already explicitly present 'in the words and deeds of the historical Jesus', and that the historical Jesus, or as I would prefer to say, Jesus in his characteristic historical reality, is only known when one apprehends in him and in his teaching the salvation that he has not merely promised in his preaching, but has also brought about by promising it.

Before we ask how this is possible, I think we ought to discuss what Ebeling says in his article 'The Quest of the Historical Jesus and the Problem of Christology'.[68]

From the very beginning, Ebeling relates the quest of the historical Jesus to christology. Since, as he says, 'the relation to Jesus is constitutive for christology, it must, if it understands itself aright, make the claim to be doing nothing else but saying who Jesus is'.[69] And notwithstanding anything that may be said about the divine nature of Jesus, he is a human being and faith in him is therefore also faith in his humanity. This faith must, therefore, be in accordance with the reality of the human being that he was, and must accordingly be concerned with the 'historical' Jesus. Ebeling goes on to say that the reality of this human being is to be sought in the fact that in him faith 'came to expression'. It is this which is 'the one absolutely decisive and all-determining characteristic in the life and message of the historical Jesus'.[70] And therefore 'the quest of the historical Jesus is the quest of this linguistic event which is the ground of the event of faith'.[71]

Ebeling arrives at this formulation because in his view the only understanding of history which is capable of understanding historical reality is 'the view of history which takes its bearings on the word-event and consequently in the linguisticality of reality'.[72] In order to understand this staggeringly simple thesis, that the historical reality of Jesus consists in the fact that in him faith came to expression, it is naturally of decisive importance to understand what is meant here by 'faith'. Hans Conzelmann has already pointed out that this formula, like Ernst Fuchs's expression, the 'attitude of Jesus', can easily be misunderstood as a mere catchword.[73] In fact, if Ebeling's formula passes into common currency in the sense of what is for the most part conventionally understood as faith – and since it is so well adapted to this purpose, this will very soon happen – it is not difficult to imagine the consequence. But Ebeling has set out in three publications what kind of faith it is which came to expression in Jesus.[74]

The first thing which Ebeling says about this faith is that it is not a faith 'which expresses itself in some kind of dogmatic confession'.

> The concrete content of faith comes on each occasion only from the concrete situation to which it refers, thus, e.g., from being affected by an illness.[75]

> It belongs to the essence of faith . . . that it has to do with something that is God's concern.

Consequently, 'in faith, word and fulfilment are bound as firmly together as in the word of creation that speaks and it is done'. Thus, 'the power of faith is marked outright as the power of God'. Anyone who believes in the sense in which faith came to utterance in Jesus is by so doing allowing God to be effective, lets God go into action, and 'it is legitimate to ascribe to his faith what is a matter for God'. It is in precise accordance with this that someone who believes in such a way is 'helpless' and 'cannot help himself'. And in so far as this helpless person knows that he relies wholly upon God, the certainty and power of his faith is 'the certainty and power of God himself. For that reason these statements would be completely meaningless, if they were not understood as referring to God, i.e. in such a way that faith can exist only in relation to God.'[76]

In this sense, therefore, faith can only exist with regard to God – only, moreover, in the sense that it is 'manifestly directed towards God in a concrete encounter with him'. This is the case with the Samaritan, the Syrophoenician woman, and the heathen centurion, to whom Jesus 'imputes faith . . . irrespective of any confession of faith – and such a faith too as he has not found in Israel'.

One can hardly doubt that the faith of which Jesus speaks is the same as his own, even though he does not speak explicitly about this.[77] Anyone who wishes to arouse faith must, as Ebeling quite rightly says, 'bring his faith into play without speaking of faith'. The question that matters is whether this faith is faith in Jesus. In any case it is certain that the Jesus of the synoptic gospels, by contrast to the Jesus of St John, did not speak of a faith in himself. Nevertheless, 'a peculiarly close connection has to be affirmed between the faith which is spoken of in the sayings of Jesus, and Jesus himself'. This means that it is 'faith in the power of Jesus', as is shown particularly clearly in the stories of healing. In general, it is related to Jesus, in so far as 'it is faith awakened by Jesus himself'. Jesus ascribes faith to those who are to be healed and can then say to them: Your faith has helped you. It is as if he was saying to those who do not know how and by what they have been healed, that it is their faith which has healed them.[78] Ebeling also understands Jesus's call to follow him in the same sense.[79]

Jesus's distinctive use of the word 'Amen' also belongs here. This word which, in contrast to the prevalent usage, Jesus puts at the beginning of his statements, signifies that he 'understood his statements, and would have them understood, as statements made before God, in which God himself is the guarantor of what is said'. By so using it, Jesus said that 'the truth and reality of his words is the truth and reality of God'. By this he means that by 'identifying himself entirely with his words' he 'surrenders himself to the reality of God', and 'lets his existence be grounded on God's making these words true and real'. The ἀμήν is primarily not at all a question of corroborating the individual saying that follows'. Rather, this word originates in 'a decision that has already been made, an assent given once for all to the reality of God, an absolute readiness to obey, an irrevocable act of being cast upon God and grounded in him'. Here 'Jesus performs a vicarious act'. For 'the obedience in which that certainty consists has vicarious power in this, that it becomes the source from which certainty flows'. This again is not something that happens only in relation to a number of particular circumstances, but concerns the very existence of those who hear him, in such a way, moreover, that he makes this existence 'a believing existence'.[80]

Finally, one can say of the faith which came to utterance in Jesus that it can never be anything but the faith of an individual person, and that only as such is it true, genuine faith. This faith is fundamentally different from that of late Judaism, in which men more or less 'took for granted both their participation in the faith of the fathers or of Israel as a whole and also the possibility of falling back upon it'. Again, associated with the fact that faith is in each case that of the individual, there is the further fact that it 'is not a partial act'. Rather, it affects the whole existence of the believer, and is therefore 'a movement, in which the whole of existence is given aim, definition and ground'. As a believer, man, 'prior to all the several partial aspects in which he manifests himself and into which he divides himself and dissipates his energies, is one and the same and a whole'.[81] A faith which instead of this was 'the blind acceptance of certain circumstances, alleged facts and dogmatic conceptions' could only be a caricature of this faith. Faith understood in this way would be bound 'to divide man, instead of being the event in which man comes to wholeness, and experiences salvation'.[82]

NOTES

1. James M. Robinson, op. cit., p. 12.
2. Bultmann, *Glauben und Verstehen*, p. 208.

3. Althaus, op. cit., p. 12.
4. Bultmann, op. cit., p. 208.
5. Käsemann, op. cit., p. 152, and 'Neutestamentliche Fragen von heute', in *Zeitschrift für Theologie und Kirche*, 1957, p. 11.
6. Käsemann, *ZThK*, 1957, p. 150.
7. *ZThK*, 1957, p. 12.
8. *ZThK*, 1954, p. 142.
9. *ZThK*, 1954, p. 129.
10. Ibid., p. 132.
11. p. 129.
12. p. 152.
13. p. 152.
14. p. 133.
15. p. 134.
16. p. 133.
17. p. 141.
18. p. 133.
19. p. 130.
20. pp. 132f.
21. p. 138.
22. p. 138.
23. p. 139.
24. p. 138.
25. p. 152.
26. p. 152.
27. Günther Bornkamm, *Jesus von Nazareth*, Stuttgart, 1956; tr. Irene and Frazer McCluskey with James M. Robinson, *Jesus of Nazareth*, Hodder and Stoughton, 1960.
28. Op. cit., pp. 12; tr. p. 14.
29. pp. 19f.; tr. 22f.
30. pp. 21f.; tr. p. 24.
31. pp. 22f., tr. p. 25.
32. p. 48; tr. p. 53.
33. p. 18; tr. p. 21.
34. p. 18; tr. p. 21.
35. Althaus, op. cit., p. 46.
36. Bornkamm, op. cit., p. 53; tr. p. 58.
37. p. 54; tr. p. 60.
38. p. 54; tr. p. 60.
39. Fuchs, 'Die Frage nach dem historischen Jesus', *Zeitschrift für Theologie und Kirche*, 1956, pp. 219f.
40. Fuchs, 'Glaube und Geschichte', *ZThK*, 1957, p. 151.
41. *ZThK*, 1957, pp. 150f.
42. *ZThK*, 1956, pp. 221f.
43. *ZThK*, 1957, p. 155.
44. *ZThK*, 1957, p. 146.
45. Ebeling, 'Die Frage nach dem Historischen Jesus und das Problem der Christologie', in *Zeitschrift für Theologie und Kirche*, 1959, Beiheft 1, p. 15;

tr. James W. Leitch, 'The Question of the Historical Jesus and the Problem of Christology', in *Word and Faith*, SCM Press, London and Fortress Press, Philadelphia, 1963, p. 288.

46. Fuchs, *ZThK*, 1954, pp. 31f.
47. Fuchs, *ZThK*, 1954, p. 33.
48. Bultmann, 'Das Verhältnis der urchristlichen Christusbotschaft zum Historischen Jesus' in *Sitzungsberichte der Heidelberger Akademie der Wissenschaften* 3, 1960.
49. Op. cit., p. 6.
50. p. 10.
51. p. 14.
52. p. 9.
53. pp. 12f.
54. p. 15.
55. p. 16.
56. p. 17.
57. p. 15.
58. p. 17.
59. p. 18.
60. p. 19.
61. p. 22.
62. p. 23.
63. p. 25.
64. p. 26.
65. p. 27.
66. p. 26.
67. p. 26.
68. Ebeling, op. cit., tr. Leitch, 'The Question of the Historical Jesus, etc.'.
69. Op. cit., pp. 14f., tr. p. 288.
70. pp. 21f.; tr. p. 296.
71. p. 30; tr. p. 304.
72. p. 20; tr. p. 295, cf. his article 'Wort Gottes und Hermeneutik', *ZThK*, 1959, pp. 224ff., tr. James W. Leitch, 'Word of God and Hermeneutics', in *Word and Faith*, pp. 305-332.
73. Conzelmann, *ZThK*, 1959, Beiheft 1, p. 8.
74. 'Was heisst Glaube', *SGV*, 216, Tübingen 1958; 'Jesus und Glaube', *ZThK*, 1958, pp. 64ff., tr. Leitch, 'Jesus and Faith', in *Word and Faith*, pp. 201-246; *Das Wesen des Christlichen Glaubens*, J. C. B. Mohr (Paul Siebeck), Tübingen, 1959, tr. Ronald Gregor Smith, *The Nature of Faith*, Collins, 1961.
75. Ebeling, *ZThK*, 1958, p. 95; tr. 'Jesus and Faith', pp. 232f.
76. Op. cit., pp. 96f.; tr. p. 233.
77. p. 97; tr. pp. 233f.
78. p. 98; tr. p. 234.
79. p. 99; tr. p. 235 n. 1.
80. pp. 99ff., tr. pp. 237f.
81. p. 100; tr. p. 239.
82. p. 101; tr. p. 240.

5

THE TASK OF CHRISTOLOGY

FROM THE fact that christology claims to state who Jesus is, and from the further fact that 'in Jesus faith came to utterance', and that this is 'the one absolutely decisive and all-determining thing in the life and message of the historical Jesus, determining everything in it', Ebeling concludes that it is the task of christology 'to bring to expression what came to expression in Jesus'.[1] This formulation cannot mean that the task of christology would be fulfilled if it succeeded in setting out the phenomenon of the coming to expression of faith in Jesus in the same way as a historian. The knowledge of this phenomenon is of course necessary for christology. For it desires to know, and must indeed know, who Jesus was in the reality of his earthly life. The starting-point of Luther's christological thought is that it must begin with the real and true manhood of Jesus. If this is correct, christology ought to assert only what is based on the manhood of Jesus, and is limited to saying who this man is.[2] Nevertheless, christology goes beyond what the historian can say. For although the latter can speak of the coming to expression of faith in Jesus, the faith of Jesus is not yet brought to expression merely by his speaking about it. But this is what ought to happen in christology.

It is now necessary to be clear about what happens when something is brought to expression. In the sense in which this term expression is applied here to the faith of Jesus, something is not brought to expression merely by being spoken about in the same way in which people, for a more or less pressing reason, discuss any arbitrary matter and share their views about it. Rather, this only happens when something which of its nature is meant to sustain the whole existence of man is brought to expression in such a way that it can no longer be evaded without

The Task of Christology

this having a decisive effect upon human existence. If what is expressed is evaded, then one is evading one's own existential life and failing to find it. As long as the phenomenon in question remains unexpressed, it exists only in obscurity, inarticulated and unreal. It is still confused with others, and so its proper nature is suppressed or falsified; consequently, it remains ineffective in its true essence. But, if it is expressed, it comes to sustain the whole existence of everyone it affects. It is this which happened when faith came to expression in Jesus; in its own way it became the one absolutely decisive and all-determining thing in the existence of Jesus.

We have described the task of christology as that of saying who Jesus is, and describing in new terms the faith which came to expression in him as that which sustained his whole existence. If this is correct, its task is not yet fulfilled with the affirmation of historical scholarship that the faith of Jesus was of the kind described above – that is, the thing which brought his existence to wholeness and sustained it as a whole, a faith which had the same effect in the existence of those who apprehended Jesus in this reality. In christology, the faith which came to expression in Jesus must be brought to expression in such a way as to make clear that it sustains our whole existence and is the decisive element in it. At the same time our own existence, in its wholeness as that which is sustained by faith, must also be brought to expression. Only then is the task of christology fulfilled. The faith which came to expression in Jesus must so take hold of us in our existence that this existence is brought to wholeness as an existence which is attentive to Jesus, and is therefore saved or, by denying Jesus, abandons itself to evil. Otherwise we are not speaking of Jesus and his faith in christological terms, but in historical terms – in the way in which one speaks of anything which has nothing directly to do with our existence, and to which one can adopt any attitude one pleases, of acceptance or rejection.

The task of christology, which consists of bringing the faith of Jesus to expression in this way, has always existed since it came to expression in Jesus himself. For once what had happened to him had been realized, it was felt necessary to understand this faith in such a way that it was possible to pass the knowledge of it on to others. What we nowadays call the primitive Christian kerygma, or the New Testament witness to Jesus Christ, was the first attempt on the part of primitive Christianity to fulfil this task. It was an attempt on the part of the Christians of the early church to bring this faith to expression as that which sustained their own existence. Once one is aware that this is the task of theology, that is, to speak of Jesus as the Christ, it is no longer surprising that the primitive Christian kerygma, particularly in the form in which it has been handed down in the New Testament epistles and in the Gospel of John, says so extraordinarily little about the historical facts of Jesus's life. Similarly, with the synoptic gospels, the historical study which believed that its duty was to seek in them the historical Jesus 'arrived, at the conclusion of its long and painful way, not as it originally hoped at the historical Jesus but at the primitive Christian kerygma as the original datum of the gospel tradition'. For, in a sentence of Käsemann which we have already quoted, they, too, present 'in the first instance the primitive Christian kerygma, and individual words and acts of Jesus only as they are embedded in the latter'.[3] The significance which Jesus had for the primitive Christian church and its faith did not lie in what he was in himself, but in the fact that he had become the 'Lord', that is, he who through his faith determined the existence of those who believed in him. If this is so, then it is also easy to understand that this significance 'became so powerful that in the very earliest period it had already absorbed into itself the historical facts of his life'.[4] Consequently, for the primitive Christian congregation, everything depended on the fact that the faith which had come to expression in Jesus, and in which they experienced the reality of Jesus, should be brought to expression by them as the faith which sustained their own existence.

But, as we have already seen, this faith is not the acceptance of certain dogmatic ideas, but affects the existence of man as an existence sustained and determined by this faith. When this faith is brought to expression as such, in it the existence of Jesus is also brought to expression. But this is only possible, in so far as his existence was an existence sustained by this faith. His existence here does not mean the detailed historical facts of his life, but his existence in the distinctive wholeness into which his faith, by bringing it about and sustaining it, concentrates it and draws it into a unity. At this point 'he himself has rendered superfluous all interest in exact biographical detail and in psychological presentation'.[5] This is what Käsemann means when he states that the kerygma pays attention to the historical facts of Jesus's life 'only in so far as they are the point of contact of eschatological events', and derive their real life from these events, so that they can no longer 'be comprehended within the category of historicity'.[6]

With regard to our christological task at the present day, underlying its distinctive features is the fact that we can no longer simply take over as our own a christology in the form in which it is contained in the primitive Christian kerygma. The first reason for this is that our existence, which the faith that came to expression in Jesus ought to sustain, has become different from that of the earliest Christians. The consequence of this is that we can no longer understand directly, that is, without translation and interpretation, the faith which is brought to expression in the primitive Christian kerygma. For if an essential element in the nature of faith is its intimate relationship to human existence, it cannot be directly understood if it is not understood within or on the basis of this relationship. It must be understood through the way it affects every individual existence, bringing this whole existence to expression at the same time as faith. Only then is it understood directly, and only in this way can it be the faith of each individual, which is the only way in which Christian faith can exist.

But if the existence which came to expression together with faith in the primitive Christian kerygma is no longer our own, then this kerygma, too, no longer affects our existence. Likewise, we can no longer understand the faith which once came to expression in that kerygma as it was meant to be understood, in such a way as for it to be our own faith. If we then suppose that this faith must nevertheless be accepted as it is found in these circumstances, simply because it is the faith of primitive Christianity, then its relationship to the totality of each individual believer's existence, which is of its essence, would have been hopelessly lost. It can be related to one's own existence only in a moral sense. Also in so far as it still resembles faith, it can do so only in the form of a legalist dogmatism – that is, in the sense that it requires the acceptance of the concepts and ideas of the primitive Christian kerygma. Here, moreover, we must remember that the primitive Christian kerygma is not the unity that it is often supposed to be, particularly when it is contrasted with Jesus's own preaching. In fact in the New Testament writings it often displays very different forms, which it took in the Palestinian or in the Hellenistic church. There is also a Pauline and Johannine kerygma, to mention only the most important. One of the main reasons for this variety is that the existence of the New Testament writers, like that of the people in the churches to which they belonged or to which they proclaimed the gospel, and to whom they brought faith to expression, was not the same.

The other reason why we cannot simply take over the christology of the biblical kerygma as our own is closely related to the first. If we no longer understand directly the faith which is brought to expression in the biblical kerygma, not only is it not related to the totality of our existence, but it has also lost its relationship to the existence of Jesus, which was something originally brought to expression in the biblical kerygma at the same time as faith in him, and was drawn by this faith into the unity in which this faith sustained it. So the impression arises that in the primitive Christian kerygma the history of Jesus, by which we mean here the historical reality of Jesus of Nazareth, is not merely 'almost absorbed', but seems not to have been retained at all. In other words, if the kerygma is misunderstood in this way, the Jesus we encounter in it is not a real historical person, but an unhistorical heavenly being, in whom faith believes by believing in the biblical kerygma we have described. If this faith ceases to be worthy of belief, because its dogmatic assumptions have collapsed, the question then arises of the 'historical' Jesus as the true and real Jesus, by contrast to this 'Christ of faith'. And theology is immediately faced and confounded by the question whether the Christ of the kerygma is still the same as Jesus of Nazareth, and whether this kerygma is reconcilable with Jesus's own preaching.

At this point the following considerations seems to me to be necessary. First of all, there can scarcely be any doubt that the primitive Christian church never abandoned the identity of the

The Task of Christology

Christ it preached with Jesus of Nazareth. Without this identity its faith and preaching would have seemed to it meaningless. Of course it is true that we know of the history of Jesus of Nazareth 'only through the kerygma'.[7] This is the sole medium through which we have access to the historical Jesus. But this medium 'in the first instance does not make this access open to us, but bars us from it'. For it shows us Jesus 'not as he is in himself', but only as the 'Lord of the church who believed in him'.[8] But this does not alter what we have just said, that for the primitive Christian church it was the real, historical Jesus of Nazareth who was the divine Lord. For this very reason it spoke in its kerygma of Jesus of Nazareth, and would not speak of him except in the way in which faith comprehends his existence in its totality, and in which the earthly Jesus in this totality of his existence is present as the Christ of faith. For the most important thing of all to it is that this Christ was the true earthly Jesus; whereas the details of his existence were not important. For the same reason, the primitive church had not the slightest interest in posing the question of the historical Jesus, far less of isolating this question in any way. It is in accordance with this that the synoptic gospels, although they recount at comparative length details from the historical facts of his life, portray him 'from the first as the Son of God'.[9]

For us, however, the question of the earthly Jesus has become isolated from these other matters. Not the least reason for this is that our existence is no longer the same as that of the members of the early Christian churches (we shall discuss this at greater length later). The question of the earthly Jesus is not merely isolated from that of the Christ of faith. As it was originally posed, and as historical study understood it until quite recently, it was actually directed *polemically* against the Christ of faith, or, as it was more usually expressed, against the Christ of dogma. It was directed against the latter as a figure interpreted by faith and exalted above earthly standards, because this was the only way in which it was felt possible to inquire about the true, real, historical Jesus. The reason for this is that this quest was determined by a kind of historical thinking which was virtually unable to think of a human being whose historical reality could be demonstrated by factual historical methods, except as a visible individual personality. And this kind of thinking in fact reached the point where it had to consider, as Käsemann remarks incidentally, 'whether the formula, "the historical Jesus", can be called appropriate and valid at all, because it arouses and nourishes almost of necessity the illusion that it is possible to give a satisfactory reproduction of the course of his life (like a biographical history)'.[10]

Consequently, Bultmann's thesis that only the 'bare fact' that Jesus had come was decisive for the primitive Christian kerygma, and that Jesus mattered for this kerygma, 'neither as a personality nor as a heavenly being', but as 'a historical event',[11] represented an extraordinary change in the quest of the 'historical' Jesus and its significance for Christian faith. This thesis is important, regardless of how one understands it in detail. But until the school of thought which is concerned with the question of the historical Jesus breaks away from the idea that the only possible understanding of historical reality is that associated with the idea of 'factual history', its present understanding of this thesis is virtually the only one possible. Paul Althaus typifies this understanding, when he says that Bultmann's thesis expressed 'a non-historical, indeed, an anti-historical attitude'.[12] Or again, Günther Bornkamm says of Bultmann's view that in it 'Jesus Christ becomes a mere historical fact, and ceases to be a person'.[13] In fact, if it is the case, as most theologians are convinced, that it is possible to understand the historical reality of a human being only in biographical terms, and therefore to think of Jesus only as a person with concrete individual features, then without doubt a thesis such as Bultmann's 'as it were breaks down the bridge between the historical Jesus and Christ who is preached'.[14]

No attention is paid to what Bultmann may mean when he states explicitly that he 'does not deny that the resurrection kerygma, is firmly rooted to the earthly figure of the crucified Jesus',[15] or when he says of the Pauline kerygma, that 'the historical person of Jesus turns Paul's preaching into the gospel'.[16] For if in the case of Jesus 'a concrete historical account' means nothing more than making his history visible in a lively portrait of his personality, this is something superfluous, and it is possible, like Althaus, to assert of these statements by Bultmann that in his theology 'they remain wholly general and abstract', and 'are not worked out at all' in concrete terms.[17] But the question

The Task of Christology

which must first be decided is whether concrete historical reality only exists in the meaning given to it by Althaus and Bultmann's other opponents, and whether this is the reality which is meant in the confession of Jesus Christ. In order to answer this question, we ought first to try to find out what is the historical reality which is intended in New Testament christology.

NOTES

1. Ebeling, *ZThK*, 1959, Beiheft 1, p. 30; tr. 'The Question of the Historical Jesus, etc.,', in *Word and Faith*, p. 304.
2. Op. cit., p. 24, tr. pp. 298f.
3. Käsemann, *ZThK*, 1954, p. 142.
4. Op. cit., pp. 132, 142.
5. Ebeling, *ZThK*, 1958, p. 103, tr. 'Jesus and Faith', in *Word and Faith*, p. 243; and *ZThK*, 1959, Beiheft 1, p. 22, tr. 'The Question, etc.', in *Word and Faith*, p. 297.
6. Käsemann, op. cit., p. 138.
7. Op. cit., p. 133.
8. p. 132.
9. p. 139.
10. p. 132.
11. Bultmann, *Glauben und Verstehen* I, p. 259.
12. Althaus, *Das sogennante Kerygma und der historische Jesus*, p. 15.
13. Bornkamm, 'Mythos und Evangelium', in *Theologische Existenz heute*, NF 26, p. 18.
14. Eduard Ellwein, *Zur Entmythologisierung*, p. 23, quoted in Althaus, op. cit., p. 26.
15. Bultmann, *Kerygma und Mythos* I, p. 144; tr. *Kerygma and Myth* I, p. 112.
16. Bultmann, *Glauben und Verstehen* I, p. 202.
17. Bultmann, *Die Theologie des Neuen Testaments*, p. 26; tr. p. 26.

6

THE CHRISTOLOGY OF THE NEW TESTAMENT

As WE HAVE already mentioned, there is not of course a single christology which is the same in all New Testament writings. But one can say that each of these christologies, albeit in a different form, bears witness to the one decisive act of God in Jesus Christ which brings salvation to the world and to men. For the divine titles which are applied to Jesus in the New Testament, and with which the primitive Christian church sought to make clear to itself the significance of what happened in and through Jesus, all refer to the same event, the same work of God, which he carried out through Jesus in the world of men and for it. The very titles make clear something which indeed can scarcely be overlooked by anyone who reads the text without prejudice. It has been the practice, especially since the period of pietism, to understand the titles in terms of an individualistic and, if I may so describe it, a personal pastoral attitude of Jesus towards men, concerned with the salvation of the soul – 'with me and you', as the saying goes. This is a misunderstanding of the whole significance of this work of God. It conceals, or at least forces into the background or to the periphery, the fact that the primitive Christian church did not see the significance of Jesus primarily in what he did for individual men, but regarded his acts as effective for the world. The two titles 'Messiah' and 'Son of man', which seem to have been applied to him in the very earliest period, already make this clear. Both derive from the eschatological hope of Judaism, and refer to the one who according to this hope was to bring salvation to the Jewish people, and with them to the whole world of men. Even in their applications in the New Testament to Jesus of Nazareth, these titles retain their reference to the future and to the salvation of the world. The original expectation of the primitive church was that Jesus would return to earth at the imminent end of the age as this Messiah or Son of man, in the power and glory of the divine office bestowed upon him, in order to judge the world and bring eternal salvation. Admittedly, it was not until after Easter that the primitive church believed in Jesus as the Messiah in this sense, and through this belief overcame the scandal of the cross, that is, of the divine curse which according to Jewish belief lay upon one who had been crucified (Gal. 3.13). For now the cross could be understood in the context of the event of salvation. This is expressed, for example, in the Gospel of Luke (24.26f.) by the statement of the risen Christ to the disciples at Emmaus, explaining what had happened to him in the crucifixion: '"Was it not necessary that the Christ should suffer these things and enter into his glory?" And beginning with Moses and all the prophets, he interpreted to them in all the scriptures the things concerning himself.'

Thus for the primitive church the coming of Jesus signified the salvation of the world, and not merely of certain individual persons and their souls. It was the salvation of the world in this sense which it expected to come with the final and imminent appearance of Jesus, the Messiah now appointed with divine power. It also lived in the faith that as this messianic community, it had been drawn even now, through the gift of the Holy Spirit through which it had become the church, into the coming of the salvation which was imminent. But this meant that its gaze, its hope, and its expectation were wholly orientated towards the future. Its every thought concerning Jesus was about him as the one who was coming to save the world. If this is understood, one can also see why the synoptic gospels are anything but *memorabilia*, and why whatever is said in them about Jesus is not meant to speak of the past, but of one who came and as such as one who is still to come. And it is therefore true, and cannot be otherwise, that

> When the earliest church proclaims Jesus as Messiah-Son-of-Man, that does not mean that it has thereby added an item to Old Testament tradition and Jesus's message. Rather, the kerygma of Jesus as Messiah is the basic and primary thing which gives everything else – the ancient tradition and Jesus's message – its special character.[1]

Thus the first and most important question is not how Jesus's personal character was constituted and what his attitude was towards different persons on the basis of his character. We hear that he performed miracles and had power over demons, but these stories are not important as an expression of his helpful and loving attitude towards individuals, but as signs of the authority given him by God, not only to preach salvation to the whole world, but also to bring it. As such signs, they are all the more important because the church never forgets that he whom it proclaims as 'the Son of man coming on the clouds of heaven with power and great glory' (Matt. 24.30), and to whom 'all authority in heaven and on earth has been given' (Matt. 28.18) is the man Jesus of Nazareth. The same is true of his preaching. When the primitive church gathered his sayings together, 'this was not because of their content, but because they were his words, the words of the future king'[2] and because they too are signs of his messianic authority: 'He taught them as one who had authority (i.e. authority deriving directly from God), and not as the scribes' (Mark 1.22), none of whom would have dared to say 'But I say to you' (Matt. 5.22), the words with which Jesus contradicted the highest traditional authority which existed for the Jews of his time. In view of all this, what is the historical reality that is the basis of the kerygma of the early church? One can only reply that in spite of the various personal features which have been preserved in the synoptic gospels, it is not the portrait of the visible and individual personality of Jesus, but the figure of a man endowed with the divine power which rules the world, such that the fact of his coming is indeed 'the decisive event through which God had called his community'.[3]

If we go on to ask whether this applies to the reality which underlies the New Testament kerygma in its later forms, we can see that there, too, the real manhood of Jesus is maintained and taken for granted. But here again, this does not mean that what is decisive and important for the kerygma, and provides the basis for faith in Jesus, is not his individual personality or biographical details; such things are only mentioned incidentally. Rather it is the whole, or as we may also say, the 'fact', of his manhood which belongs to the kerygma. That is, on the one hand, his human birth and origin (Gal. 4.4; Rom. 1.3), and on the other hand, the fact that like all men he is subject to the law: he was 'born in the likeness of men' and 'found in human form' (Phil. 2.7f.). This again points to his death on the cross, and to the fact that he was 'made to be sin' and became a curse (II Cor. 5.21; Gal. 3.13). This process goes so far that even his preaching, as it is handed down in the synoptic gospels, plays virtually no part in the kerygma of Paul, in that of John, or in the other epistles. It is easy to understand why this is so, when one remembers that the coming and existence of Jesus possessed a significance for the salvation of the whole world which overshadowed everything else.

In the kerygma, as it is formulated in these writings, Jesus is above all the one who has set the world free from the powers which have enslaved it, and man with it, under their rule. Consequently, the principal title which is given to him here is that of the *kyrios*, the 'Lord of the world'. Theologians do not agree whether this title derives from the religious usage of Hellenism or is the Greek translation of the divine title in the Old Testament. However this may be, it is clear in any case that this title certainly does not signify in the first instance lordship over the individual man who has attained faith, nor even over the church. It is only understood in its whole and sublime significance when it is realized that it signifies dominion over the cosmic powers and over the whole world which, with the help of these powers, rules the men who live in it. This is why it is 'the name which is above every name, that at the name of Jesus every knee should bow, in heaven and on earth and under the earth' (Phil. 2.9f.). When the kerygma acknowledges him as the mediator of creation, 'through whom are all things and through whom we exist' (I Cor. 8.6; John 1.1ff.; Heb. 1.3; Eph. 3.9), it is referring to this all-embracing dominion of Jesus Christ. As he is the mediator of creation he is pre-existent, and is

> the image of the invisible God, the first born of all creation; for in him all things were created, in heaven and on earth, visible and invisible, whether thrones or dominions or principalities or authorities. All things were created through him and for him. He is before all things, and in him all things hold together. He is the head of the body, the church; he is the

beginning, the first born from the dead, that in everything he might be pre-eminent. For he (God) was pleased, that in him all fullness (the life-creating presence of God) should dwell, and through him to reconcile to himself all things, whether on earth or in heaven, making peace by the blood of his cross (Col. 1.15–20).

The peace which Jesus set up as this Lord is on the one hand reconciliation between God and man, while on the other hand it is the peace which this has made possible between the Jews and the other nations, whose opposition ran for the Jews like a dividing wall through the whole of the world at that time. This is particularly clear when this passage in the Epistle to the Colossians is seen side by side with the very similar passage in the second chapter of the Epistle to the Ephesians. Here we read that Christ is our peace, because he has made one both Jews and Gentiles, who were 'alienated from the commonwealth of Israel, and strangers to the covenant of promise' and were therefore without 'hope and without God in the world', and has

> broken down the dividing wall of hostility, by abolishing in his flesh (that is, as the man who he was) the law of commandments and ordinances, that he might create in himself one new man in place of the two, so making peace, and might reconcile us both to God in one body through the cross, thereby bringing the hostility to an end. And he came and preached to you who were afar off, and peace to those who were near; for through him we both have access in one Spirit to the Father (Eph. 2.12–18).

The redemption and salvation which is given to the world by the abolition of the hostility of men against God and between the two parts into which the world was divided – the Jews who had the law and the Gentiles who did not have it – have been brought about by the victory which Jesus won over the cosmic powers, and by his breaking of their power over men, who were unable to overcome it themselves. For they were revealed by him as powers which have only cosmic authority, that is, as being only created, and not divine and creative in nature. Christ made these cosmic powers, 'a public example ... triumphing over them in him' (Col. 2.15). Not the least of these cosmic powers was the law, as is evident both from the remark in the Epistle to the Ephesians that the law was the wall which divided the Jews and the Gentiles, and also from that in the Epistle to the Colossians, that in his triumph over these powers Christ cancelled the bond of death with his accusing sentence and nailed it to the cross. So the Epistle to the Ephesians reads:

> You (the Gentiles), who (according to the sense one should add, *without* the Law) were dead through the trespasses and sins in which you once walked ... and us (the Jews), even when we (*with* the law) were dead in our sins, (therefore, both you and us) he made alive together with Christ and raised us up with him, and made us sit with him in the heavenly places in Christ Jesus, that in the coming ages he might show the immeasurable riches of his grace in kindness towards us in Christ Jesus (Eph. 2.1–7).

To understand aright these powerful statements, which take in the totality of the world, the cosmic powers which prevail in it as well as the fate of all the men who dwell there, the Jews and the nations (Gentiles), the living and the dead, it is of the utmost importance to be clear about the particular kind of reality of which they speak. These statements assert no less than what has happened through Jesus Christ has brought so profound a transformation in the world that it is possible to say with Paul that the world has become wholly new, and that the old world has been brought to an end: 'The old has passed away, behold, the new has come' (II Cor. 5.17). But it is essential to understand that this is not meant to be taken in the sense of a cosmological dualism, for which, as for example in Hellenistic gnosticism, there are two worlds different in essence, which are in conflict, an evil world and a good world, a material world and another world of the spirit. Such an understanding would be in contradiction to the belief that the world is the creation of God. But this belief is held as strongly in the New Testament as in the Old.

It is true that to a large extent a dualistic pattern underlies the thought of the New Testament. Thus the God who is revealed in Christ is opposed by his enemy Satan as the God of this aeon (II Cor. 4.4), and the wisdom of this world is foolishness with God (I Cor. 3.19). The 'inner' man is opposed to the 'outer', who wastes away as the inner man is renewed from day to day (II Cor. 4.16). One can say of the thought of the Gospel of John that its background is entirely the dualistic pattern of light and darkness, truth and lie, life and death. But although these dualistic concepts, of which the New Testament, and Paul and John in particular, makes use, derive from the kind of thought that was widespread in the Hellenistic world, yet in the New Testament, almost without exception, they are not used in the cosmological sense which is theirs in their original setting. For in the New Testament they speak not of two worlds which of their nature are essentially different from each other: rather, they refer to one and the same world, which is good or evil depending upon how it is understood by the men who live in it. If it is understood as God's creation, then in it, in accordance with its created being, the invisible nature of God, his eternal power and deity, which calls nothingness into being, can be apprehended (Rom. 1.20; 4.17). In this case it is good. But if it is understood as a world, the nature of which is that it supports and maintains itself in existence, so that the creature is exchanged for the creator, and the honour and worship which belong to the creator alone is given to the creature, it is evil, and subject to ruin and futility (Rom. 8.20). For then it bars men who venerate and trust in it from access to God the creator.

The evil world is transformed into the good; the world complete in itself, and basing its claim to be the world on its own nature, is transformed into a world which offers to the creator all honour for its being what it is; the old world is transformed into the new. This transformation is possible only if a man experiences himself, in his very innermost being, as existing from God and not from the world. For it is only in this way that he is able to apprehend God as the creator, and the world as his creation. Thus in essence this change is not really a change in the world. What changes is rather the attitude of man to God; but his attitude to the world also changes thereby. Here it must be observed that it is possible to know of God, and yet to fail to give him due acknowledgement as God, because he is not honoured *as* God, and not thanked *as* God, so that the knowledge of him is not made evident (Rom. 1.21, 28). This is what Paul says of those who exchange the glory of the immortal God for the transitory creation, and have therefore fallen prey in their hearts to wickedness and have exchanged the truth about God for a lie, by serving the creature rather than the creator (Rom. 1.21ff.). A man honours God *as* God and thanks him *as* such only when he honours the eternal deity of God which calls nothingness into being, and believes in him as him whose work is to make the dead living and the ungodly righteous (Rom. 4.17; 4.5).

This transformation of the old world into the new, the setting free of the world from enslavement to wickedness and transitoriness, and its restoration as the untarnished creation of God, has come about in Jesus Christ – or, more precisely, in Jesus's attitude to God. But this is the same as to say that it has come about in the attitude of God to Jesus, the attitude through which Jesus lives his life. And here we repeat that it has come about through the power of this attitude, which is the attitude to Jesus of God whose eternal power is altogether lifegiving. Thus what happened in Jesus was brought about by the God through whom alone the world is the world, his creation. This transformation of the old world into the new is the meaning of the dominion over the world which God has given to Jesus, by giving him the name which is above every name, at which every knee should bow, in heaven and on earth and under the earth (Phil. 2.9f.). For neither this transformation of the world which has come about in Jesus, in and as a result of his relationship to God, nor the dominion over the world which is thereby given to him, are matters which concern Jesus alone as his private affair. They affect both him and the men who live in this world, and it is for the latter that they have been carried out.

The way in which this transformation is carried out by Jesus is expressed in the New Testament in the concept of the atoning sacrifice (e.g. Rom. 3.25f.), or in the closely linked ideas of the vicarious sacrifice (e.g. II Cor. 5.21), or the ransom (Gal. 3.13; 4.5). These and other similar expressions signify a representative liberation from the powers through which the world imprisons under its dominion the men who pay it religious veneration. All these expressions are not genuinely Christian, but are adapted from the religious language of the time. They derive from the pre-Christian sacrificial cult. Consequently, in their original meaning they are strange to us, and are therefore difficult or simply impossible for us to understand. In fact, they conceal rather than make clear to us the significance they had in the New Testament, when they were adapted to the event which took place in and through Jesus. We can perhaps best describe this significance as follows. As a result of what Jesus did, the old world was transformed for him into the new and in this transformation dominion over the new world was accorded to him. He thereby took responsibility upon himself for men, who by exchanging the creator for the creation had transformed God's creation into a world subject to wickedness and transitoriness. As their brother he took this responsibility upon himself, by accepting as one of them his part in the fearful sentence of doom that they had drawn upon themselves, and united himself to them not as a lord who seeks to be served, but as one who accepted lordship 'to serve, and to give his life as a ransom for many' (Matt. 20.28).

At this point it becomes clear why these christological statements which, in the form in which they are made in the New Testament, are concerned with the salvation and damnation of the whole world, never lose sight of the humanity of Jesus Christ and what happened to him as a human being. For we must interpret the way in which all the forms taken by the New Testament kerygma are penetrated by references to Jesus's human birth, his death on the cross and his passion and blood, in terms of this intimate connection between the man Jesus and other men. Only by being wholly and utterly equal with them can he take on himself responsibility, as he does, for men and for the world, as it has become through men's forgetfulness of God. And men in their turn can relate what came about in him and through him to themselves, as something done for them, only when they can acknowledge him as their equal. But this is only possible if they recognize as their own the fate which he took upon himself as *his* own in responsibility for them. This again can only happen if he, as Paul says (Gal. 4.4), is a man like them, born of a woman and subject to the law like them.

The rule of Jesus over the world, and the transformation which this brings about of the old world into the new is the most important factor in the reality which is the context of this event. It is not the cosmological reality in which, as for example in gnosticism, the world of *hyle*, matter, understood as having a substantial existence of its own, replaces the equally substantial world of *pneuma*, spirit. Rather, it is the reality of an event which has taken place in the relationship between a man, the man Jesus of Nazareth, and God. This relationship is not a metaphysical relationship between two natures, a human and a divine nature, but one which is exercised in the obedience of the man towards God. This obedience actually takes place between Jesus and God. For by Jesus's becoming 'obedient unto death, even death on a cross', his humanity was fulfilled (Phil 2.7f.). Thus Paul can sum up the redeeming work of Jesus Christ in the following sentence: 'By one man's obedience many will be made righteous' (Rom. 5.19). The Epistle to the Hebrews likewise describes this obedience as the sacrifice which Jesus, as the high priest installed by God, offered to him: 'In the days of his flesh, Jesus offered up prayers and supplications, with loud cries and tears, to him who was able to save him from death . . . although he was a Son, he learned obedience through what he suffered' (Heb. 5.4–8).

Jesus gave himself up in faith to the will of God and let this will be carried out in him (so we may more precisely describe the obedience that is described here). We can accordingly say of this event that it can only be apprehended in faith. What has taken place here in and through Jesus is only accessible to faith, and this explains the characteristically contradictory statements which the kerygma makes about how the reality of this transformation of the old world into the new is present for those who believe in it. It states of this reality both that it is present and also that it is in the future. We have already heard that Jesus achieved victory over the cosmic powers and had consequently broken their irresistible authority over men. In this sense salvation and the new life which it has brought about already exist in the present. Thus it is Christ, as the Epistle to the Colossians (1.13) says, who 'has delivered us from the dominion of darkness and transferred us to the kingdom of his beloved Son'. But, immediately before this statement, the Epistle to the Colossians speaks of this salvation as in the future by describing those who believe as those whom God 'has called to share in the inheritance of the saints in light' (Col. 1.12).

We can see how this is to be understood by looking at the statements in the opening verses of the third chapter of this epistle. Here believers are exhorted not to set their minds on things on earth, but, as those who have been raised with Christ, to

> seek the things that are above, where Christ is, seated at the right hand of God. . . . For you have died, and your life is hid with Christ in God. When Christ who is our life appears, then you also will appear with him in glory. Put to death therefore what is earthly in you (Col. 3.1–5).

This makes the contradiction quite clear. Salvation is described on the one hand as present, and on the other hand – and, as it were, in the same breath – as future. But this passage also makes still clearer the specific character of the reality in which salvation takes place. Those who believe are addressed here as those who 'have been raised with Christ'. This they are in so far as they are no longer citizens of the old world – as such they are 'dead' – for, as has been said previously, they have been 'delivered from the dominion of darkness and transferred to the kingdom of his beloved Son'. But at the same time they are exhorted to set their minds no longer on 'things that are on earth'. The verses that follow explain what this means, by using two 'catalogues of vices' to describe what believers are to do for their part. These catalogues of vices must be understood as schematic: their principal purpose is to list what were traditionally described in missionary preaching as the characteristic gentile sins. They are used to refer to a mode of thought and endeavour which is opposed to that which is required in the beginning of the passage: 'Seek the things that are above, where Christ is.'

Thus with regard to the reality of the salvation brought about by Jesus, it finally becomes clear from these apparently contradictory statements, that salvation is present, while still in the future, that this reality is of the same kind as that which took place in what happened between God and Jesus. We can perhaps begin by saying that in this reality salvation is something already brought about by Jesus in his relationship to God, and that of God to him, and that it has thereby become a possibility for men and for their world. For, as we have already seen, it is for men that what took place between God and Jesus was intended. When we speak here of a 'possibility', we must note that the salvation realized by Jesus Christ is in no sense automatically imparted to the men for whom it has been brought into being. Certainly the possibility exists of their partaking in it. For it has been brought about by his submitting himself for them, and indeed for everyone, to the sentence of doom which loomed over them all. Yet only if they apprehend it does it exist for them as the reality which it is 'above, where Christ is, seated at the right hand of God' (Col. 3.1). That Christ sits at the right hand of God means that in the name and in the eternal life-giving power of God he exercises dominion over the world, a dominion in which the old world is transformed for him into the new. Thus the way in which the salvation brought into being by Jesus is a reality makes intelligible what at first sight seemed so strange: the statement, constantly repeated in the New Testament, that salvation, as it has been realized by Jesus Christ, is both already present and also still in the future. That is why it can be said of those who believe that their new life is 'hid with Christ in God', and therefore 'not to be sought on earth', but is nevertheless present and real – for they are addressed as those who 'have been raised with Christ'. Yet it is also true of them that they live upon earth, and that although they have been set free from enslavement to the powers of the world, they still have to fight against them and must, therefore, be exhorted not to set their minds upon 'things that are on earth'. Or, as Paul says very pointedly in the Epistle to the Philippians, he whom Christ Jesus has made his own, now presses on 'to make it my own' (3.12).

All this makes it clear that the reality of salvation is not the same as a natural reality. Just as salvation through Jesus is realized in the decision which he made to take on responsibility for men, so it can be apprehended by the men for whom he realized it only in a responsible decision. For as long as man lives upon earth, there always exists for him besides this salvation the other possibility, that he should seek that which belongs to this earth, and so fall prey once again to the powers which Jesus has conquered. Consequently, this salvation is not something received once for all, but must always be apprehended in a renewed decision. A frequent and astonishingly obstinate misunderstanding of this is to suppose that this participation is only possible from time to time, and that in fact salvation is only present in such a reality experienced from time to time. This is not so. Rather, it means that this participation is rather like loyalty, which is not something present once for all, unless it is confused with mere familiarity. If loyalty is genuine, it too requires a constantly renewed decision.

NOTES

1. Bultmann, *Die Theologie des Neuen Testaments*, p. 43; tr. p. 42.
2. Op. cit., p. 8; tr. p. 8.
3. p. 43; tr. p. 43.

7

THE HISTORICAL BASIS OF NEW TESTAMENT CHRISTOLOGY

WE HAVE tried to find out, from an examination of New Testament christology, whether the basis of the primitive Christian kerygma is the personal history of Jesus, in the sense of the visible features of his individual personality, and his preaching as understood in relation to his personality, or whether this basis is to be sought in what happened to the world through Jesus. The first view is widespread and more or less taken for granted at the present day not only in theology, but probably even more in the preaching of the church. It is the inevitable view once Jesus is seen as concerned above all with the salvation of the souls and the bodily well-being (the healing of the sick) of individual human beings who encounter him. This view has been held almost universally since the days of pietism. The salvation brought about by Jesus is necessarily always sought in his personality and in its distinctive individual features. The real content of the kerygma is not the portrait of this historical personality, and therefore it cannot appear in these circumstances as anything other than empty. We have seen, however, that the event which the primitive Christian kerygma proclaims is concerned in the first instance with the salvation of the world. This, moreover, is true not only of the form of the kerygma which we find in the epistles of the New Testament, but also in that which is handed down to us in the synoptic gospels. Thus we can sum up what we have learned about the christology of the New Testament kerygma as follows: The dominion of Jesus Christ over the world, and the transformation of the old world into the new which is brought about by him through this dominion, in which the world is reconstituted as the creation of God and thereby saved, is the eschatological event which came about through Jesus's coming into the world, and this event consequently contains everything which is said of Jesus in the New Testament kerygma.

The question which we must now ask is whether this event is historical. If this appears to be so, we would then have to ask what kind of event this history is. We have already posed this question indirectly in trying to find out the kind of reality which is the context of this event, and we saw that this reality is not of such a kind that in it two different and substantially existent worlds can be exchanged for each other. This negative answer, that the reality in which this transformation of the old world into the new was carried out by Jesus Christ was not in any sense a natural reality, corresponds to the positive statement that it is a reality of history. What this means has already been made clear in what we said about participation in this event. This is something that is not accorded automatically to man; he can only partake of it through a decision which must be constantly renewed. This is so because even the believer still lives 'in the world', for he is not taken out of the world once for all by faith. Nor may he leave the world (I Cor. 5.10); rather, 'everyone should remain in the state in which he was called' (I Cor. 7.20). We understand the whole force of what this signifies when we realize that the world in which the believer lives is *one*, which is capable of being both the 'old' and the 'new' world. Because this is so, there is an unceasing threat of 'to live in the world' becoming 'to live by the world'. But if man does not live only 'in' the world, but also 'by' it, that is, if he places his trust in it and makes the things of the world (Rom. 8.5; I Cor. 7.33) his most important concern, then it is the 'old' world. In such a trust and concern the powers of the world win back the authority which they had over men before they believed. Thus it is historical man who partakes in this transformation of the old world into the new, which was realized by Jesus through his attaining dominion over the world by the conquest of the cosmic powers. Historical man means here man who does not live above or outside the world, but lives a historical life within it, never free from the necessity of decision. He is consequently retained by faith in the world, that is, in the 'calling' (the better translation is 'situation' or 'state of life', e.g. – as Paul has in mind here – that of a circumcised person or a slave') in which God has called him, so that 'there he may remain with God' (I Cor. 7.24).

But we must now go on to answer the question of the historicity of the transformation brought about by Jesus of the old world into the new. We have already said that the ideas and concepts in which the New Testament writers describe this are borrowed from the cosmological dualism which was widespread in the Hellenistic world. But in the way in which they are used in the New Testament, they no longer describe two worlds which are substantially different from one another, but one and the same world, which is the creation of God. While men no longer recognize this world as the creation of God, it is deprived of the creative power of God, and as such a world, it is now left to its own devices and falls prey, in spite of all the might within it and indeed because of this, to 'futility and decay' (Rom. 8.20f.). Again, with irresistible force, it entangles in this catastrophe the men who live in it, because they have not 'maintained' the knowledge of God which they had (Rom. 1.18ff.), so that they have placed the trust which was due to the creator in his creation. The sentence of doom upon this monstrous perversion, which has been passed in this way upon man and his world, can only be averted if its cause is removed. But this cause is not a concrete catastrophe, however it may be conceived, but nothing other than that which Paul expresses by saying that men by their wickedness have suppressed the truth (Rom. 1.18), by exchanging the truth about God for a lie (their religious veneration of the world) (Rom. 1.25). This exchange cannot be undone except by the truth of God itself. But it is the very truth of God, which with the 'eternal power and deity' of God (Rom. 1.20) has allowed the lie for which men have exchanged God's truth to become powerful over them, so that they can no longer escape from it. The only way this sentence of doom can be averted is for someone who like other men lives under this sentence of doom to succeed in bringing the lie to light as such in himself, that is, in the fate that came on him in his own life. He can only do so by allowing the sentence of doom which is passed inescapably upon the lie to be fulfilled in himself to the bitter end. And this is the only way in which the world can once again be revealed as God's creation.

The primitive Christian kerygma proclaims that this has

happened in Jesus Christ. Paul has found the most powerful expression for this when he says that Christ has 'become a curse for us' (Gal. 3.13). This curse is the sentence of doom which has been imposed upon the whole world as a result of the perversion of truth into the lie, and which is concentrated in Christ into a single figure which now stands for everything that is subject to this perversion. Paul says the same elsewhere, when he states that God 'for our sake made Christ to be sin' (II Cor. 5.21). Here one must remember that for Paul sin is not in the first instance something done by man. For him sin is more than anything else the fateful power which has come into being through the ominous confusion of creator and creature, and which together with the powers of the law and death brings ruin over men and their whole world, so that they cannot escape it. So when Paul says that Christ has been made sin for us, he means that the sin which rules over all of us to our ruin has hurled itself in the form of this power upon this one person, so that he has become, as it were, the very embodiment of this sin. He says the same in Rom. 8.3.: 'God sent his own Son in the likeness of sinful men.' All the statements of the New Testament kerygma which tell that Christ died for our sins (I Cor. 15.3), that he himself carried up our sins in his body to the tree (of the cross) (I Peter 2.24), that he suffered for our sins (I Peter 3.18), that he is the lamb of God, that he bore the sins of the world (John 1.29), and many other expressions, all repeat again and again the same statements, that the whole life and being of Jesus, his purpose and his endeavour, is determined by this sentence of doom which prevails throughout the world. It lies upon him, who was 'born of woman, born under the law' (Gal. 4.4), as it has lain on no one else amongst those born of women. For it lies upon him *for* the others. The meaning of this 'for', which refers to his representative capacity, carries the sense of a responsibility for everyone, for the whole world. To take on responsibility for another means to take the other's place. If this person is someone who is guilty, then it means to take responsibility for his guilt. This again means to take the guilt of the other and the sentence which follows from it upon oneself as one's own, as though one had deserved it oneself.

If we attempt to make what Jesus has done for the world

intelligible with the aid of the concept of the responsibility with which he has taken the guilt and the pain of man upon himself as his own, then it is of decisive importance to be clear what this responsibility means, in the sense in which it is taken on not only *for* someone, but also *in the sight of* someone. For only when someone is there to whom one has to give an account of one's responsibility, is it a true and full responsibility. And only when we ask to whom Jesus must give an account of his responsibility do we perceive what it was that made Jesus able, according to the primitive Christian kerygma, to take the responsibility for the world upon himself, and where he received the power to bear this responsibility. Just as the primitive Christian church took for granted that he who took this responsibility upon himself was a real, true man, it was equally certain that what came about in this man Jesus of Nazareth, and through him, was done by God. It was God who 'sent' him into the world (John 3.17; Rom. 8.3; Gal. 4.4) and by whom he was 'given up' (John 3.16; Rom. 3.25; 8.32). But the primitive Christian church was equally certain that what God did in and through Jesus did not take place without Jesus's own will. Just as Paul says of Jesus that he was given up by God, he can likewise say – and here is speaking of the same event – that Jesus 'gave himself for our sins to deliver us from the present evil age' (Gal. 1.4; 2.20). Or, as we read in the Epistle to the Ephesians, 'he gave himself up for us, a fragrant offering and sacrifice to God' (5.2), or in the Epistle to the Hebrews: he 'offered himself' (9.14). And in many other passages, the same thing is said in a similar way. These statements are not alternatives, that it is God or Jesus who acts, but both are true and equivalent.

In the previous chapter we referred to the fact that Paul can sum up the whole redeeming work of Jesus in the statement: 'By one man's obedience many will remain righteous' (Rom. 5.19). Of course this obedience must be understood in accordance with what happens through it. For what happens through it is not anything which can be done in general by men in the world. This obedience brings about a transformation which takes in the totality of the world: the 'old world' becomes the 'new'. Whether the world is the 'old' world, that is, the world which is subject to futility and decay, which for those who live in it still remains the world, and which therefore draws men with irresistible force into the doom which prevails within it; or whether it is the 'new' world, God's creation, in which men have freedom for God as his sons and therefore receive their life from his life-creating deity (Rom. 8.21) – whether the world is one or the other, the world of death or of life, of truth or of the lie, depends not upon any situation which originates within itself, but simply and solely upon whether someone who lives in it lives by the world or lives by God. But a person can only live *in* the world, but not *by* it, if while living in it and knowing that he is responsible for it, he lives by responsibility in the sight of God. With this responsibility his existence is nothing other than a full and unqualified answer to the call of God, in which God calls into existence things that do not exist (Rom. 4.17), so that in this way this man can 'reflect the glory of God and bear the very stamp of his nature', as the Epistle to the Hebrews says of Jesus (1.3). Thus if we say that the transformation of the old world to the new takes place in the obedience of Jesus, in which he takes upon himself responsibility for the world in responsibility *in the sight of God*, then at the same time we are saying that Jesus carried out what he did through the eternal creative power of God. For only through this can the world be the creation of God.

We believe that all this is no more than Jesus says of himself in the Gospel according to John, like a refrain running through the whole gospel. He says that he did not come 'of himself', but that God sent him. 'Truly, truly, I say to you, the Son can do nothing of his own accord' (5.19, 30; 8.28). He does not speak of his own authority; the Father who sent him has given him commandment what to say and what to speak. He knows that the Father's commandment is eternal life (12.49). 'The words that I say to you I do not speak on my own authority, but the Father who dwells in me does his works' (14.10). The 'works' referred to here are not so much the individual acts which the evangelist narrates of Jesus, but the one work in which he fulfils his mission from God. This constant repetition of 'not from himself' has not only a negative, but above all an extraordinarily positive sense. One can perhaps express this best by saying that Jesus possesses the whole existence which God has given him in being sent by God. This is already evident in the fact that in this gospel the name of God is 'the Father who sent me', so that one can say of Jesus, as he appears in the Gospel of John, that his being consists of his being sent by God. Consequently, it is said of him, 'My food is to do the will of him who sent me, and to accomplish his work' (4.34).

As far as the historical character of this event is concerned, one must of course say that it is not historical in the sense of a 'factual historicity' which can be affirmed on the basis of some kind of documentary evidence. For if, as we have attempted to show, the saving event proclaimed by the primitive Christian kerygma is something which has taken place between Jesus Christ and God, there simply cannot exist any documentary account which would be capable as such of providing a reliable testimony to it. We have already seen that we can sum up what took place between Jesus and God by saying that it took place in Jesus's obedience towards God. But there cannot be a single eye-witness to confirm that Jesus truly acted obediently towards God, and indeed with such an obedience that through it alone the work of transforming the old world into the new was possible. This follows from the very nature of such an event. Here only faith can bear witness and, moreover, only such a faith as can make possible for the believer's faith an obedience which is in accordance with that exercised by Jesus, and for the sake of which Jesus himself exercised his obedience. The obedience through which Jesus was able to bring about this change and avert the sentence of doom through which God's creation is perverted into a world subject to futility and ruin, is of such a nature that in it Jesus could take upon himself, by the power of God, a responsibility for the whole world, and so could accept for himself the fate of the world. In the words of the New Testament, he became a curse for us, and died for our sins. There is no question that all this is not an event which takes place visibly and demonstrably like the historical events with which the historian deals, and for which there would, therefore, be appropriate documentation by eye-witnesses, by means of which one could have an historically reliable knowledge of this event. Rather, the event which was proclaimed by the primitive kerygma takes place in the obscurity of faith, in which it is accessible only to faith, and from which it is not possible in any way for it to emerge.

But as we have seen, many theologians are of the opinion that the kerygma would remain empty and would be nothing more than a myth, if it did not possess some degree of 'factual historicity' which could be confirmed by the documentary evidence of eye-witnesses, and 'traced back to history which has taken place as a matter of fact'.[1] According to this view, it is necessary to 'trace it back to history which has taken place as a matter of fact', because faith is only possible through 'such historical traces left by revelation' or 'signs', which are 'the forms which revelation imposes upon history' and which it 'draws up into the event of salvation', and the historical knowledge of which 'is accessible even to unbelievers'.[2] Two things are here distinguished in the kerygma, though at the same time it is said of them that they are associated with one another 'in an inseparable unity'. On the one hand there is 'the account of an event which happened in human history at a time and place which can be determined', while on the other hand there is 'the indicative and cohortative testimony of the significance of this event for salvation and judgement'. It is considered that in this way 'the kerygma of the apostles and the church always contains an historical content as well'.[3] In the word of preaching which can be believed on the basis of this historical event, the historical content of the kerygma then takes on 'a reality which affects us'.[4]

This understanding of the event which is proclaimed by the kerygma, and which forms its basis, is clearly quite different from our own. We believe that this event must be understood exclusively as one which took place in the obedience of Jesus between him and God. We have already said that of its nature, this event cannot be made visible in historical terms. It is accessible to faith alone. If one sought to draw from this the conclusion that this event was not historical, this would mean that one did not take the humanity of Jesus seriously, that is, as that in which God reveals himself as he who acts historically with men. Consequently, the historicity of this event lies in the fact that it took place between the man Jesus of Nazareth and God, and that what took place here was carried out in the responsibility of this man for the world and the men in it. Since this event occurred in the life of a human being who as such lives in the world, it naturally follows that it also takes place in the form of visible happenings, and that in this life things happen in which this event is concentrated in a particular way, as its decisive turning points, as is the case in particular with the crucifixion and resurrection of Jesus. This explains why the New Testament kerygma, particularly in the form which it takes in the theology of the apostle Paul, is concentrated upon these two events. But it would be false if this were taken to mean that it was these events in themselves, as they took place as a matter of 'factual historicity', which form the true event of salvation. One would then have to say that the apostolic kerygma 'derived its origin' from them as from historically ascertainable facts. This is asserted by Althaus and many other theologians. But if these happenings form part of the event which, in our view, is the content of the kerygma, then they, too, must be understood in terms of this event. That is, what took place in them in accordance with their proper historical meaning is in fact the event of Jesus's obedience towards God, and nothing else. The latter is taken here, of course, in the full sense in which we have tried to understand it.

As far as Jesus's death on the cross is concerned, this means the following. In the language of the New Testament, Jesus suffered death on the cross for our sins. Thus for example Paul says that God gave Christ Jesus to the world as an 'expiation by his blood', or, as one may also translate it, as one who expiated by his blood, as a result of which sin was forgiven (Rom. 3.25). The background of this statement is the concept of sacrifice, through which the sins of those for whom it is offered are expiated. Here, however, the concept of sacrifice which underlies the sacrificial cult is essentially abolished. For the cultic sacrifice is offered by man to God in order to placate him. But here it is God who offers Jesus, and in such a way that Jesus sacrifices himself in the fulfilment of God's will. But the intention of the will of God here is not that in his hostility towards sinful men he should be placated by them, but that men should be reconciled with him and cease from their hostility towards him, which Paul expresses by saying: 'God, who through Christ reconciled us to himself' (II Cor. 5.18). The Epistle to the Hebrews shows very clearly how inadequate the concept of sacrifice is for what the New Testament tries to express through it. There the intention is to express the significance of that which took place on the cross within the framework of the concept of sacrifice. The only sacrifice which is in any way comparable with that of Jesus on the cross is that which Abraham set out to make with his son Isaac. For in order to do this Abraham had to exercise obedience to the point of sacrificing himself, the father of Isaac, and not only himself as Isaac's father but, much more, himself as him for whom Isaac had become the fulfilment of what God had promised him with regard to the whole world. This sacrifice is similar to that which God demands of Jesus, in so far as it could only be offered if Abraham were ready for an obedience which comprehended his whole existence, as he had received it in the promise of God. But it was dissimilar in so far as the obedience which led to the sacrifice that Jesus offers did not remain, as in the case of Abraham, at the point of readiness, but had to be exercised to the point of the death of him who sacrificed himself.

In order to be able to make intelligible what happened to the world and the men in it through Jesus, we introduced the concept of responsibility, in which Jesus took upon himself the fate of the world. Accordingly, we can say of that which took place on the cross that, as a consequence of this responsibility, Jesus finally came under the power of the futility to which the world is subject as a sentence of doom which can neither be remitted nor escaped. The reason for this punishment is the sin of man. And this sin is the exchanging of the creator for the creation, of which Paul speaks in the first chapter of the Epistle to the Romans. In this exchange the truth of God is suppressed by the wickedness of men (Rom. 1.18) through which they pay to the creation, that is, to the world, the religious veneration which is due to the creator. We speak here of a sentence of doom, in order to show that for those who come under the consequences of this exchange, it is impossible either to reverse them, or to recognize them. Paul expresses this when he says that under the power of sin men have exchanged the truth of God for a lie. This lie is that the creation is the creator (Rom. 1.25). Anyone who exchanges truth for a lie in this way does so in the belief that in the lie he has the truth, and so long as he regards the lie as the truth, he cannot recognize it as a lie and therefore cannot reverse the exchange which he has made. Where anything like this happens, doom hangs over him with irresistible force.

By taking on himself the fate of the world in responsibility for it, Jesus subjects himself to the sentence of doom which hangs over the world. On the cross, this doom comes upon him. But in being carried out upon him, it is also carried out upon the world, which has brought him to the cross. In each case, however, this takes place in a quite different way. In the first instance, the difference between the two is that the attitude of both to this sentence of doom is fundamentally different. The world and the men in it, upon whom it comes through Jesus's death on the cross, which they have brought about, do not know that they are doing what they do under the power of a sentence of doom which governs them. They are likewise ignorant of what they are doing, that is, carrying out this sentence of doom upon him whom they crucify. But Jesus, by taking upon himself this sentence of doom in responsibility for those upon whom it has been imposed, sees through the exchange of truth for the lie, in which it originates, from which it derives its power, and through which it dominates men, so that he lets it come upon him in full knowledge of the fact.

When the kerygma proclaims that Jesus suffered death upon the cross for our sins, 'for' here does not only mean that the sentence of doom which originates in sin is being fulfilled both in Jesus and in the world. It does of course mean this. Indeed, this is why the cross is the sign of the curse which Jesus has become for us (Gal. 3.13). One cannot be too profoundly aware of what this means, for the power of the evil which here comes over Jesus, and over the world, is the measure of the obedience that Jesus must exercise in taking this evil upon himself in responsibility to the world. What this means can only be understood on the basis of the force and power of the sin in which the evil which is revealed upon the cross originates. We followed Paul in describing sin as the exchanging of truth for a lie (Rom. 1.25). If we translate according to the sense, this is the exchanging of the God who is truly God for one who is not truly God. The God who is truly God, according to Paul, is the God who bears witness to himself as such by being he who 'gives life to the dead and calls into existence the things that do not exist' (Rom. 4.17). But the God who is not truly God is the creation, that is to say the world, to which men pay the veneration which is due to the creator alone by placing their trust in it and by living not only in it but by it. By making this exchange they actually withhold from God his deity, that is, his status as creator, and at the same time deny the world its creatureliness, in which alone it can be what it is in truth, the creation of God. The consequence is the most horrible perversion imaginable, the perversion into nothingness of the being to which God the creator has called what does not exist. What God has called into being is now all that it still can be without God and left to itself, that is, nothingness closed in upon itself. Men are thrown back upon their own wisdom, which is nothing other than the world closed in upon itself, and they are now all that they can be when they are deprived of the life-giving deity of this God. That is, they are dominated by death; their only remaining destiny can be death, and this is so. Consequently the word of God which calls them to life and which alone gives life that lives for the sake of life, has become the curse which delivers over to death what belongs to death. This is the uttermost profundity of evil, and in it Jesus sacrifices himself by taking on himself the fate of the world and responsibility for it. In responsibility for a world which has become meaningless, he experiences as his own the futility of the world, and the fate of men who are entangled in this futility. Because he undergoes this knowingly, he undergoes more profoundly than it can be experienced by any man, the sentence of doom which is imposed along with this futility upon the men who live in the world. For men, entangled in this sentence of doom, are able neither to recognize it nor to avert it. And this Jesus does in obedience.

For Jesus to do this in obedience means that he knows that, in his responsibility *in the sight of God*, he is responsible for the world. What does it mean for him to know that he is responsible in the sight of God, in the obedience in which he takes upon himself responsibility for the world? If this obedience is not understood in a moral sense, but in the sense which we have already tried to make clear, as an obedience which affects the very being of man, then it signifies that in the wickedness which comes from the world and envelops him as one who shares in the fate of the world, Jesus experiences the God who calls into existence the things that do not exist. When we say this, we are referring to the resurrection of Jesus – and in fact this is the only way in which one can speak properly of it. That is, we are speaking of it in its intimate connection with what took place on the cross. For it is only in relation to the cross that one can properly understand what took place in the resurrection. One is not yet speaking of what took place on the cross as faith acknowledges it and knows of it if one speaks only of the bodily death of Jesus and the temporal end of his life. In the same way, one is not yet speaking of his resurrection as faith believes in it, when one says only that in it someone who was dead in the body once again came to life. What Jesus underwent on the cross is, as we have tried to show, infinitely more than merely his bodily death. If he died for our sins, as the primitive Christian kerygma asserts, then what overtakes him in this death is not merely human mortality in general, not merely death as a natural fact or as an untimely end to his earthly life, but death itself, which is deprived of its power as the 'last enemy' when Christ 'destroys every rule and every authority and power (which the world exercises over men when it is the object of religious veneration)' (I Cor. 15.24f.). This death is the futility, the condemnation (Rom. 5.18) which as a consequence of sin prevails over all life and death with inescapable force. But as a result of Jesus giving himself up in obedience to this futility, it is no longer the futility of the world which asserts itself against God and tries to be the world without his 'eternal power and deity'. Just as surely as the eternal will of God is mighty in the obedience of Jesus and in the responsibility with which he takes this futility upon himself, so with equal certainty this futility becomes that which does not exist, but which God calls into existence, and the Crucified, who was crucified for us and became sin (Gal. 3.13 and II Cor. 5.21), becomes the 'first born from the dead' (Col. 1.18), to whom God 'gives life' (Rom. 4.17). What happens here is expressed in the Epistle to the Ephesians in the language of a hymn: God has made known

> the immeasurable greatness of his power in us who believe, according to the working of his great might which he accomplished in Christ when he raised him from the dead and made him sit at his right hand in the heavenly places, far above all rule and authority and power and dominion, and above every name that is named, not only in this age but also in that which

is to come; and he has put all things under his feet and has made him the head over all things for the Church, which is his body, the fullness of him who fills all in all (Eph. 1.19–23).

NOTES

1. Althaus, op. cit., pp. 32, 33.
2. p. 19.
3. p. 16.
4. p. 28.

8

FAITH IN THE PRIMITIVE CHRISTIAN KERYGMA

IT WAS THE question of the historical basis of the primitive Christian kerygma which led us to consider the christology of the New Testament. In order to answer this question, we sought to obtain a clear understanding of the historical event of the so-called act of salvation, in particular the crucifixion and resurrection of Jesus. We said that what happens in these two events, upon which the primitive Christian kerygma concentrates, is historical in so far as it takes place in the obedience of the one man Jesus of Nazareth, who in this obedience takes responsibility for the world upon himself, and in carrying out this responsibility receives dominion over this world. But we have so far left open the question of how the news of this event comes to the men for whom it all happened, and how this news can be believed by them. Present-day theology tries to answer this question in two different ways, though in both cases the conviction is that this event is historical. The difference between the two answers is that the first, which we have already discussed in another context, proceeds from an event which can be confirmed in its 'factual historicity', an event in which, it is believed, the apostolic kerygma has its origin and basis.[1] The second of these two answers – which is the one which we shall attempt to give here – proceeds from a different kind of event. We assert that while it cannot be 'confirmed by historical research', it is nevertheless historical, in such a way that to demonstrate its historicity is one of the most important tasks which theology has to fulfil at the present day.

According to the first of these two answers, the account both of the history of Jesus's life, and also of the most important events in it, has come to us through the apostles, on the basis of their 'historical closeness and connection to the history of Jesus'. It is considered possible subsequently to confirm what happened by the aid of the historical study of the testimony of the apostles. In this sense this 'historical closeness and connection', which refers principally to the position of the apostles as eye-witnesses, is regarded as providing the 'specific authority' of the apostolic preaching. In other words, this authority 'depends upon the "authenticity" of the apostolic witness, that is, upon the historical threads which go back to the *witnesses* of the history of Jesus, including the resurrection'.[2] But this statement, that the authority of the apostolic witness 'depends upon its "authenticity"', has an ambiguous meaning to which we must draw attention for it has important consequences for everything that follows.

From the context in which this statement is made, it necessarily follows that the authority which 'depends' on the 'authenticity' of the apostolic testimony is limited to what is accessible to the 'closeness and connection' which is explicitly described as 'historical'. At best, such a 'historical closeness' can only impart 'knowledge about a factual historical event', such as the crucifixion of Jesus. But such knowledge, as we are explicitly assured, is not 'of itself a certainty concerning the event of salvation in the cross of Christ'. Rather, this latter certainty is a matter of faith. But factual historical knowledge is not faith; as is rightly said, it is the outcome of 'retrospective historical study and reflection, which is something other than the act of faith'.[3] This means, then, that it can have no bearing on anything other than the pure fact that a man called Jesus of Nazareth was crucified, and that after the death of this man a congregation was formed which believed in him as the Messiah, whom God had raised from the dead. Neither the 'historical closeness' of the apostles to these events, nor retrospective historical knowledge tracing its way back to them, can produce any certainty about whether and in what way this man really showed himself by his death on the cross and by his resurrection from the dead to be the Christ. For knowledge of this kind is by common consent the result of 'a historical exercise'.[4] But such an exercise cannot show, with regard to the events which it may be able to confirm took place as a matter of historical fact, that God either did or did not reveal himself in Christ.

Thus the authority of the apostolic witness, which derives from the 'historical closeness' of the apostles to the history of Jesus is limited to matters of bare historical fact within this history. It is remarkable how this authority is tacitly claimed for the whole extent of the apostolic preaching, that is, not only in respect of 'the question of the historicity of its factual content', but also in respect of its 'testimony to the significance as salvation and judgement' of the event which is narrated. To some extent, the psychological reasons why this is done are comprehensible, when one considers the fundamental importance which is accorded to the 'purely historical event' in this theory. This significance is manifest when events which are a matter of purely factual history are constantly referred to as the 'genuine history' or as the 'history that really happened'.[5] According to this theory what happened as a matter of ascertainable historical fact is the 'basis' and 'origin' of the kerygma.[6] It is consequently also held that 'historical inquiry into the factual historical basis of the kerygma seems to be imperative'.[7] Without this the kerygma would become 'empty' and would lose the 'authentication' which is necessary to it.[8] Likewise, it is said of faith that its 'basis' is 'the kerygma as it is traced back retrospectively to the history which took place as a matter of ascertainable fact, and to this extent, therefore, is this body of ascertainable fact itself'.[9] Finally, we even read that it is the 'worldly reality of ascertainable facts' which 'bears the event of salvation'.[10] In order to understand this, one must bear in mind the exclusive and decisive significance accorded here to the ascertainable factual nature of this historical event, and one must also remember that underlying this theory there is a concern to prove that what is proclaimed by the kerygma of the primitive church is not a myth[11] but a real historical event. The prevailing opinion, moreover, is that such a proof is only possible if the factual historicity of this event can be scientifically assured. If all this is borne in mind, then it is comprehensible at least in a psychological sense that the authority of the apostolic witness, which it possesses from the apostles' 'historical closeness and connection to the history of Jesus', with regard to any particular historical narrative, is summarily claimed for everything else to which it sets out to bear witness. The underlying idea, which of course is never uttered, is perhaps this: if the apostolic testimony possesses authority with regard to the events which it narrates, then one can also rely on this authority with regard to its statements about the event of salvation. One need scarcely say that this conclusion is invalid. Since only faith is able to apprehend the event of salvation, so an authoritative testimony to the latter can only have the authority which comes to it from faith. This, in its turn, means that this authority can be accorded to faith only on the basis of this event as the event of salvation. Thus regardless of what authority the kerygma may possess on the basis of its purely historical content, on which, it is suggested, everything else must be based, this cannot possibly be the authority which the kerygma must have for faith. It can only have such authority as a testimony to the events of *salvation*.

Thus when this theory ultimately comes to the question of how faith is possible in 'God's action as such in what has happened as historical fact', then the only answer it can give apart from very incidental references to the 'conscience'[12] and 'the miracle of the Holy Spirit',[13] is: 'Here one must believe, here the question whether this proclamation (i.e. of the 'saving significance' of this event) is valid is unbelief in itself'.[14] And in so far as the kerygma is intended to be 'a witness to the significance as salvation and judgment' of what has happened as a matter of factual history, it can be so only 'in the indicative and cohortative'.[15] Does this mean anything more than 'in the assertion that this is the case, and in the exhortation to believe what is asserted'?

This is one of the two answers to the question of how the account of what happened, which is the basis of the kerygma and the faith, comes to the men for whom this event took place, and how this account can be believed.

We shall now try to give another answer to this question. We shall proceed, as we have said, not as in the first answer from an event which can be ascertained in its 'factual historicity', but from an event which by its very nature takes place between Jesus and God in a way which is not historically ascertainable.

In the previous chapter we have already tried to clarify the nature of this event by looking at what the primitive Christian kerygma claims to have happened in the two incidents which it sees as the central events, and therefore as those which provide the basis of faith – the cross and the resurrection of Jesus. We have taken the ideas and concepts which are used in the New Testament to make this event intelligible, and have tried to transpose them into another set of concepts which are closer to our modern thought. We have to do this, first because it can be clearly seen from the way these concepts are used in the New Testament that in their original, cultic sense they do not provide in the New Testament an adequate expression for what they are intended to denote, and that consequently, in the way they have been used in the New Testament, they have already been 'demythologized', as we would say today.[16] The other reason why we must attempt to translate these concepts is that for us at the present day, without a study of comparative religion in some profundity, they are completely unintelligible.

In our attempt to carry out the task of translation, through which we hope to render this event intelligible to ourselves, the following concepts are available to us: obedience, responsibility, fate, the exchanging of the creator for the creation, doom, futility, and faith in the God who calls into existence the things that do not exist. The most important of these concepts is that of faith, for all others derive from it the particular meaning which they have in the context we are to discuss here. This is faith in the God who calls into existence the things that do not exist. We understand this faith, and the God in which it believes, in the same way as Paul, when he speaks (Rom. 4.1ff.) in these terms of faith and of the God of this faith. Paul is concerned here to make intelligible the faith through which, as he has already stated (3.28), man is justified before God. In order to do this, Paul points to Abraham, whom he regards as the father of all those who in this way achieve righteousness before God, regardless of whether or not they possess the 'law' which was seen by the Jews as the sole way to righteousness (Rom. 4.9–14).

For 'Abraham believed God, and it was reckoned to him as righteousness'. And in fact this happened 'before he was circumcised', that is, before he had fulfilled the 'law' (Rom. 4.3, 11). Thus Paul contrasts Abraham, as one who had faith in God, with 'one who works' and whose wages are not reckoned 'as a gift', but receives them 'as his due' for what he has achieved. 'And to one who does not work, but trusts him who justifies the ungodly, his faith is reckoned as righteousness' (Rom. 4.4f.).

It seems to me to be perfectly clear that what Paul is seeking to express here and in other passages by means of the concepts of 'righteousness' and 'justification' is precisely what we would express in the phrase 'to suit someone', or, in what I regard as more formal language, 'to behave to someone in accordance with their nature'. If I 'suit someone' or 'behave to him in accordance with his nature', then my behaviour towards him is wholly determined by him and his nature, and I allow him to be towards me and treat him as the person who he is by nature.

Now Paul says that God's nature is that he is he 'who gives life to the dead and calls into existence the things that do not exist'. This means that in accordance with his divine nature God shows himself as God only to someone whose attitude towards him is not determined by what he has achieved, and who therefore does not believe, like 'one who works' that he can make a claim upon God on the basis of some achievement required by the 'law', and of what he has become through this achievement. If one adopts this attitude towards God, then one simply does not 'suit' him at all; one is not in accordance with him as the God that he is by the fact that he calls into existence the things that do not exist, and brings to life those who in themselves, even in spite of the best and greatest works which they achieve in accordance with the law, are dead. For this is not to trust that God is capable of this, and to fail for some reason to accept that, before God, one can only be someone who without any qualifications relies on his life-giving deity and upon his grace. Thus the only person who can 'suit' God is one who acknowledges and is, therefore, able to profess that with all that he is and has and is ever able to be and have, he is nothing before God, but yet in this very nothingness puts his trust in God, and relies on God to show himself, in his human futility and in this alone, as he really is. When a person believes in God in this way, that is in complete reliance upon him, he truly acknowledges him *as* God, and so thanks and serves him *as* the God who he really is, and giving him the honour which is due to him as the creator, letting him be who he really is and therefore really honouring him as God.

Thus of all the concepts which we use to make intelligible to ourselves the event which is the basis of the primitive Christian kerygma, it is this faith in God who calls into existence the things that do not exist, which gives meaning to the others, and

Faith in the Primitive Christian Kerygma

provides the sense in which they in their turn must be understood in the context of this event. This is particularly true of obedience, for, as we have said, everything we are discussing takes place in obedience. Obedience towards the God who calls into existence the things that do not exist means first and foremost to trust in this God with one's whole existence, and to live it out in faith in him, so that in everything which is done in this existence, a place is left for the creative power of God, and everything which takes place in it, takes place within and through this power.

But it would be a misunderstanding of this faith, and of what takes place within it, if it were regarded as concerning only the existence of an individual, and, if I may so put it, his private relationship with God. The God who calls into existence the things that do not exist is never the God of particular individuals, be they few or many, but the God who is the creator and Lord of the world. Anyone who takes this God seriously, must also take seriously the world, as God's creation, and as the place within which he lives according to the will of God. Consequently, there is no salvation or damnation for man which is not closely identified with the salvation and damnation of his world. But a person who is obedient is trusting himself and his whole world to God. Therefore the obedience of which we have spoken does not exist unless there is a responsibility in the sight of God for that person's world, a responsibility implied by his obedience. This responsibility may take a double form, as that in which man is responsible *for* his world *in the sight of* God. If in this double form it was based at every moment on the obedience from which it can venture to trust, without any reserve, in the God who calls into existence the things that do not exist, then this responsibility would make it possible for man to see into and penetrate the sentence of doom which hangs over him and the world as a result of the exchanging of the creator for the creation.

To understand this, it is necessary to know what this sentence of doom is, and how it is possible to see into and penetrate such a sentence. Paul describes the sentence of doom we are talking about as follows: Although men knew of God, they did not honour him as God, that is, as the God who he is; consequently, in their thinking they have become subject to that which is futile in itself. Since they knew of God, since the creation of the world, so Paul believes, they were able to perceive the invisible nature of God, namely his eternal power and deity, by which he creates everything from nothing. They would have done so had they properly understood what he created, that is, if they regarded and treated it as created. But instead of this, they relied upon the creature, which is nothing without the creator, and honoured it instead of the creator (Rom. 1.19ff.). In order to understand this statement, which is very complex, and therefore very difficult, it is useful to realize that here Paul is speaking of two different ways of knowing God. In a brief sentence in the Epistle to the Galatians he distinguishes them as follows: 'Now that you have come to know God, or rather to be known by God' (Gal. 4.9; cf. I Cor. 8.3). The first is the knowledge through which, according to Paul, the whole world knows of God, but in which – this would be the other way of knowing him – it does not truly know of him as God, that is, by knowing that as something which does not exist of itself, it has been called into being by God. This other kind of knowledge takes place in what Paul calls being known by God. When a man is known by God, God takes him, as Luther sometimes expresses it, into his 'use', that is, into the use which is in accordance with his being as God, his eternal creative power and deity. But if men who have this first knowledge do not 'attest it' by allowing themselves, in the second kind of knowledge, to be taken by God into the 'use' which is in accordance with his deity, then God gives them up to a 'base mind' (Rom. 1.28). Relying on the creature instead of the creator, they are subject to futility and all imaginable wickedness, and perversion. The worst thing, and what is truly damnable, is that as a result of exchanging the creator for the creature, which is what all this amounts to, they now take on themselves on behalf of the creation, that is, for the world and its powers, the responsibility which they owe to God alone. This perversion of responsibility, through which men have become inescapably subject to futility (for they are held fast by this responsibility, although it is basically perverted) forms the sentence of doom which is passed upon them and upon their world through this sinful exchange.

For a sentence of doom to be averted and its power broken, it is necessary for its reason to be known. If it is possible to translate into other terms the primitive Christian kerygma, with the aid of the ideas and concepts which we have proposed, we can now say that the primitive Christian kerygma, as it is handed down to us in the New Testament writings, proclaims that Jesus Christ has succeeded in averting this sentence of doom, by taking upon himself and exercising, in the power of faith and obedience, this twofold responsibility – he knew himself to be responsible in *the sight of God* and *for* the world. In this way he exposed himself to the fate which is imposed upon the world and upon man in this sentence of doom, and drew it upon himself. In the power of his obedience he then dared to entrust, to the God who calls into existence things that do not exist, himself and his own existence, fulfilled as it was by this responsibility on behalf of the world, and subject as it was to the world's futility. By so doing he simultaneously recognized the basis of the sentence of doom and at the same time brought it to utterance in the world, which was so ensnared in this sentence of doom that in everything that it thought and did, and not least in its religious devotion, it unwillingly grew increasingly entangled in it. And he did this by attesting that the faith which the men of this world had not been able to sustain was that through which alone the sentence of doom could be averted. We have already said what happened through his doing this, when we discussed the cross and the resurrection of Jesus.

We set out to discuss in this chapter how knowledge of the event which is the basis and content of the Christian kerygma comes to those for whom it all happened, and how this knowledge can be believed. The only answer that can be given to the first of these two questions is that knowledge of this event has come to us through the primitive Christian kerygma, and that is, through the testimony of the writings of primitive Christianity. But, as we have tried to show, in the very matter to which it bears witness, this testimony cannot be submitted to historical control of any kind. This is so, because such a testimony to events of this nature cannot exist, so that any attempt to provide a historical authentication of this event would be a failure. For of its nature it is an event which can only be perceived by faith, and no other testimony to it is possible except that given by faith. Is this the case here? Is the only possible explanation how knowledge of these events came down to us that it came through the primitive Christian kerygma as the testimony of faith? For that is what the kerygma is, and recent scholarship is recognizing it to be so with increasing unanimity. If this is so, we are bound to ask whether, in order to believe in these events, we have to rely upon the faith of the New Testament witnesses. This would mean, of course, that we would have to believe in that faith to be able ourselves to believe in these events, so that our faith could be based only on that of those witnesses, and only indirectly, through their mediation, on the events themselves. We can only give an answer to this question by posing a further question. How in general, that is, both for the New Testament witnesses and for us, is faith in these events possible? In other words, what would be the nature of a faith which was in accordance with these events?

We have already said that the only possible witness to these events is a faith which makes possible for the believer the same obedience for the sake of which Jesus exercised obedience himself. These events, moreover, can only be perceived by such a faith. The New Testament expresses these events by saying that Jesus died 'for' our sins. We interpreted the word 'for' by saying that Jesus took upon himself, in responsibility for us, the fate which lies upon men as the consequence of sin. Jesus, as Philippians 2.5ff. puts it, took the form, or as it is better translated in accordance with the sense, the nature or being of a slave, by being born in the likeness of men, and humbled himself, by becoming obedient to death, even death on a cross. Or, as the same idea is expressed in Rom. 8.3: 'God sent his Son in the likeness of sinful flesh and for sin.' Thus by dying for the sins of men or, as we may express it, by taking upon himself the fate of men who are subject to the futility of the world, Jesus equates himself with men and becomes equal to them. What men, therefore, are in reality, men enslaved to the sentence of doom imposed upon them and upon their world, is manifested in him. But this can only be perceived by those who now recognize in the image and in the fate of Jesus Christ their own image and their fate; who therefore recognize that the burden which lay upon him and which he bore is that which lies upon them; and who, now that he has been drawn in their place under the sentence of doom which is imposed upon them, realize that this is the burden which lies upon them.

Without such a recognition of one's own image and fate in the image and fate of Jesus, there can be no knowledge of what happened when Jesus came into the world and was crucified. For example, when Paul says, 'I have been crucified with Christ' (Gal. 2.20), he can only say this because in the man whom the Jews brought to the cross he recognizes himself. This does not mean, of course, that Paul is identical with Jesus. He recognizes himself in him in the sense that he recognizes the fate which this man met on the cross as the same as that which is destined for him, and which, if it is to be fulfilled in him and to be recognized by him in this way, would be seen to be the same abandonment by God which came upon this man on the cross when death overpowered him. Consequently, there can be no knowledge that Jesus died for our sins, unless we recognize that the sentence of doom to which he has exposed himself in responsibility for his brethren is the same as that which has been imposed upon us in our failure to attest the knowledge of God which we had by believing that God is he who calls into existence the things that do not exist.

The New Testament text expresses the fact that without this recognition of ourselves in him who died for our sins there is no possibility of faith in him. Numerous statements all say that 'those who belong to Christ Jesus have crucified the flesh with its passions and desires' (Gal. 5.24). Naturally, when Paul uses the word 'crucify' here he does not mean that those who belong to Christ have suffered exactly what Christ suffered on the cross, or must allow the same to happen to them. But he does mean that they must fight against the men who, in the crucified Christ, they have recognized themselves to be. This is what the Epistle to the Ephesians means when it says:

> You were taught in him, as the truth is in Jesus. Put off your old nature which belongs to your former manner of life and is corrupt through deceitful lusts, and be renewed in the spirit of your minds, and put on the new nature, created after the likeness of God in true righteousness and holiness (4.21ff.).

By attesting that he has recognized himself and his fate in the crucified Jesus in this way, man is also able to recognize what has happened in the resurrection of Jesus, and to believe in it as something which affects him. And just as what took place on the cross took place between Jesus and God, in that Jesus took upon himself in obedience towards God responsibility for men who, together with their world, are subject to futility, so also what took place in the resurrection took place between Jesus and God. By exposing himself in faith on the cross in the uttermost degree to the fate that comes upon this futility, as his own fate, he experiences in it the God who calls into existence the things that do not exist. For as surely as the external will of God is mighty in the obedience and the responsibility through which Jesus took upon himself the fate due to this futility, this futility itself becomes that which does not exist, which God calls into existence. And he who, by obediently taking upon himself the fate of men who are enslaved to the power of sin, accepted for himself the futile existence of these men, became him whom God 'highly exalted and bestowed on him the name which is above every name', and made him Lord over all 'in heaven and on earth and under the earth' (Phil. 2.5ff.). What is true of the knowledge of what took place on the cross is also true of the knowledge of what took place in this way in the resurrection, and of faith in it. This knowledge likewise exists only when we, who have recognized ourselves in the crucified Christ and so have comprehended the cause of the sentence of doom which brought him to the cross for our sake, learn and find courage, in the power of his obedience and faith, to believe with him in the God who gives life to the dead and calls into existence the things that do not exist. It is only in this faith that it can become true for us that 'by the great mercy of the God and Father of our Lord Jesus Christ, we have been born anew to a living hope through the resurrection of Jesus Christ from the dead' (I Peter 1.3).

As in the case of what happened upon the cross, what is decisive here is the knowledge that it is God who is acting in his creative power in Jesus Christ, that is, in his obedience, in his responsibility, and most of all in his faith, in which Jesus is who he is and does what he does. Because it is God who acts in the faith of Jesus, or as we may also say, for whose action in him Jesus makes room by his faith, this faith is faith in the God who, above all else that is said and believed concerning him, confirms his eternal creative power and deity in him who is brought to nothing before him. And therefore, Jesus, who believes with this faith, this 'one man', is 'the free gift in grace' of God (Rom. 5.15). With this in mind, Paul can say of what took place in and through Jesus, that 'all this is from God, who through Christ reconciled us to himself' (II Cor. 5.18). That is, when God caused this man Jesus to be born, this came about for the sake of men, who otherwise would be hopelessly cut off from God in the fate to which they are condemned because of their sin. And we may go on to echo another saying of Paul, that in this one man, God 'predestined' those whom he has called to faith in Christ 'to be conformed to the image of his Son, in order that he might be the first-born among many brethren' (Rom. 8.29). What happened between God and Jesus happened for the sake of them and their faith. All this happened in order that the sentence of doom, which had been imposed upon them and the world because of their sin, might be averted. Consequently, there can be no knowledge of this, and no faith in it, except where we recognize ourselves and our fate in the image and fate of him whom God sent into the world in the same form as us, that is, in the form 'of sinful flesh' (Rom. 8.3).

Now that we have gone as far as this in explaining how the knowledge of the events which are proclaimed in the primitive Christian kerygma comes to those for whom they happened, and how this knowledge can be believed by them, we must answer another question concerning these events and faith in them. This is the question which lies behind the attempt which we discussed at the beginning of this chapter to see the necessary 'basis' of the kerygma and of faith in the 'worldly reality of historical fact', by which 'the events of salvation are borne',[17] for, it is asserted, 'the events of salvation take place within a historical process which is their element. One must know about this factual historical process', because 'certainty' about this factual historicity is part of faith, and consequently faith cannot 'dispense with the process of *historical authentication*';[18] for this is the only way in which it can be certain of the reality in which it believes. We can most easily make clear what is at issue here by trying to clarify once again the difference between this answer to the question of the basis of faith and our own. In this first answer, two kinds of event are distinguished. The first, as we

4

have seen, is referred to as 'genuine', the 'history that really happened', and consists of events which can be ascertained as having happened as a matter of historical fact or as 'reality which is a matter of factual history' by historical scholarship. This kind of event can be distinguished from another, which is termed a 'saving event' or 'event of salvation', and which, whatever further assurance may be given of it, can only be perceived by faith.

But nothing of consequence is said about the nature of a saving event, what happens in it, and what is signified by the statement that such events 'take place in an historical process which is their element'. The statement that the kerygma is the 'testimony to a historical revelation', because it 'can be shown to originate from genuine history' has not the slightest relevance to history which has any kind of relationship to revelation. For what is called 'history' here is, by common consent, not concerned with what happened in revelation, but only with a process which belongs to the worldly reality of factual history, as it can be known through historical scholarship. It is this process to which the attribute 'genuine history' is applied, and from which it is alleged 'revelation can be shown to originate'.[19] But one could only speak of 'historical revelation' by interpreting the events which take place in revelation, that is the true events of salvation as such, which are the object of faith, as historical events. But this is not possible for the very reason that the attribute 'history', or 'genuine history as it really happened' is restricted to the 'factual historical process', in its 'factual historicity', about which one can only obtain certainty by the method of historical scholarship. It would necessarily follow that, as we have already seen, there would be no other basis for the faith which alone can 'recognize' the true saving events than the assertion of the saving significance of these events, the exhortation to believe what is asserted, and the warning that whoever fails to do this, is guilty of unbelief.

This is one answer to the question of the basis of the kerygma and of faith in it. By contrast, that which we are attempting to give here proceeds from what takes place in revelation itself, and is concerned to show that the events with which we are dealing are not of such a nature that they can be confirmed by historical method, but can be perceived only by faith. But this faith is not one which can be based on an assertion and an exhortation to regard the assertion as true. Rather, it is only possible on the basis of participation in something that happens, and in fact in the events which are the basis of the kerygma. But in accordance with the nature of these events, the nature of this participation is such that one can say of it that in it one experiences faith. For in this faith, man is drawn into events which face him with a decision. He must decide whether he will admit that his existence is such as it is. That is, to quote again the Epistle to the Ephesians, it is 'your old nature which belonged to your former manner of life and is corrupt through deceitful lusts' (Eph. 4.22), and that in this old nature he is in an intolerable contradiction to the man who is 'created after the likeness of God in true righteousness and holiness'.

From what we have already said, it is clear that the meaning of the expression 'deceitful lusts' is misunderstood if it is taken only in the conventional moral sense. It covers every sense, including – something of course of great importance – a very lofty and ethical sense, in which man, as one who fails to show faith in the God who calls into existence the things that do not exist, has fallen prey to the futility of a creation deprived of its creator, and who is therefore compelled by these desires to gain and to assert his position in the world, and also in the sight of God, through what he is capable of himself. The experience of faith itself, which we merely outline here, affects the most profound basis and depth of human existence, and unless this experience is present in what happens to man in faith, the faith we are describing does not exist. What happens here is the same as what was meant when we described how the knowledge of what happened on the cross and in the resurrection of Jesus is only possible when man recognizes his own image and fate in the image of the crucified Christ and in the fate which came upon him on the cross. If he recognizes himself in this, and admits that what he recognizes is his own personal reality, then it is no longer possible for him to doubt it once he has recognized it. Nor can he have any doubt about the historical reality or about the true humanity of the man in whom and in whose fate he has attained this recognition. Here and here alone can we seek the criterion by which to tell whether what took place in and through Jesus is a myth or not. We must, of course, repeat that there is no other possible way for men to become aware of this reality and truth, either in themselves or in the man on the cross and Golgotha, except the way of faith.

NOTES

1. Cf. above pp. 17ff.
2. Althaus, op. cit., p. 30.
3. p. 36.
4. p. 39.
5. pp. 18, 31.
6. p. 31.
7. p. 13.
8. p. 31.
9. p. 32.
10. p. 36.
11. pp. 13, 33.
12. p. 18.
13. p. 45.
14. p. 18.
15. p. 16.
16. Cf. my book *Entmythologisierung und Schrift*, 3rd ed., Stuttgart; tr. *Demythologizing and History*, SCM Press, London, and Scribners, New York, 1955.
17. Althaus, op. cit., p. 36.
18. p. 35.
19. p. 18.

9

THE PREACHING OF JESUS

IN THE PRECEDING chapters we have discussed the primitive Christian kerygma from the point of view of its christology and the nature of its historicity. We have discovered the following. We saw that this christology proclaims a set of events which took place between Jesus and God, and which concern the salvation and damnation of men and of their world. In so far as the person of Jesus is present in it, it is not, as in the traditional christology of the church, the second person of the triune God, in whom divine and human nature are united, and who in the power of the union of God and man, understood in this sense, redeems the world. But neither is Jesus, as he appears in the christology of the primitive Christian kerygma, understood as he usually is at the present day, particularly in recent christology influenced by pietism. He is not seen as a saviour concerned in the first instance with the salvation of the soul of individual human beings, a saviour in whose visible concrete image and individual personal features it is believed 'the fatherly countenance of God' can be perceived. Rather, in the christology of the New Testament the purpose of Jesus is presented as that of a man who, in the obedience towards God which determines and sustains his whole existence, has the power and the authority to take upon himself responsibility for the fate which is imposed upon man and his world, and, by taking it as his own, to allow it to be fulfilled in himself and so to avert it.

In so far as this christology contains features in the person of Jesus which go beyond what is human, as for example the pre-existence of a being who took part in the creation, his miraculous birth, and many other such elements, their significance is to make visible what is implied by the obedience of Jesus towards the will of God, when it is understood in its full sense. That is, such features signify that what happened in and through Jesus does not have its origin within the context of this world, but in the decree and eternal creative power of God, and that it is a cosmic event in the sense that it affects the whole world of man. But the meaning of these statements is never such as to detract from the significance of the humanity of Jesus or to do away with it. He is and remains the historical man Jesus of Nazareth, and it is to him that the statements of the primitive Christian kerygma are intended to apply. This is also the case when the primitive Christian kerygma speaks of Jesus as having been carried up to rule in heaven at the completion of his earthly work, and ascribes divine titles to him. Thus, for example, at the beginning of the Epistle to the Romans Paul uses what is probably a formula which was current in the primitive Christian congregation before his time, when he says that Jesus was 'designated Son of God in power . . . by his resurrection from the dead' and confesses him, with the rest of the Christian congregation, as the 'Lord', who as a man 'was descended from David according to the flesh'. He says this without any special emphasis which would have resulted from any explicit reflection upon the humanity of Christ. There was no need for such explicit reflection, because it was taken for granted by the primitive Christian congregation that everything which they said about the Christ in which they believed was said of the man Jesus of Nazareth. And thus the identity of the Christ who is exalted to be the Lord with the earthly Jesus was no problem for them.

There is, moreover, in the New Testament no trace of the doctrine of the two natures, with which the theologians of the early church later tried to resolve this problem, and in which they provided the church with the dogmatic structure which dominated christological thought until the beginning of the modern period. But since then, owing as much as anything to the historical thought which came into being with the modern period, the Christ of the traditional thinking of the church ceased to be credible, and the quest of the Jesus who was a real historical human person became increasingly urgent.

In the chapter in which we discussed the task of christology, we pointed out that when the question of what Jesus was really like was originally posed, it was not directed against the Christ of dogma, but once critical historical scholarship had posed the question of the historical Jesus, it was henceforth understood to be directed in this polemic sense against the Christ of the church's traditional christology.[1] And we also noted that a more or less conscious but completely unjustified identification was made between the Christ of traditional christology and that of the primitive Christian kerygma. Our attention was also drawn to the following points. If we no longer have a direct understanding of the faith which was brought to expression in the primitive Christian kerygma, then not only is it no longer related to the totality of the existence of those who 'believe' with a faith which has now become faith in a dogma: it has also lost its connection with the existence of Jesus in its totality. If this happens, then the Christ of the primitive Christian kerygma inevitably ceases to be a true historical person, and becomes an unhistorical heavenly being.[2] We noted, moreover,[3] that it follows that the question of the historical Jesus, as it is posed by critical historical scholarship, assumes a mode of thought which can scarcely think of a real historical human person other than as an individual and clearly accessible personality. And because the primitive Christian kerygma, in the form in which we find it in the Gospel of John and the New Testament epistles, says virtually nothing about the personality of Jesus, and equally little about his own preaching, it is easy to get the impression that the Christ of this kerygma is as unhistorical as that of the traditional dogma of the church. The question of the historical Jesus led increasingly to the view that continuity between the Christ of faith and the Jesus of history seemed impossible. Similarly, the proclamation of Jesus as the Christ seemed to be irreconcilable with Jesus's own preaching. If this were inevitably the case, it would be an intolerable situation for Christian faith.

But we have tried to show that the primitive Christian kerygma regards the Christ which it professes as the man Jesus of Nazareth, and not as any kind heavenly being similar to the gnostic redeemer, and that it takes for granted that he is Jesus of Nazareth, to such a degree that it was hardly ever thought necessary to reflect upon the matter, except under the pressure of the gnostic ideas which found entry here and there into the early church. Furthermore, we tried to show that the events which are proclaimed by this kerygma are historical in nature.

If this is so, then the question of the historical Jesus, as it is posed to us by his own preaching, which is still to some extent recognizable in the synoptic tradition, must be asked in a new way. We must ask whether the events which the kerygma proclaims as having taken place between the man Jesus and God are reconcilable with Jesus's own preaching. This is a different question from those which have hitherto been asked about the historical Jesus, above all because it is not prejudiced from the start by a polemic against the Christ of traditional church dogma. Accordingly, it seems possible sometimes to use the statements of the kerygma, in so far as they are concerned with these events, to help us to obtain an understanding of Jesus's own preaching.

Thus, the question of the relationship between the preaching of Jesus as the Christ and Jesus's own preaching, as it must now be asked, is as follows: Does the kerygma understand Jesus aright in what it says about what took place between Jesus and God? Must the statements in the kerygma about Jesus as the Christ first be reconciled with his own preaching, or do they in fact say the same? We must not, however, exclude the possibility that with the aid of the christological statements of the kerygma, we may possibly obtain a more correct understanding of Jesus's own preaching than that which is obtained when the latter is not merely isolated from the kerygma, but is interpreted from the first polemically, as though it were opposed to the kerygma, the christology of which is more or less unconsciously equated with that of the traditional dogma of the church. In this way one can avoid the danger, almost inevitable when the preaching of Jesus is taken in isolation, of regarding it not as the gospel, but as law.[4]

We need scarcely remark that in the attempt to understand the preaching of Jesus anew, which we described in Chapter 4, 'The New Quest of the Historical Jesus', certain steps have been taken in the right direction. But the decisive question, in a full understanding of what is at issue here, is whether the preaching of Jesus is in accordance with the christology of the kerygma with regard to its principal distinguishing feature. That, of course, is that the event between Jesus and God does not concern, or at least does not primarily concern, the salvation of the individual human soul, but the salvation of the world of men.

The Preaching of Jesus

Accordingly, the decisive element in the kerygma is not the personality of Jesus, such as would enable him to have this concern for the individual soul, but the fact that he is the God and Saviour of the world of men.

If we ask this kind of question about Jesus, then we must inevitably first ask what is the nature of the relationship of Jesus to the world, which underlies such a statement concerning him. If we pose the question in this way, we realize that the relationship of man to the world which is assumed in these events between Jesus and God was something new at that period. Before Christian faith came, it did not exist. Hitherto, the nature of man's relationship to the world had been such that he was responsible *to* the world and its law. Now, however, he has become responsible *for* it. The gods whom man hitherto considered himself obliged to serve and worship were deities of the world, that is, representatives of the world and its ordinances, through which and by which it is the world, and through which men live their life by the world. It is this pre-Christian attitude to the world which Paul, for example, has in mind when he says that before faith came we were confined under the law, kept under restraint (Gal. 3.23), or when he speaks of the changing of the creator for the creature, and the ungodliness and wickedness, that is, the sin of men, upon which the wrath of God has been revealed (Rom. 1.18). Consequently, the world against which we are warned in the New Testament as that which 'is in the power of the evil one' (I John 5.19), and to which we ought not to 'conform' ourselves (Rom. 12.2), is not the world in itself, but the world which is the object of men's religious veneration, and to which, with the powers that dominate it, the *stoicheia, dynameis, archai*, etc., they regard themselves as responsible. Consequently, the 'ungodliness and wickedness' which Paul speaks of as the real sin of man, is only understood in its full sense when one realizes that it refers to the religious worship of pre-Christian mankind. The same is true of the law, which Paul attacks so passionately, because through its works men suppose that they can become righteous in the sight of God. The truth, however, as he says, is that those who 'rely on works of the law', that is, who believe that they can justify themselves and their lives in the sight of God through this law and its works, 'are under a curse' (Gal. 3.10). Thus, the law here is the law of the world as the object of religious veneration, to which men believe that they must hold themselves responsible. By so doing, in the blasphemous error in which they exchange the creator for the creature, they conform themselves to the world which they assume to be divine, instead of 'conforming' to him who is the true God, the creator of the world and of themselves, *to* whom they are responsible *for* the world.

This new understanding of the relationship of man to the world, that is, that he is not responsible *to* it, but that he is responsible *to* God *for* it, and also for its remaining God's creature and not being put in place of God through a responsibility exercised *towards* it, expresses a perception of immense significance. It sets in motion a change which in truth affected the whole history of the world, and is so great that we know of no other such in the whole of history.

This perception, and the change which it brought about, is the assumption underlying everything which is proclaimed in the primitive Christian kerygma. That is, that Jesus as the Christ is he who, in a responsibility exercised towards God, took upon himself responsibility for the world and for the evil brought upon it as a result of the sin of the men who live in it, and thereby averted the sentence of doom. And we must now ask whether this responsibility for the world on the part of man is first found in the primitive Christian kerygma, that is, whether it is a perception which was first achieved by the primitive Christian church, in accordance with which it transformed the gospel of the kingdom of God, as Jesus proclaimed it, into the kerygma of the Christ who is the *kyrios*, the Lord of the world. Or was it Jesus who achieved this perception and lived it out in his life? If so, the kerygma would be the proclamation of the fact that Jesus, by realizing this perception in the name of God in his life, to the point of death, became Lord of the world. The answer to this question can only be found in the preaching of Jesus, by trying to see whether we can understand this preaching in terms of the questions asked above. We must first ask how the relationship of man to the world is seen in his preaching – whether it is still the ancient pre-Christian relationship, or that which we saw was the assumption of everything which is said in the primitive Christian kerygma.

The Preaching of Jesus

One of the most important discoveries, if not the most important of all, which has been made by the critical historical study of Jesus's preaching is that of its thoroughgoing eschatology.[5] The word eschatology was originally used to refer to the expectation, characteristic of Jewish apocalyptic, of an end of the world which at the present time was still to come, and was thought of in cosmic terms, and of the renewal of the world which would come about with it. This end of the world was to take place at some future time, when, as we read in the second Epistle of Peter where the thought is still wholly that of Jewish apocalyptic, 'the heavens will pass away with a loud noise, and the elements will be dissolved with fire', whereupon 'new heavens and a new earth' are to be awaited.[6] But when the word 'eschatological' is applied to the preaching of Jesus, it no longer means the expectation of a cosmic end of the world which at the present time has not yet come. Consequently, the decisive element is not the temporal future in which it is expected. The great, all-embracing crisis still remains – not, however, as in apocalyptic eschatology in the form of the cosmic events of the end of the world as it exists, and the equally cosmic renewal of the world which follows. Rather, this great transformation is an event in which not only did the world as it exists come to an end, but something new began as well; thus through it everything becomes different. In the preaching of Jesus this 'something new' is called the kingdom of God. Its coming, and that which happened to the present world through it is the true eschatological event. What we may call the eschatology of Jesus deals with this. Since this coming of the kingdom of God is now already happening, the eschatological event which is placed in the eschatology of Jewish apocalyptic only in the temporal future, that is, at the end of the cosmic world which was still to come, is here brought forward into the present. And therefore the end which is, on the one hand, the end of the present world and, on the other hand, the inauguration of the kingdom of God, also took place in the present, so that participation in the eschatological event is already possible for men in the present.

It is true that this participation is of the only kind which is possible as long as the present world, the end of which is now under way, together with the beginning of the kingdom of God, has not yet wholly passed away. Thus, while participation in the kingdom of God is something that takes place here and now, it is nevertheless something which must be a matter of constant concern in faith, vigilance and expectation. This is the reason for the strict exhortations to watch and wait. Men must realize that they are like the doorkeeper whom his lord commanded to watch when he went on a journey and left home (Mark 13.34f.). And 'no one who puts his hand to the plough and looks back is fit for the kingdom of God' (Luke 9.62). The situation of someone who becomes aware of the coming of the kingdom is like that of the man who found treasure hidden in a field, and hid it, and 'in his joy he goes and sells all that he has and buys that field' (Matt. 13.44).

What we have said so far about the eschatology of the preaching of Jesus has made clear a further and very important difference between it and the eschatology of the Jewish apocalyptic. This difference is that – unlike the latter – it does not imply a change from one world to a completely different one. For what is brought about by the kingdom of God is not a new cosmological world, which can be thought of as following the cosmological destruction of the former world. What is brought about by the kingdom of God is rather a fundamental new attitude of man to God, which is wholly determined by the rule of God over men, and through which the relationship of man to the world in which he lives is also fundamentally changed. The coming of the kingdom of God is not a cosmological event, and neither is the passing away of the present world which begins with it. What is beginning to come to an end is rather the dominion which the world has hitherto exercised over men.

Of the other things which remain to be said about the kingdom of God, the first thing we must mention in the present context is that the coming of the kingdom brings a judgment upon the present world. For the coming of the kingdom reveals that this world is opposed to the rule of God. The nature of this opposition is that under the rule of the world not only are certain things done which are against God, but that this world dominates, in particular through the religious practice which is characteristic of it, man's relationship to God in such a way that this is in fact not directed towards God as man claims, but towards the world. Through this judgment the world loses the right to the rule which it has hitherto exercised over men, and therefore the end of this rule has begun.

Thus the eschatological message of Jesus faces men with this judgment, which is passed upon the present world with the coming kingdom of God, and also faces him with the decision whether he is to submit to this judgment or not. This is the situation in which a man finds himself when, becoming aware that the kingdom of God has come even now, he understands at the same time that the present world in which he has not only lived hitherto but in which he is still living, is passing away. It explains why Jesus's preaching is characterized as much by an unconditional demand as by the eschatology which determines every statement in it.

If what we have said concerning Jesus's eschatology is correct it implies that the world which the eschatological preaching of Jesus described as passing away is the same world which, in the primitive Christian kerygma, was said to be under a sentence of doom, through which it was subject to 'decay and futility' (Rom. 8.20f.), because man had exchanged the creator for it, the creation. It was, therefore, the world as it had become as a result of the pre-Christian attitude of man towards it. The most obvious manifestation of this attitude was the pre-Christian cult. If we now consider what Jesus says about cultic religion, we can see whether what we have said about the eschatology which is found in its preaching is correct, and clarify it further.

What he says concerning keeping the Sabbath holy is a particularly clear comment on this religion, for it was one of the most important cultic commandments of Jewish religion. The same is true of his comment on cultic purifications. The first saying is that, 'The sabbath was made for man, not man for the sabbath' (Mark 2.27), and the second is that, 'Not what goes into the mouth defiles a man, but what comes out of the mouth, this defiles a man' (Matt. 15.11). What is significant in these sayings is not that they contain a warning against any particular cultic action, or are meant as instructions about the right way to carry these actions out. Rather, their significance is that such sayings reject cultic piety as such altogether. And the reason for this is not only that it cannot be used to become righteous before God, who demands more than merely the fulfilment of a cultic commandment, but because through it a true attitude to God, in accordance with both the nature of God and the nature of man, is made impossible. The most pointed expression of Jesus's view of cultic piety is expressed in the woe uttered against those who were its official and particular guardians:

> Woe to you, scribes and Pharisees, hypocrites! for you cleanse the outside of the cup and of the plate, but inside they are full of extortion and rapacity. . . . Woe to you, scribes and Pharisees, hypocrites! for you are like whitewashed tombs, which outwardly appear beautiful, but within they are full of dead men's bones and all uncleanness. So you also outwardly appear righteous to men, but within you are full of hypocrisy and iniquity (Matt. 23.25ff.).

Why does Jesus speak of hypocrisy here? If his words are taken as an accusation of subjective hypocrisy, in the general terms which he uses they would be a scarcely tolerable exaggeration, even if they were taken as a caricature, a mode of speech which Jesus uses quite often. It must be accepted that Jesus knew that amongst the pious observers of the law in his age and amongst his people there were men who were wholly serious in their piety. Thus these words cannot very well refer to a subjective hypocrisy, but rather must be saying of cultic piety that it is equivalent to hypocrisy in so far as it is not what it seems to be.

What, then, takes place in cultic piety? There is no cult without sacred things, sacred vessels, gestures, prescriptions and laws. All these are things of this world, which, because they are cultic, are separated from the rest of the world; they are sacred things, as opposed to secular, and may only be used for the cult. Nevertheless they belong to the world, and moreover to the world as it is. As things in which the fundamental, that is, cultic, ordering of this world finds its expression, they serve in a particularly high degree to maintain in existence the world within which they are sacred. But if it is supposed that one is serving God with them in accordance with religious prescriptions laid down to this end, then God himself, whether one wishes it or not, and whether one knows it or not, becomes a God who, like the things of religion, and the laws for their use, belongs to the present world. The more seriously and strictly one observes these laws, the more God, like the worship which is offered to him, is made worldly. Jesus stated with cutting sarcasm that the object of this piety is in truth not God, but the world as it is. He described what it makes of a person when he accused the scribes and Pharisees of doing all their pious works

> to be seen by men; for they make their phylacteries broad and their fringes long, and they love the place of honour at feasts and the best seats in the synagogues, and salutations in the market places, and being called rabbi by men (Matt. 23.5ff.).

One must not take the sting out of the accusation which Jesus makes against the devout by understanding it as ordinary vanity. More than that is at issue here. These people supposed that in what they were doing they were serving God. In fact, they were serving the world and the piety which is appropriate to this world, and through which its existence is assured. And they were thereby carrying out the exchanging of the creator for the creature which we have already described, and in which, as we have seen, the knowledge of God which they possessed – for their cultic piety was proof of this – was not affirmed as the knowledge of God as he is in truth (Rom. 1.28). It is this, the failure to affirm a knowledge which one has, which Jesus called hypocrisy. Thus the scribes and Pharisees were hypocrites, Jesus said, because they 'neglected the weightier matters of the law, justice and mercy and faith' but pretended that what they did in accordance with the public ordinance, that is, that they 'tithed mint and dill and cummin' (Matt. 23.23) was the fulfilment of God's commandment. Furthermore, the devout Jewish observers of the law, in the pride of their Jewish faith in God, boasted that by contrast to the so-called Gentiles they had a true knowledge of God; while in fact, with their cultic and legal piety, they were guilty of the same exchanging of the creator for the creature as the Gentiles.

They do this in their piety not only in so far as it was a cultic legalism, but also because it was an ethical legalism. The law in this sense was the particular pride of the Jews. Through the law, which God gave them through Moses, and through the gift of which he chose them as his people, they had – in the words of Paul, who himself, until his conversion, was a devout Jewish observer of the law – 'the sonship, the glory, the covenants, the giving of the law, the worship and the promises' (Rom. 9.4). In the history of Israel, this law increasingly changed from the law of the God who is the God and Lord of the whole world, into that of the religious world of the Jewish people. This world, and participation in it, rested upon the law. Anyone who fulfilled the commandments of this law and therefore made himself a place in the religious and moral ordering of this world, would prosper in it, and would boast of his righteousness, that is his due place in this world, before God and men. One must be aware of this background to realize what a monstrous thing Jesus did when he attacked what 'was said to the men of old' with the words, 'But I say to you . . .' (Matt. 5.21ff.). Here he was attacking the law with which the world of the Jewish people, as God's chosen people, stood or fell, and therefore he was also attacking this world as a world guaranteed by God through this law.

But these words, 'But I say to you . . .', mean more than this. For in what he went on to say, he replaced that which 'was said to the men of old'. He removed the law – as something belonging to the world, fitting man into his place in the ordering of the world, and maintaining his life in the world if he fulfils it – from the relationship between man and God. Such a law, without which there cannot be any kind of world in which man can live, consists of a greater or lesser series of commandments, which demand or forbid various kinds of action. But the relationship to God as Jesus understood it has nothing to do with this kind of law. For this relationship to God is like a tree: only a good tree brings forth good fruit, while a rotten tree brings forth rotten fruit. Consequently, 'the good man out of the good treasure of his heart produces good, and the evil man out of his evil treasure produces evil' (Luke 6.43ff.). This is not meant in the sense of predestination. Rather, it says that man can only stand before God in his whole being, in his whole existence. For God is concerned with the being of man. Here no law is of any use, because if it consists of commandments which are capable of being carried out, its aim can be only the carrying out or otherwise of individual acts.

In his great antitheses Jesus said:

You have heard that it was said to the men of old, 'You shall not kill; and whoever kills shall be liable to judgment'. But I say to you that everyone who is angry with his brother shall be liable to judgment (Matt. 5.21f.).

This saying is misunderstood if it is taken to mean that the judgment can be avoided if a rising anger against one's brother is suppressed. This was so with what was said to the men of old: anyone who refrained from killing escaped the judgment. Here, however, the case is different. Even if one succeeded in suppressing one's rising anger, one would already have been angry with one's brother and would, therefore, already be liable to judgment. Indeed, the point of the saying is to reduce the law as such to absurdity. It becomes absurd if it is realized that what is done on the basis of the commandment, and is called for by the commandment, can never be what is required by the law as the will of God. By so expressing the matter, we make it clear that there are two different experiences of the law here. One is that in which the law is experienced in the context of the world; the demand that it makes is that man should fit himself into his place in the ordering of the world. A practicable law, requiring that one should carry out or refrain from any particular action, can help one to attain what is demanded. The other experience affects man in his relationship to God. What this demands cannot be achieved on the basis of a commandment, that is, through any particular action. But the demand as Jesus understands it is that of the second experience of the law.

This is perhaps made most clear in Jesus's saying concerning almsgiving. Here Jesus warns his hearers against allowing their piety 'to be seen by men', in order to be praised by them. Anyone who acts in this way 'will have his reward', and therefore 'has no reward from the Father in heaven'. When one gives alms, the left hand should not know what the right hand does (Matt. 6.1ff.). Thus not only should one not allow one's piety to be seen by other people, but not even by oneself. It is this that Jesus is saying when he says that the left hand should not know what the right hand does. This can only mean that an act of almsgiving which is not to have 'no reward from the Father in heaven' must on no account be carried out in the intention of fulfilling a prescribed commandment. Of course in all this one must bear in mind that the sayings of Jesus, whatever individual matter they may be speaking of, are directed, in accordance with the eschatological character of his preaching, to one single issue. This is the relationship between man and God. Nothing is further from his intention than to lay down in his sayings any kind of code of ethics, that is, commandments and instructions such as are needed for the thousand multifarious circumstances and matters in and through which men satisfy the possibilities of a life lived in and derived from the world. When someone came to Jesus and asked him to settle a dispute about inheritance between him and his brother, he refused, saying, 'Man, who made me a judge or divider over you?' (Luke 12.13f.). That Jesus's concern in his preaching was man's relationship to God can be seen, in his sayings concerning almsgiving, from what he says about the 'reward' which one has 'from the Father who is in heaven' for alms given in the right way. There is another reward, but the one excludes the other. This is the reward received by those who give alms 'that they may be praised by men'. It is this praise from men which is the reward, and is both in accordance with the intention with which the alms are given, and also with the authority which lays down the commandment on which one is acting. Of course one alleges and presumably supposes oneself that with this gift one is serving God, but in fact one is serving the world, for almsgiving belongs to the religious laws of the world. And instead of the expected reward from God one receives the reward of the world. This means that an action carried out on the basis of such a law remains within the world and does not reach God. Naturally, what is said concerning the reward which one will have with the 'Father in heaven' does not mean that true almsgiving should be done *on account of* this reward. For if one gives in this way, the left hand is only too aware of what the right hand is doing. What, then, is the 'reward from the Father in heaven'? What is it with which the 'Father who sees in secret' will reward almsgiving in secret? Or in other words, what is the nature of the relationship to God which Jesus is expressing in this saying, and which cannot be realized on the basis of the law?

There is another saying of Jesus about almsgiving which provides an answer to this question. In this saying Jesus compared the tiny gift which a poor widow puts into the alms box, with the great gift which is given by rich people. Jesus says of the widow that she put in more than the others. For whereas the others gave 'out of their abundance', she gave 'out of her poverty . . . everything she had, her whole living' (Mark 12.41ff.). Thus, whether the giving of alms is right is decided not by how great or small the gift is, but whether it is such that through it, regardless of whether the giver contributes much or little, he is brought into the position of having to rely upon God. To rely upon God, to know that one is dependent upon him, and therefore to let him be one's God, is to have faith. And so it is faith understood in this sense which alone is capable of fulfilling a relationship to God appropriate to what he is and to what man is in the sight of God. Only through such faith, and through what is done as a result of it, can man make a place in himself for God. And therefore in an act of almsgiving which takes place in the concealment of this faith, and not as a pious work required by the prescription of the law, God's manifestation of himself to the giver as his God, can also come about, for of its nature this, too, can only come about in concealment. And it is this which is the 'reward from the Father in heaven'. Consequently, what is required in the saying concerning almsgiving is the faith through which one makes room in oneself for God in his deity and his divine action.

In order to understand the nature of this demand, that is, in order to understand that in its true sense it is not a requirement of the *law*, one must bear in mind two considerations. The first is the tacit but fundamental assumption underlying the demand made by Jesus with regard to almsgiving. We can see what it is from the first of these sayings, which Luther translates: 'Take care of your piety' (as the Greek word *dikaiosyne* is properly translated here). The Jews to whom Jesus was speaking took for granted that almsgiving was an exercise of their piety, and that they were doing it for God. In what Jesus says about almsgiving he calls this automatic assumption into question. Consequently, he gives the warning: 'Take care of your piety', that is, that it should really be done for God, and be in accordance with his deity. But to do this, means to trust that to one who turns to him, God will manifest himself as his God, and will do this before any action on man's part. But if one supposes that what matters in piety is what man does, then this piety is not carried out, as it must be, for God above all, but as a human action. In this case, in whatever way alms are given, they are given 'in order to be seen by men'. But the law which is being followed in this kind of action, whatever one may say of it, is that of the world in which one lives, and by which one understands oneself; and in it one is relying upon this world. In order to make the meaninglessness of this kind of action as clear as possible, Jesus says of it that because those who practise this piety do so for the sake of the world, they 'sound the trumpet before them', in order to draw attention to the pious action with which they are fulfilling the law of this world. They thereby show themselves to be mere hypocrites, who pretend to serve God, and in fact have no object beyond themselves and their own actions and, therefore, the world in which they live. But there is no room here for him who is God in truth, and for him to act. Consequently, what Jesus is demanding in his saying on almsgiving is something which a person can do only in the faith that God is always ready to manifest himself to him as his God. Thus the action which is demanded is not of the same kind as is demanded by the law. Rather, man is being called upon to let God do what he will do for everyone who lets him be his God.

The second consideration we must bear in mind in order to understand the nature of this demand is that – like the rest of Jesus's preaching – it is eschatological in nature. Since this preaching proclaims the coming of the kingdom of God, it also proclaims the end of the present world, which has already begun with the coming of the kingdom of God. As we have seen,[7] the end of the world here is the judgment which is passed upon this world, because the world dominates the relationship of man to God through its own characteristic piety, laid down by a worldly tradition which is presented as the commandment of God. It thereby totally corrupts this relationship. This is the situation in which Jesus proclaims his demand, and on the basis of which it must be understood.

An enormous change was brought about by the preaching of Jesus. How far beyond normal standards is the issue in the decision of man in response to it, can be seen in sayings like the following: 'If your right eye causes you to sin, pluck it out and throw it away; it is better that you lose one of your members than that your whole body be thrown into hell' (Matt. 5.29f.). Such sayings, not to say outbursts, which are isolated from any context, show with what unrestrained passion the demand of Jesus calls upon men to repent and turn away from this present world with its hypocritical piety, which teaches men to honour God with their lips, that is, in the empty way which corresponds to the tradition of this world, while their heart is far from him (Mark 7.6). And we see how Jesus calls men, with all the urgency of the final hour, to the kingdom of God which is now coming and which alone, when it is accepted in his gospel, can save them out of this world which is coming to an end.

The most pointed summary of the nature of the right relationship to God is given by Jesus in the saying: 'Whoever seeks to gain his life will lose it, but whoever loses his life will preserve it' (Luke 17.33). Life here must not be understood simply as life in the ordinary sense. We must realize that the saying speaks of two kinds of life. Jesus is speaking, on the one hand, of life lived on the basis of the world and, on the other hand, of life lived through God. The life which people try to gain is the life which they think they can gain with the aid of cultic piety. They seek to gain it by doing what is regarded as pious in the world in which the law of this piety prevails, and by which life is sustained within it. Of course the idea behind this piety is that the life gained by it is the same as that which is lived through God. But this, the life lived through God, is the very thing which is lost in this way. But, on the other hand, whoever gives up the life which he previously supposed, following the piety of the present world, was life lived through God, will in fact gain the life that is lived through God.

What is the meaning of this abandonment of life, and how does it come about? The answer may perhaps most easily be found in looking at the saying which sums up, as the 'greatest commandment', everything which Jesus has to say about the relationship of man to God:

> You shall love the Lord your God with all your heart, and with all your soul, and with all your mind, and with all your strength. The second is this: You shall love your neighbour as yourself. There is no other commandment greater than these (Mark 12.30f.).

The most important thing in this saying seems to me to be that in it the relationship to God and that to one's neighbour are intimately linked. One's relationship to one's neighbour is, one might say, taken up into that with God. Not of course that both are the same. It is rather that the relationship to one's neighbour derives the particular meaning given it here from the relationship to God. This means that the second commandment interprets the significance of the first. I cannot love my Lord without fulfilling his will. For it is only in this way that he can be my Lord in the way in which he wills. The second commandment sets out what he wills.

The nature of such a love for one's neighbour is made clear in what Jesus says elsewhere about love. One of these sayings reads:

> Love your enemies, do good to those who hate you, bless those who curse you, pray for those who abuse you. To him who strikes you on the cheek, offer the other also; and from him who takes away your cloak, do not withhold your coat as well. Give to everyone who begs from you; and of him who takes away your goods do not ask them again (Luke 6.27–30).

The other side of the picture is presented in the saying which comes shortly after:

> If you love those who love you, what credit is that to you? For even sinners love those who love them. And if you do good to those who do good to you, what credit is that to you? For even sinners do the same. And if you lend to those from whom you hope to receive, what credit is that to you? Even sinners lend to sinners, to receive as much again (Luke 6.32–34).

The difference between the relationship to one's neighbour which is described in the first saying and that which is described in the second is clear. The second saying describes the relationship between men which is normal in the present world in accordance with its rules, and by which this world is maintained in being. Here the way in which one person acts towards another is such that one expects part of the good that one does to the other. But in the relationship which the first saying describes, the reverse is true. It speaks of an action which is characterized by the fact that the expectation which is the basis of the kind of action described in the second saying is here altogether excluded. Of course one must not rob this first saying of its meaning by taking it as advice on how to bring someone who hates one to do good to one, by doing good to him through refusing to resist. For what would be the difference between this attitude and the other? Such ideas are in any case quite remote from what Jesus is saying here.

This becomes clear at once when one considers the difference between the two attitudes to which Jesus is referring. This difference is clearly his concern in these sayings for they deal with the difference between the relationship to another man which is determined by God, and one which knows nothing of God. In the second group of sayings the conclusion is each time: 'What credit is that to you?' or, as one may also translate it, 'What good are you to get out of it?' Credit or good from whom? The idea seems to be that in such a relationship one cannot speak at all of credit or good in the proper sense, either with regard to God or with regard to men. For nothing more is happening here than the exchange of two things of equal value. Activity of this sort is as it were complete and finished in itself; it remains within its own sphere and nothing new happens as a result. God never has anything to do with what happens here; one has no need of him in order to behave in this way. The situation is quite different in the case of the relationship described in the first group of sayings. Whereas that of the second group of sayings is wholly determined by the expectation of receiving 'life for life', the action described in the first group takes place as it were in a vacuum, without any such expectation. But whereas in the second case one's debt with the other person is settled, in this first case 'your reward will be great, and you will be sons of the Most High' (Luke 6.35). What does this 'great reward' consist of?

We do well to recall here the saying that whoever seeks to gain his life will lose it. In the light of this saying, we can understand what is meant by this 'losing'. Whoever loves his enemy and does good to him who hates him, no longer lives by trusting in the present world with its ordinances and its permanence; he abandons the life which he gains through this world, and through the fulfilment of its ordinances – he 'loses' it. Here he is doing the same as the widow who 'out of her poverty put in everything she had, her whole living' into the alms box. We must remember, also, that the words of Jesus are not intended as commandments which require one particular action or another. Whatever particular thing they are referring to, they always have in mind one thing alone, the relationship to God which lets him be who he is. The enemy whom you love, the person who hates you, and to whom you should do good, etc., are all extreme examples which Jesus uses to show what the attitude and action of man must be for it to be possible to say that his reward for this will be great, or, as Jesus himself puts it elsewhere, that in it the 'losing' of life takes place, in which life is 'gained'.

Consequently, the 'great reward' which Jesus promises for such action consists in imparting to those who 'lose' the life which they have sought in the present world in accordance with its ordinance, the presence of the kingdom of God, and 'entry' into it, through this very 'losing' of their lives. This is the meaning of the sayings which call the poor, the hungry, and those who mourn, blessed because theirs is the kingdom of God, because it is they who shall be satisfied, and shall laugh (Luke 6.20ff.), or the sayings which promise to the little children that they will inherit the kingdom of God (Mark 10.14), and to the tax collectors and the harlots, that they will go into the kingdom of God before those who keep the law (Matt. 21.31), and to those who ask, seek and knock, that they will receive, that it will be opened to them, and that they will find (Matt. 7.7f.). Those who are spoken of here are all people whose trust in the present world, in which the devout believe that they possess life, has been lost in some way or other. It is for this reason that they can be ready for the kingdom of God which is at hand. And this kingdom is present, as soon as it is awaited in such a way that one's hope is no longer set upon the world which is coming to an end.

What Jesus intends in all these sayings is hopelessly misrepresented, if it is supposed that the 'losing' of life and the 'gaining' which is promised as a result, are so related to each other that the 'gaining' of life follows the 'losing' of it in time, so that life is 'gained' only in the future. Rather, the 'losing' which is spoken of in the first part of this saying does not come about only after someone seeks to gain his life, for he loses it from the very first in making this attempt and as a result of it. And likewise, the 'gaining' of life takes place directly in the 'losing' of which the second half of the saying speaks. But this is only possible because both the 'losing' and the 'gaining' takes place through and within the kingdom of God. For the 'losing' takes place, as we have seen,[8] in the experience of the judgment upon the present world; and the 'gaining' is only possible through the grace of God. But judgment and grace are so closely linked in the act of God that one takes place in the other. It is because this is so, and is the fact which the preaching of Jesus claims to reveal, that it is eschatological preaching. And consequently the relationship between 'gaining' and 'losing' is such that one 'gains' one's life by 'losing' it, and there is no interval of time between one and the other. Rather, the 'gaining' takes place in the very same present moment as the 'losing'. Because the life that has been 'gained' is present in the presence of the kingdom of God, its being present is something that can only be perceived in faith. That is, the coming to an end of the present world is only provisional in so far as this world still exists as the temptation for man. Thus the 'life that is gained', which is equivalent to his salvation, is never present without this temptation, with which faith has to battle so long as it remains faith. For faith ceases to be faith when the temptation that comes from the present world ceases to be present and disappears.

That can mean two things. Either that faith is still only the arbitrary affirmation of a dogmatic assertion, or else that it has been transformed into what Paul calls 'knowing face to face', in which 'I know as I am known', as opposed to knowledge 'in part', or in the dim image in which one can see in a mirror (it is of course a metal mirror which Paul has in mind; I Cor. 13.12). Thus the existence of salvation in the present moment, which takes place through the presence of judgment, is such that it can exist only in faith. The point of this 'only' is not to do away with the presence of salvation; rather, it makes clear that salvation is constantly threatened by the temptations of the world which is coming to an end. In so far as the presence of salvation is of this nature, it points to a consummation, not of course of salvation in itself – for this, as something bestowed by God alone, is always whole and complete – but of the extent to which it is present. This consummation can only take place when the present world finally comes to an end. This can only come about through man's death. Yet nothing new happens in death with regard to salvation itself, but only with regard to the threat that comes from the present world and its temptations. Of course death is the severest threat to salvation, and the hardest test which faith must endure. That is why salvation is revealed in its purest presence, unassailed and invulnerable, in the endurance of this test. Only in this way, on the basis of the presence here and now of the eschatological event, can one also speak of an event which is still to take place in the future, the final end of all things.

NOTES

1. Cf. above, p. 49.
2. Cf. above. p. 48.
3. Cf. above, p. 49f.
4. Cf. Conzelmann, *Zeitschrift für Theologie und Kirche*, Beiheft 1, pp. 5, 13.
5. Cf. my book *Verhängnis und Hoffnung der Neuzeit*, Stuttgart, pp. 174ff.
6. Cf. Käsemann, 'Eine Apologie der urchristlichen Theologie', *ZThK*, 1952, pp. 272ff.
7. Cf. above, p. 102.
8. Cf. above, p. 102.

10

THE PREACHING OF JESUS AND THE PRESENT WORLD

DID THE primitive Christian church come to realize the responsibility of man for the world – which we recognized as the assumption behind everything which is proclaimed in the primitive Christian kerygma – only by transforming Jesus's gospel of the kingdom of God into the kerygma of the Christ, who, in the responsibility which he took upon himself for the world, became its *kyrios*? Or did Jesus recognize this responsibility for the world previously and take it upon himself? We asked these questions at the beginning of the previous chapter. In order to answer them, we examined his preaching. We took as our starting-point the discovery of recent scholarship that this preaching was completely eschatological. By contrast with the apocalyptic eschatology current in the Judaism of his time, the transformation of the world which Jesus proclaimed was not merely something which was deferred until the final end of the present world, but something which was already taking place at the present time in the coming of the kingdom of God. Whether man participates in the coming kingdom of God or not depends upon whether he is able to break away from the present world. It is faith in the approaching rule of God which makes it possible for him so to break away.

What is decisive here is that what takes place in the transformation of the world which Jesus proclaimed is not, as in Jewish apocalyptic eschatology, a passage from one cosmic world to another different one, from an old to a new world, but a new attitude of man to the world in which he lives, which is fundamentally different from the old. Man is responsible for this new relationship, through which the world is reconstituted in the sense that the salvation which comes with the kingdom of God is present in it. He remains responsible for it, moreover, as long as he lives. This new relationship of man to the world, with which the transformation of the world as we understand it here is concerned, differs from the old principally in that it is no longer the present world and its ordering which determine the relationship of man to God. In consequence, this relationship to God is no longer perverted into an abysmal hypocrisy, such as came about through the domination of the present world over man. Thus Jesus's eschatological message of the coming kingdom of God calls upon man, in readiness for the kingdom of God, to forsake the domination of the present world and its ordinance, which it exercises through the ritual piety which is in accordance with this domination. As a result, man, who was responsible *to* the world through ritual piety, becomes responsible *for* it. That is, he becomes responsible for its no longer dominating him through its characteristic piety and so separating him from God.

Thus we can say that it was not the primitive Christian church which first realized man's responsibility *for* the world; Jesus had already done so. But this is only to answer the first question we asked and not the second – did he also, as primitive Christian preaching states, realize this responsibility in his life and thereby become the *kyrios* of the world? Again, only Jesus's own preaching can give us the answer to this question. We must consider what he says in it about himself, the bearer of this proclamation.

If we are to do this, then we must constantly make a distinction between what the preaching of the primitive Christian church says about this matter, and what Jesus's own preaching says. Without exception, the statements of the church on the subject all proceed from the belief that by taking on a fate imposed upon the world and the men who live in it as his own, in responsibility for them, he averted this sentence of doom and so became Lord of the world. In order to affirm that he carried out this task, and did so through the power of God, and that God then accepted and confirmed this responsibility as that in which the sentence of doom was averted, the primitive Christian church spoke of Jesus, even in his earthly life, with the divine titles which are appropriate to such a Messiah. It therefore spoke of Jesus and his work in the way that was possible after he had carried it out.

• • •

The Preaching of Jesus and the Present World 119

The first question is whether Jesus himself claimed for himself and his preaching any of these messianic titles. It is difficult to decide whether or not he did so, because it is difficult to dispute that he claimed for his preaching an authority which – to say the least – was very close to that of a Messiah, in the sense in which the Jewish people had long awaited the coming of such a Messiah. He did so by claiming that the kingdom of God had been directly inaugurated in his preaching, and that whether or not men accepted or rejected his preaching, and therefore himself, was equivalent to a decision upon their salvation or damnation. So at least we must understand the saying of Jesus that, 'I saw Satan fall like lightning from heaven. Behold, I have given you authority to tread upon serpents and scorpions, and over all the power of the enemy; and nothing shall hurt you' (Luke 10.18f.). The saying, 'He who is not with me is against me and he who does not gather with me scatters' (Matt. 12.30), has, indisputably, the same reference. And he can also say; 'Blessed are the eyes which see what you see. For I tell you that many prophets and kings desired to see what you see, and did not see, and to hear what you hear, and did not hear it' (Luke 10.23f.).

But what is the basis of the authority which Jesus claims for his preaching and for himself? According to the view current at the time, the Messiah had to show that he was authorized by God through particular 'signs', that is, through miracles. That is why the Pharisees came to Jesus and tried to test whether he was really the Messiah, by requiring him to authenticate himself by an appropriate 'sign from heaven'. But he rejected this, and referred them to his preaching and to the repentance which he called for (Matt. 16.1–4). In the same way, he withdrew from the crowds which were gathering about him because of the healings and other miracles which he carried out, and also instructed those he had healed to keep silent about what he had done for them (Mark 1.35ff.; 1.44). He did do miracles, but not in order to show that he was the Messiah. As far as the authority of his preaching was concerned, he was not able either to appeal, as was customary in the Judaism of the time, to any recognized office or ministry which he held, which would have been the guarantee that his preaching was in accordance with what was regarded as the truth in the present world in which he lived. As a result, there was nothing to which he could appeal, except what he preached. But, in the world in which he preached, it was for his preaching that an authentication was required which would be acceptable in that world.

This was the situation of Jesus with regard to the world to which he preached the coming of the kingdom of God; and for him, no other position was possible with regard to the present world. That necessarily followed from what he preached. We have seen that his message of the coming of the kingdom of God stands or falls by its proclamation, at the same time, of the the coming to an end of the present world and its ordinance. If Jesus had had anything with which he could satisfy, in accordance with the ordinance of this world, the demand for a proof of the authority and truth of his preaching, this would not have been a proof of the truth of his preaching, but rather an unmistakable sign that it was not true. It would have meant that his preaching would not have been of the coming kingdom of God. If this is the situation in which Jesus found himself with regard to the present world, then it is clear that the present world and the kingdom of God which he preached, completely exclude one another, and are irreconcilable alternatives. It is this that his preaching asserts. Here, indeed, one is dealing with two masters, both of whom one cannot serve at once. 'Either he will hate the one and love the other, or he will be devoted to the one and despise the other. You cannot serve God and mammon' (Matt. 6.24).

In this study of the preaching of Jesus, we are trying to find out what it said about him who uttered it. An extraordinarily important conclusion can be drawn from what we have already said. The decision Jesus demands in his preaching he takes on his own account by the very fact of having preached it. That is, it is of the nature of what he preached, that he is only capable of preaching it by making for himself, in the very act of preaching, the decision between two irreconcilable alternatives, the present world with its ordinance and the coming kingdom of God. On Jesus's own lips, that is, in connection with his message of the kingdom of God, the saying which is so central to his preaching, that whoever loses his life will gain it, is not a wise saying which can be applied to various occasions, and which someone can hold to be true without having already realized it. In the form in which Jesus uttered it, it can never be uttered by anyone who does not abandon his life, as it is lived in the present world, in reliance on the ordinance which prevails within it, by placing his trust in the coming of the kingdom of God and so receiving the life which is in accordance with the kingdom. To understand properly what this means, it is necessary to bear in mind that Jesus proclaimed his message of the coming kingdom of God in the midst of the present world and under the ordinance which prevails in it. It is likewise necessary to understand quite explicitly what this meant for him. It meant that by what he preached, not only did he come into direct opposition to this world and its ordinance, but also aroused the opposition and hostility of this world against him and his preaching.

The opposition of the present world to Jesus is made deeper by the fact that his conflict with it does not affect one or another individual aspect of it, which might be changed without affecting its stable existence. Rather, it is the profoundest basis of this world which is threatened by the preaching of Jesus, that is, its cultic and legal piety. It is this aspect of it which Jesus attacks most passionately; for it is this which maintains what is most characteristic of it. As we have seen, he dismisses this piety as an abysmal hypocrisy. The charge is all the more pointed, and goes all the deeper, because as we have seen, it is not meant merely in a subjective sense. If this were the case, then it would apply only to the way in which this piety were practised by particular individuals, whether few or many. But his criticism is aimed at the essence of this piety. For however it is practised, whether with fanatical seriousness or with conventional casualness, its essential basis is that it claims to serve God and the life which men have to receive from God through its practice. But, in fact, it serves the world that is constituted by it, and the regard that one receives through it in the eyes of the world. It is this that Jesus calls its hypocrisy. This charge is appropriate to those who are the guardians of this piety, because for what they call the true service of God they appeal to the prophets. But the prophets have already unmasked this piety as idolatry. Consequently their veneration of the prophets, whose authority they claim for themselves and for whom they build tombs, is nothing but hypocrisy (Matt. 23.29-33). Jesus found himself in an opposition to the present world which was unconditional and exclusive, and this was in exact accordance with the irreconcilable conflict and hostility between the present world and him and his preaching. Consequently, it was virtually certain that between them, sooner or later, a dispute would arise which led to catastrophe.

But the fact that Jesus proclaimed his message of the coming kingdom of God in the midst of the present world, and under the domination of the ordinance which prevails within it, implies another statement which we must consider further. This concerns Jesus's relationship to the men who live in this world. Here one must distinguish between his different attitude to two groups. On the one hand, there are the authorities of the present world, whose task and passion it is to watch over the piety which is enforced in it and maintains it in being, the 'scribes and Pharisees', to use the stereotyped phrase which is constantly repeated in the synoptic gospels. On the other hand there are those who likewise live in this world but who, for whatever reason, are not at home within it, and do not belong to it and trust in it in the same natural way as the others.

The former, the scribes and Pharisees, are those who by their strict observance of the ritual and legal prescriptions, and equally strict exhortation to follow them, make particularly clear the nature of this piety. For it is against them above all that Jesus makes the charge that 'they do all their deeds to be seen by men', and in this way hope to achieve respect and honour in the world which is theirs (Matt. 6.1; 23.5). They are the true representatives of the present world, and its domination over the men who live in it. Their whole thought and activity is directed towards maintaining this world in being: 'You traverse sea and land to make a single proselyte, and when he becomes a proselyte, you make him twice as much a child of hell as yourselves' (Matt. 23.15). This is because they put the commandments of their own world in the place of the word of God. Thus they deprive the latter of its validity and lead the people astray into honouring God only with their lips, while keeping their hearts far from him (Mark 7.1–13). Instead of showing men the way into the kingdom of God, they close it to them; they neither enter themselves, nor allow those who would enter to go in (Matt. 23.13). As we have already heard, they may well be zealous to follow pious sophistries, by scrupulously tithing mint, dill and cummin; but the weightier matters, justice and mercy and faith, they neglect (Matt. 23.23).

It is this which leads to such atrocious perversions such as that which enables someone, by appealing to the laws of this piety, to avoid the most elementary duties towards his father and mother, by declaring that that with which he is able and ought to support them, he has consecrated to God as a pious offering, so that it is no longer possible for him to give it to his parents (Mark 7.9–13). They do the same to the commandment concerning the sabbath. The guardians of this piety, who were lying in wait for Jesus in order to accuse him when he healed a sick person on the sabbath, were sorely embarrassed by Jesus's question whether it was permitted to do good or to do evil on the sabbath (Mark 3.1ff.). Consequently, those who claimed for themselves the authority of Moses, the highest which existed amongst the Jewish people, received this bitter condemnation: 'Woe to you, scribes and Pharisees, hypocrites' (Matt. 23.23). For with ther piety and the 'tradition' which they put forward as the commandment of God, they made it impossible for themselves and those who listened to them to recognize the reality in which God calls for obedience to his command.

Jesus's attitude towards the other group of people was completely different from this. Whereas the woes applied to the one, the beatitudes were spoken of the other. This group is not so closely defined as the first. The most diverse figures appear in it. We have already tried, albeit only provisionally, to find a possible way of identifying them as a second group by contrast to the first. That is, that they are those who, for whatever reason, are not at home in the present world as it exists, and who in some way are excluded from it. Jesus himself once summed them up by referring to them as 'sinners'. He said he had come 'not to call the righteous, but sinners' (Matt. 9.13). One of the most offensive things in Jesus's attitude to the guardians of traditional piety was that 'he eats and drinks with tax collectors and sinners' (Mark 2.15f.). Thus they regarded him as 'a glutton and a drunkard, a friend of tax collectors and sinners' (Matt. 11.19). For by doing this, he put himself into the company of those who were most scrupulously avoided by the devout.

Jesus quite openly used the expression 'sinner', in the sense in which his opponents understood it, and so made the opposition which lay between him and them acute to a degree which was unbearable to them. For they naturally understood the word 'sinner' in the sense of their own piety. Here, 'sinners' were those who, because they did not or could not keep the ritual laws, because their calling did not make it possible for them to do this, lacked full rights or any rights at all in the world of this piety. According to this view, however, those who had undergone some misfortune were also 'sinners', for according to the view of divine retribution which was prevalent, 'whenever a man met with any unusual misfortune or distress, the question inevitably arose as to the latent cause of his sufferings'.[1] Thus in the Gospel of John, Jesus is asked by his disciples, 'Who sinned, this man or his parents, that he was born blind?' (John 9.1f.). According to this view, the eighteen people who were killed by the tower in Siloam falling on them, were more guilty than all the others who dwelt in Jerusalem (Luke 13.4). Jesus understood himself to be sent to these 'sinners', and not to those who in the present world are accounted 'righteous'. And the significance of his sending is not at all to call the 'sinners' to become righteous in this world through 'penance'. For he is not calling them into the world as it exists, but out of it into the kingdom of God, which stands in direct opposition to it. He calls them into this kingdom as those, who because they are excluded from this world as it exists, are closer to the kingdom of God than those who in this world are the 'righteous'. Consequently, 'Many that are first will be last, and the last first' (Mark 10.31). Amongst those who are last, and who will be first, Jesus names 'the tax collectors and harlots' (Matt. 21.31); it is scarcely possible for us to realize how scandalous this was in the eyes of the piety of the time.

But it is not only such as these, excluded because of their public sinfulness from the world as it exists, who belong to the group of those to whom Jesus understands himself to be sent in this sense. This group also includes the poor, those who in some bodily or spiritual way are wretched, the hungry and thirsty, the lonely and sick, the blind, the lame, the lepers, and finally those who are lowly, and children, who are nothing or not yet anything in the present world.

The question has constantly been asked, whether Jesus was referring to these persons in the real sense or only in a metaphorical sense. For example, was he speaking of those who are actually poor, or, as in Matt. 5.3, only the 'poor in spirit'? This question seems to me to have been posed falsely. There is no doubt that it is not absolutely obligatory to take a list of persons of this kind in the literal sense. They are examples which Jesus names, and what is said about them is true: by contrast to the 'righteous' of the present world they are near to the kingdom of God. But the same is also true of those of whom they are only examples. But it is one of the characteristics of Jesus's thought that he always chooses as examples very elementary cases, such as those who are actually poor, or those who are bodily blind and lame, in order to make unmistakably clear to us that he is speaking of something which is as offensive as it is incomprehensible to the thinking of the present world, and in order to point repeatedly to the irreconcilable contradiction between the present world and the coming kingdom of God.

What does it mean to say that people of this kind, the tax collectors and harlots, like the poor and wretched, are close to the kingdom of God? If the picture we have given of the preaching of Jesus is correct in its main outlines, then it cannot have been Jesus's opinion that those who live under a disadvantage in the present world, because they are not fully recognized in it, are to be compensated in the coming kingdom of God for what they have previously lacked. Nor do the sayings signify that to be poor and wretched, to suffer misfortune and to be sick is in itself an advantage – as if for example, by bearing this in patience and humility, one might be led to seek and to attain through it an inner happiness. If what Jesus says is understood in the context of the eschatological message of the coming to an end of the present world and the coming of the kingdom of God – and this is the only way in which it is possible to understand it in the sense in which he meant it – then such statements mean that all such people have at any rate the advantage of not being so bound to the present world as the others. For them, one might say, the world is not so comfortable, not so self-contained, as for the others who 'have their reward'. Consequently, they have ears to hear about the coming kingdom, while the others cannot hear because they are entangled in the present world and can only understand what has a meaning within it.

But again, this ability to hear does not mean that because

people are poor and wretched, they can automatically hear this message aright. Once again, we must bear in mind what it means for Jesus to proclaim his message of the coming kingdom of God in the midst of the present world and under the domination of the ordinance that prevails within it, and for him to proclaim it, we must add, to men who live in this world. Jesus's conflict with this world and with the piety which dominates within and over it could not have been so sharp and implacable as it was, if he had not known how great the power is which this world exercises over those who live in it, and as long as they live in it. When he spoke of it, he spoke of 'Satan', the 'strong man', whose house no one can enter and plunder his goods unless he has first bound the 'strong man'. Only then can he plunder his house (Matt. 12.29). But another form of this parable states that it is possible for this 'unclean spirit', when he is driven out of his house, to return. 'And when he comes he finds it empty, swept and put in order. Then he goes and brings with him seven other spirits more evil than himself, and they enter and dwell there; and the last state of that man becomes worse than the first. So shall it be also with this evil generation' (Matt. 12.43ff.). We have already quoted the saying of Jesus which speaks of the authority 'to tread upon serpents and scorpions, and over all the power of the enemy' (Luke 10.19).

In order to understand the power which this world possesses, one must bear in mind that its basis and source lies in the piety which prevails within it as the world that now exists. This piety in its turn owes its domination to the fact that it is this piety which constitutes this world as such. That is, by means of the law which belongs to it, for those who live in the world it makes the reality in which they find themselves an all-embracing entity which possesses its meaningful – that is, worldly – unity, which makes it a world, in the law which prevails throughout the totality of human reality. In this way, the men who fulfil this law receive their life from this secular entity. When one remembers that this ritual and legal piety imposes this law upon men in the name of God, the creator and Lord, one can judge how utterly irresistible is the domination with which it holds men imprisoned in the dominion it has set up.

The power which the present world has over the men who live in it lies in its being closed in itself, in what I might term its 'religious totalitarianism', in which it tolerates absolutely no one and nothing within itself which does not belong to it, and which does not serve it, by receiving from it its life and its meaning. Perhaps it is this 'religious totalitarianism', which the present world as it exists derives from its characteristic ritual and legal piety, to which Jesus is referring in the parable quoted above when he says that the 'strong man' must first be bound before it is possible to break into his house, that is, in the world dominated by this piety. In other words, the power of this piety must be broken. The only way this is possible is for the nature of this piety – what Jesus calls its 'hypocrisy' – to be unmasked. A mere doctrinal enlightenment is not sufficient to do this. This already existed within Judaism, at least in so far as voices were present within it which echoed the Old Testament prophets and said such things as: 'It makes no difference whether one does little or much, so long as one's heart is fixed upon heaven (i.e. God)'. or: 'Whosoever in his dealings and behaviour with the creatures is actuated by faithfulness is accounted as having fulfilled the whole Torah'. Or it was taught that what mattered was 'so long as men are of good will their sins are absorbed by their good deeds, while, conversely, the good done by a man of ill will is worthless'.[2] But in accordance with the characteristic thought of Judaism, such doctrines always remained merely individual sayings included amongst the whole series of traditional opinions. The doctrines of the rabbis were always simply placed side by side. They were 'faithfully preserved, indeed, verbatim, wherever possible, with the name of the rabbi who first uttered it'.[3] But they are and remain isolated opinions amongst others, and so they do not affect the whole, and cannot break down its worldly structure. And in this way, the domination of ritual and legal piety continued to be taken for granted by those who lived in this world.

Although when someone for some reason is excluded from the closed world of this piety the possibility of his hearing the message of the coming kingdom of God is much greater than for anyone else, he can only truly hear it when this message is proclaimed in the present world in such a way that the totality of this world is brought into question by it. This means that the law of its piety must be broken down as obviously and clearly as its domination in this world is now obvious. It was this which took place through Jesus's attitude to the 'sinners', those who were excluded from this world on the basis of its law. Not only did he refrain from scrupulously avoiding fellowship with them, as this law demanded; he explicitly sought it. We have already said that the fact that he did this was for the leaders of the Jewish people, who regarded themselves as responsible for the existing piety and therefore for the ordering and the continued existence of their world, one of the most scandalous things in Jesus's attitude. But for the 'sinners', who by the very fact of their exclusion from a world so completely closed in upon itself experienced its irresistible power over them, the encounter with this man who sought their fellowship by 'calling' them who were sinners was something utterly incomprehensible. But this incomprehensible attitude itself had the power to make the possibility of 'hearing', which they possessed as those who were excluded from the present world, into real 'hearing'. This was all the more the case in that this man who dared to unmask the perversion of the piety which excluded them from the world, forgave them their sins and did so in the name of God, whose kingdom he proclaimed as now coming. All this was wholly different from a merely doctrinal enlightenment concerning the piety which prevails in the present world. Rather, it was a historical act of quite extraordinary significance. For in it the relationship of man to the world, and therefore the world itself, was transformed in its very essence.

NOTES

1. Bultmann, *Das Urchristentum im Rahmen des antiken Religion*, Zürich 1949, p. 76; tr. R. H. Fuller, *Primitive Christianity in its Contemporary Setting*, Thames and Hudson, 1956, p. 70.
2. Bultmann, op. cit., p. 72; tr. p. 67.
3. Op. cit., p. 69; tr. p. 64.

II

JESUS'S PREACHING IS WITHOUT AUTHENTICATION IN THE PRESENT WORLD

WE HAVE already seen that when Jesus said he had come to call 'sinners' (Matt. 9.13), this did not mean to call them to become 'righteous' in the present world. For such a calling could only mean to fulfil anew the law of the piety which prevails in the present world. But from everything which we have already learned about his preaching, it is impossible for the call of Jesus to mean this. Rather, he called those who 'have ears to hear', and in his experience these were, above all, those who in the judgment of the present world were 'sinners', and were therefore excluded for ever from this world. He called them to turn away from it and towards the coming kingdom of God which he was proclaiming. The break which Jesus made with the piety of the traditional world goes so deep that the basic language of this piety received a completely different meaning when he used it. Consequently, no agreement was possible between him and the representatives of this piety in any decisive matter. It is true that they both used the same words, but in them they were speaking two completely different languages. How could these devout men understand Jesus when he said of those who for them were simply the 'last' – that is those who were condemned without question in their world as 'sinners' – that equally without question they would be the 'first' in the kingdom of God which he was proclaiming? What could it be other than a dreadful and incomprehensible blasphemy to those who professed this piety when they heard Jesus say, 'There will be more joy in heaven over one sinner who repents than over ninety-nine righteous persons who need no repentance' (Luke 15.7).

These and similar sayings of Jesus, and indeed his whole preaching, are misunderstood if one does not realize that the men who were openly condemned as 'sinners' by the traditional piety were not sinners to him. And therefore, in such a statement as 'I am come to call sinners', the word 'sinner' is used in a sense completely contradictory to that of the judgment of the devout about those to whom this word refers, and signifies that he, Jesus, does not regard them as 'sinners'. This is made perfectly clear if one translates the Greek word not as 'call', but as 'invite', which is the meaning which it in fact possesses here. Thus Jesus first of all used the word 'sinner' in precisely the sense in which the devout understood it, while at the same time he was rejecting this meaning in what was for the devout a most abrupt and most scandalous way.

But one would not be doing justice to what Jesus was saying here if one did not notice that the word 'sinner', as he used it, has yet another sense. This comes not from the world as it exists from which they were excluded, but rather from that into which he called the people whom he had in mind here, or more precisely, invited them, that is, the kingdom of God. This meaning remained incomprehensible to the devout Jews, at least as long as the kingdom of God which Jesus proclaimed as coming remained hidden from them, that is, as long as they supposed that by contrast to the 'sinners' whom Jesus was inviting they belonged to the righteous whom he was not inviting, in a way in which to them must have appeared completely unreasonable. Thus the men Jesus had come to call were those who, in the judgment of the devout, were in fact 'sinners', and this is why he called them such, so that the devout might know who he was calling. Although they were not 'sinners' for him in this sense, they were nevertheless in need of the grace of God. But in this they were not distinct or separate from any other person, whoever he might be. The only thing which distinguished them from the 'righteous' is that as those who were excluded from the present world, they were nearer to this grace than the righteous. Jesus's attitude to them was in accordance with this. He took them to himself and did not withdraw from them (Luke 15.2). There is nothing which divided them from him. When a chief tax collector showed an unusual desire at least to see Jesus as he passed by in the street, and therefore climbed into a tree,

Jesus invited himself into his house. For the men of the ancient world this was a particularly close association, which in this case was extraordinarily offensive to devout Jews – and when they were in his house, Jesus said to this man: 'today salvation has come to this house, since he also is a son of Abraham', that is, someone to whom the promise given to Abraham applied (Luke 19.1ff.).

It was scarcely possible for Jesus to take the part of these 'sinners', and to unite himself with them more decisively than in the way in which he passed judgment upon the Pharisee and the tax collector in the parable. He first portrays the Pharisee as an exemplary person in the terms of Jewish piety, who, when he went into the temple to pray, thanked God for making him someone who fulfilled his religious duties beyond the usual measure, and was, therefore, not like other men, extortioners, unjust, adulterers, or even like the tax collector who happened to be in the vicinity. But Jesus contrasts him with the tax collector, who with the prayer 'God, be merciful to me a sinner!' was able to say everything that moved him. He says of the two, the Pharisee, who for every Jew was without question righteous, and the tax collector, who according to the judgment of Jewish piety was equally without question a sinner, 'This man went down to his house justified rather than the other' (Luke 18.10ff.). How did Jesus come to pass such a judgment upon these two men, and why did he place himself, as he does with this judgment, on the side of the 'sinner', so becoming, as his opponents rightly saw, their equal? If we recall the sayings that the last will be first and the first last (Matt. 19.30), we can say that he made such a judgment because the tax collector, who was conscious of his sin – the parable says explicitly of him that he, 'standing far off, would not even lift up his eyes to heaven, but beat his breast' – was one of those who are last, while the Pharisee was convinced that he was one of those who are first.

But here again, we would not be doing justice to Jesus's words if we understood the expression 'to be last' only in the sense of Jewish piety, that one who is 'last' in this way is someone excluded from the world of Jewish piety. Of course this is so, and because of this such a person is one of those for whom it is possible to become 'first' in Jesus's sense. As long as this is only a possibility, however, such people still remain under the constraining influence of the world from which they are excluded. This possibility only becomes a reality when such a person is no longer 'last' merely in the sense of Jewish piety, but when he becomes last in a completely changed and much more profound sense. What this means is expressed, in the parable of the Pharisee and the tax collector, in the tax collector's prayer: 'God, be merciful to me a sinner!' Anyone who, like this tax collector, knows that he is dependent upon the grace of God, and cannot find salvation anywhere except in his grace, is one of the 'last' in the extreme sense that by comparison with it the piety of the Pharisee, and the world from which the 'sinners' are excluded, becomes an insubstantial thing. But because of this he now becomes 'first', or, as Jesus said of the tax collector in his parable, righteous. But he becomes righteous in a sense completely different from that of the traditional piety, and quite incomprehensible to it. For this righteousness can never be possessed, as something well earned, after the manner of that piety. Anyone who receives it does so as one who knows that he is 'last', and that this is how he becomes righteous in the sight of God. This is something given to him by pure grace, which is nothing but grace.

Thus what determined the attitude of Jesus to those to whom he had come was what he had to preach to those who, although they were excluded from the present world, still lived in it under the domination of the piety which prevails in it. This was his message of the coming kingdom of God. We have already seen that as a result of the completely exclusive opposition between it and the present world, Jesus's message was only possible in so far as he directly took for himself, in the act of his preaching, the decision that must be made in the face of the irreconcilable alternative which this opposition produces. With this decision he at once placed himself on the side of those who were excluded from the present world. For with this decision, he excluded himself from this world, and was therefore himself one of them. It is impossible to exaggerate the exposed position in which his existence was placed as an inevitable consequence of this. We have already seen that there was nothing in the present world on which he could call to authenticate his preaching and the decision that came with it. He, like his message, was completely alone in the face of the world in which he was living. For even those who believed his preaching and followed him were people so constituted that they were anything but an authentication for him in this world. If there was anything over and above what he preached which could still be an encumbrance to him, and could make his whole preaching incredible in the sight of the present world, they could. All that could sustain him, the sole and only thing on which he could rely, was therefore the coming kingdom of God. This is so much the exclusive basis of his preaching that one can say that what speaks in him is the presence of the kingdom itself. It seems to be this which the gospels mean when they say of those who heard him, 'They were astonished at his teaching, for he taught them as one who had authority, and not as the scribes' (Mark 1.22 and parallels).

The difference between the teaching of Jesus and that of the Pharisees is that the teaching of the latter was bound to the present world and the quite unquestionable authority of the ordinance prevailing within it. In accordance with the principle of Jewish piety, that the whole of life ought to possess the 'character of ritual holiness',[1] this ordinance had to take in all the variety and complexity of the phenomena of life. Thus the task of the scribes' teaching was to find as far as possible, for every conceivable individual case, the necessary prescriptions which corresponded to this ritual and legal piety. It was consequently unable to avoid giving the impression of a weird scrupulosity and a triviality which was as insecure as it was meticulous with regard to the observation of the ordinance of the present world. This can perhaps most clearly be seen in the fact that the number of prescriptions constantly grew, and the proportion of prohibitions amongst them was extraordinarily large.

One can say of the authority for which Jesus's preaching came to have a reputation amongst those who heard it, that it represents the positive side of the fact that it was quite impossible for him to give proof of his authority as a teacher within the structure of the present world. For he could call upon none of the authorities that exist within it. Or – to put it even more pointedly – where he seems to be doing this, he does so in such a way that the authority to which he is appealing, instead of being for him, is thereby made to speak against him. Thus, for example, in Matthew 11.2ff. he refers the disciples of the Baptist, who had sent them to ask him whether he was the promised Messiah, to the prophet Isaiah: 'The blind receive their sight and the lame walk, lepers are cleansed and the deaf hear, and the poor have good news preached to them.' Then, however, by referring this to himself in the words, 'And blessed is he who takes no offence at me', he claims to apply this promise of the prophet to his own ministry in such a way that it could not but seem anything but a blasphemy to a pious Jew. But those who 'have ears to hear' – who were on the one hand those who 'labour and are heavy laden' under the burden of this legal piety (Matt. 11.28), and, on the other hand, those who are 'not yet skilled'[2] in its confusion and sophistry – perceived in his automatic and sovereign disregard for the existing authorities the authority which this man claimed for his preaching. And they noted that the teaching of this man, unlike that of his opponents, was not committed to the service of the present world and the ordinance which prevails within it.

Jesus described the nature of this authority himself in the parable of the labourers in the vineyard. The master of a vineyard sent workers into his vineyard at various hours of the day, from the early morning until an hour before sunset. He agreed with the first labourers he hired upon a wage of a denarius a day. To those who he hired later he said, 'Whatever is right I will give you'. All he said to those he hired last was 'You go into the vineyards, too'. But when evening came, regardless of the different lengths of time for which they had worked, the master paid all of them the same wage which he had agreed with the labourers he had taken on in the early morning. When those who, as they said, had borne the burden of the day under scorching heat grumbled to him that they had received the same wage as the last who had worked for only an hour, he said to one of them: 'Friend, I am doing you no wrong; did you not agree with me for a denarius? Take what belongs to you, and go; I choose to give to this last as I give to you. Am I not allowed to do what I choose with what belongs to me? Or do you begrudge my generosity?' (Matt. 20.1ff.).

This parable compares two completely different modes of thought. The one is that of the workers who have worked all day, and find it a cruel injustice that for the work which they have carried out they receive no more wage than those who have done incomparably less than them. For this is the ordinance in the working world in which they live and think – that the wage shall be in accordance with the work. The other mode of thought, completely incomprehensible to these labourers, is that of the master of the vineyard. Of course he pays the labourers he hired in the early morning their wage, in accordance with the agreement he has made with them and which they had approved, and pays them what he owes them. But at the same time he regards himself as free, as the master of what he owns, to do with it as his generosity suggests. The surprising thing is that the labourers who call upon their rights, and dispute his right to follow his generosity, place themselves in the wrong, because their thinking in terms of what is fair leaves no place for generosity, which makes them envious.

One can scarcely be wrong in seeing the purpose for which Jesus tells this parable in his wish to justify his own attitude to 'sinners' in the sight of his pious opponents. He does so by presenting them with the idea that the authority on which his action is based belongs as much outside the world of their piety as the generosity of the master of the vineyard was offensive to the labourers who were obsessed with the idea of fairness. The god in whose name the Pharisees and scribes rejected the preaching of Jesus and his attitude was the god of the present world and its ordinance. Just as the relationship of man to this god is bound up with the ordinance of this world – for only someone who adapts himself to this ordinance and fulfils its prescriptions is righteous in his sight – so also the relationship of this god to men is subject to the ordinance of this world. It is true that according to the Jewish belief he is the Lord of this world. But, comparing him with the master of the vineyard in the parable, he cannot do what he chooses with what belongs to him for he has made himself and his will subject to this world and its ordinance – for this is the nature of this god and the piety which serves him. One must remember this in order to understand how monstrous it seemed to those who believed in this god, for Jesus to say that God 'makes his sun to rise on the evil and on the good, and sends rain on the just and on the unjust' (Matt. 5.45). For if this god does not follow the existing order of the world, he ceases to be credible. His credibility depends on it being true that someone who cannot point to the achievements which the ordinance of this world requires does badly in it, while one who fulfils this ordinance does well. That is why those who are devout in the manner of this world were also convinced that they could tell with certainty, from the misfortune that someone had suffered in this world, that he had sinned. And in fact the learning of the scribes included the ability to calculate 'the punishment applicable to particular sins . . . down to the last detail. . . . Wherever a man met with unusual misfortune or distress, the question inevitably arose as to the latent cause of his misfortune.'[3]

Jesus would have nothing to do with such calculations. The God on whose authority he based the authority of his preaching and his attitude is not subject to the ordinance of the present world. In the kingdom of this God, human achievements count for nothing. Such achievements would be necessary within the world; but before God all that can ever be said of them is: 'When you have done all that is commanded you, say, "We are unworthy servants; we have only done what was our duty"' (Luke 17.10). Thus the authority to which Jesus appeals has its validity in the fact that it cannot be authenticated in any way by anything which belongs within the present world and is of value in it. There is only one thing which authenticates it, and that is the coming kingdom of God which Jesus preaches, and which is in exclusive opposition to the present world, since in its coming a judgment comes upon this world and its authorities. We have already said that if there had been anything within the ordinance of the present world which could have served Jesus as an authentication for his preaching, it would not have been a proof of its truth, but an indisputable sign of its untruth.[4] The kingdom that he would then have been preaching would never have been the final end of the world as its exists, but only one of the many changes in some particular aspect of it which are constantly taking place in everything, but never change the enduring condition of this world. His preaching would then have been based on this world, and on the ordinance which maintains it in being. Its significance could only have been that of the formation of a new party in it, with the task of spreading the ideas and views of Jesus, in order to bring through them an appropriate change within the existing world. The exclusive opposition between the coming kingdom of God and this world would not then have existed in reality. To assert this opposition would only have been a propaganda element which could have been used in the dispute between different parties, in an attempt to give the desired force and penetration to the view of one's own party.

But if Jesus did not preach merely a change of this kind in the present world, which had to be authenticated within it, but really preached the coming kingdom of God through which the final judgment is passed upon the present world, then the authentication for this preaching cannot be sought anywhere but in God himself. It can be sought, moreover, only in a God who is not subject to the present world and its ordinance. Now, as we have seen in our study of the preaching of Jesus,[5] the God whose will Jesus proclaims is in fact the God who reveals himself as such only to those who – in faith in him – dare to lose the life which they have lived hitherto, in reliance upon the present world and its ordinance, and who in losing this life gain that which God gives them in his coming kingdom. It then becomes clear that this kingdom is not some new kind of present world, to which, with its ordinance, this God would be as much subject as he was subject to the old. It is easier to understand what Jesus had in mind when he spoke of the kingdom of God if we remember that the Greek words *basileia Theou* (literally translated, kingdom, kingly rule of God) as Jesus used them did not have the meaning of a sphere ruled by God, but signified the dominion, the lordship of God in the sense of his rule. Just as the kingdom of God as Jesus proclaimed it is in opposition to the existing world and its ordinance, so also the dominion of God must be understood as a rule which is opposed to the dominion exercised by the present world over the men who live in it. These two kinds of dominion are exclusive: either the world as it exists at any time rules over men, or else God does. But in Jesus's proclamation of the kingdom of God, his thought reaches out beyond the world which had hitherto been the ultimate reality which existed, and was therefore thought of as God's eternal world and ordinance. This means not only that the existing world of Judaism ceased to be the ultimate reality, as it was thought to be by the piety which prevailed within it; it also means that the kingdom of God which was preached by Jesus may in no sense be thought of as analogous to this world, that is, as possessing in itself an ordinance with which it assures its permanent existence for eternity and dominates those who live in it. Consequently, the sole authority to which Jesus appeals for his preaching is God, as he rules in the freedom of a deity which is subject to no ordinance in the present world. This is the God to whom Jesus points in the parable of the master of the vineyard, who claimed for himself the right to do as he chose with what belonged to him.

This is also the reason why Jesus rejected any responsibility in the sight of the present world and its authorities for his preaching, and held himself responsible for what he said and did solely to the God whose kingdom was now coming. For it is this God to whose will, now no longer concealed by the pious tradition of this world, he was responding in his preaching and in the 'sign' he gave of it, his attitude to the 'sinners' who are excluded by the guardians of the present world. This responsibility ignores the ordinance of the world, which no one has hitherto denied to be that of God. It recognizes only God as him to whom, and to whose will, he has to answer directly. This God is Lord of the world in such a way that like the master of the vineyard in the parable of the labourers in the vineyard, he has the right to do what he chooses with what belongs to him. He is thereby seen, as the true Lord of the world, to be in irreconcilable conflict with the dominion over the world which traditional piety, with its commandments, has falsely arrogated to itself. And this responsibility makes clear the ultimate significance of everything which takes place in the preaching of Jesus. Through it one responsibility is opposed to another, that of Jesus to that of the religious leaders of his people. For one can hardly deny that the latter felt themselves responsible for the maintenance of the world in which they lived, and for the men who lived with them in it. It was through this very responsibility that they excluded those who did not fulfil the ordinance of this world. And it is likewise this responsibility which obliges them to defend the pious ordinance of their world against Jesus's preaching of the coming kingdom of God, which by common consent would bring this world to an end; for they were convinced that this preaching would only bring evil upon the world.

But by contrast to Jesus's responsibility, theirs was of such a nature that in regarding themselves as responsible for the maintenance of the world in which they lived, these men were responsible *to* it. This means that the world with which they were dealing was one which dominated them in this responsibility, and which they were serving by the scrupulous maintenance of its ordinance. They were consequently so overwhelmed by it, and by their responsibility *to* it, that the true responsibility *for* the world, which can be owed *to* God alone, remained inaccessible to them. Of course the 'scribes and Pharisees', we must repeat, knew that man's principal responsibility is to God – otherwise they could not have been the successors of the Old Testament prophets. But their world of ritual and legal piety had established itself so firmly about them that they were unable to hear the voice of God except in his commandments. The greatest and most urgent demand, which must be fulfilled from day to day, from hour to hour, and from one activity to another, was that of living their daily life in all its detail on the basis of the piety which underlay them. Because they could only hear these commandments, the responsibility which man owes to God was unintentionally transformed into one required of him by a world which presses ever more closely and more irresistibly upon him through the constant immediacy of its prescriptions. Once the proclamation of the coming kingdom of God had been heard in his world, a proclamation acknowledging no responsibility except to God, with what follows from this, it was inevitable that the world should regard this proclamation and the actions associated with it as the most impious blasphemy. And in fact, in and through this responsibility, Jesus was proclaiming the fall of the false god, who was in fact the world which this piety venerated, and whom he saw as Satan falling like lightning from heaven (Luke 10.18).

NOTES

1. Bultmann, *Das Urchristentum* etc., p. 70; tr. *Primitive Christianity*, etc., p. 65.
2. W. Bauer, *Wörterbuch zum Neuen Testament*, Berlin 1937, p. 810.
3. Bultmann, *Das Urchristentum* etc., p. 76; tr. *Primitive Christianity*, etc., p. 70.
4. Cf. above, p. 120.
5. Cf. above, p. 120f.

12

JESUS AND HISTORY

JESUS accepted a responsibility in which he proclaimed the kingdom of God and demanded a renunciation of the present world which was coming to an end. This meant no less than that for the first time in the life of mankind, as far as we know, history was made which was no longer the account of what had happened at some time within the framework of an eternal, unchanging world. As this new kind of history took place, the existence of the world and that of man as well was drawn into it. For one cannot speak of history in this sense until the world in which man lives ceases to be the final and all-embracing reality. It must no longer provide the eternal and unchangeable ordinance to which he strives to adapt his actions and thoughts, in order to gain security for his own continued existence from the permanence of this world, and to participate, in spite of his own transitoriness, in its enduring qualities. In the mythical age, this unchangeable ordinance of the world, or, in other words, its existence as the world which embraces all reality, was represented by the gods. At a later period, when intellectual enlightenment had made the myth of the gods increasingly difficult to believe, philosophical thought tried to replace them by eternal truths, through which it was thought possible to make sure that the world continued in existence. This happened above all in the case of the Greeks, and the course they took is still having its effect at the present day, if not on history writing, at least on philosophical thought concerning history and the nature of history. Wherever we hear of anything which is supposed to be supra-historical, this is due to the influence of this kind of thinking.

As long as the idea of the world as the final and all-embracing reality is still in force – whatever form it may take and however much it may be modified – and so long as it is still supposed that man can only be aware and certain of the meaning of his existence by participating in the eternal significance of the world and in its unchangeable being as such, it is impossible to reach an understanding of history such as Jesus preached as the reality of human existential life. For in the former conception, history exists as an event which takes place within the world as the final and all-embracing reality, and in the framework of its eternal and unchangeable ordinance; but the world is not affected by it. For as the reality which it is understood to be here, the world remains outside history, or can be said to be supra-historical, above history. That is, it is not itself involved in what happens in history; the world itself remains outside the changes which are characteristic of these events. The same is true of men, in so far as their existence derives its meaning from the world understood in this sense.

What happened in Jesus's proclamation of the coming kingdom of God was the proclamation of the coming to an end of the world as it had hitherto been understood, as the final and all-embracing reality. That is why he preached 'repentance', calling upon men to turn their backs finally and radically upon this world. It is consequently better to avoid this translation of the Greek word *metanoia*. For the sense which the word 'repentance' has taken on in common usage conceals rather than expresses what Jesus was saying. Jesus meant by it a new kind of thinking, through which the relationship of man's whole existence to the present world is reversed. By calling for this new kind of thinking, he is calling the men who live in the present world and place their trust in it to turn decisively away from it. He is not commanding them to turn away from the world altogether, though a widespread and obstinate belief exists that this is what he was saying. For Jesus was not an ascetic. What he required was a turning away from the whole of the world as it existed at the time, the world in which the men to whom he was speaking actually lived. But as we have seen, what was characteristic of this world is the way in which those who lived in it thought of it as the world. That is, they considered its existence as the world, the ordinance and law which constituted and maintained it as the world, as consisting in its being for those who lived in it and trusted in it the final and all-embracing reality on which their salvation and damnation depended. When he spoke of repentance, Jesus was demanding that men turn their back on this way of thinking about the world. And since, as we have seen, this way of thinking about the world was expressed in the piety practised by the Jews of his time, and because the thought of the men who lived in this world was, one might say, firmly anchored by it, so Jesus, in his call for repentance, called for a radical turning away from this piety, and therefore for a turning away from the structure of the world which it presupposed and guarded. Thus what took place, and was meant to take place, in this turning away, was the total transformation of all things, manifested above all in the fact that those who were the first in the present world would be the last in the coming kingdom of God, while those who in the present world were the last would be the first in that kingdom (Mark 10.31 and parallels).

In order fully to understand what this signifies, we must bear in mind three things which are of decisive importance for the understanding of Jesus's preaching, but to which inadequate attention, or no attention at all, is very often paid. The first is that neither the negative nor the positive aspects of Jesus's preaching relate to man in isolation from the world. Rather, when he speaks of man, he always speaks of the world in which man lives, for without this world he does not exist. Secondly, the preaching of Jesus refers to man as him on whom the way the world is the world for him in fact depends; that is, it depends upon him what the structure of the world is like for him. It is man's fault if the world is such that it exercises an unlimited domination over him, as happened through the piety of late Judaism; a domination which, while it is regarded by man as the rule of God, in fact makes it impossible for him to know God as God, and as such as the Lord of the world. Thirdly, we must remember that Jesus's preaching of the coming kingdom of God, and of the coming to an end of the present world, is of such a nature that it cannot be authenticated by anything which is valid within the present world. Only if due significance is accorded to these three points is it possible to understand what is said at the beginning of this chapter – that through Jesus's preaching of the coming kingdom of God, history can be seen to be the mode of human existence, and of the way in which the world exists as such.

.   .   .

We have stated, then, that we do not regard history as an event which takes place within the framework of a world order which always remains the same and never changes, within a world which exists and remains the same for eternity. We think of it rather as an event, a change into which both the world and also man in his existence are drawn. This event takes place between man and the world on the basis of decisions which man has to make, and which are concerned with how the world, as it is constituted as such, is to be his world at any time. A historical event of this kind affects the world with regard to the way in which it is constituted, which does not remain the same, once for all. A historical event also concerns man, who is responsible through his decisions for the way in which his world exists.

Thus when Jesus himself calls upon those who like him live in the present world to repent, this means, as we have seen, that they must turn away from this world and from the way in which it exists as the world. Thus, above all, they must adopt a new way of thinking about the piety which prevails within the world and maintains it in existence as it is. Jesus himself turns away from this world by uttering this call; by the basis which he gives to his call. He does so because it exists in a way which signifies the damnation of the men who live in it. And as we have seen, he does this without being able to appeal to any authority which holds good within this world. In all this, he himself is acting historically in the sense in which we understand the word. That is, his whole existence becomes historical. For it then becomes an existence which cannot be authenticated either by anything which holds good in the present world, or by anything which could hold good in any imaginable world. In other words, we call the existence of Jesus historical because for him there is no world *to* which he could be responsible for his existence – whatever kind of existence it possessed, and whatever the nature of the ordinance which prevailed within it. For it is not possible to be responsible to that *for* which one is responsible.

Thus, in this sense, the existence of Jesus is historical, and in it history has been shown to be a completely new mode of human existence. But our exposition of the preaching of Jesus, which, as we saw, determined his existence, showed that the reason for this essential impossibility of finding any authentication for it in any world that existed was that he was responsible to God alone for the world. If this is so, then the historical thought current at the present day forces us to ask whether this responsibility in the sight of God does not raise the existence of Jesus out of and above history. This would in fact be the case if the God in whom Jesus found the sole possible authentication for his preaching had revealed himself to him outside the historicity of his existence. This would have happened if Jesus had claimed for himself and for his preaching a special calling by God, as was done by the Old Testament prophets, or if he had been able to appeal to the knowledge of hidden decrees of God which had been imparted to him alone. But he refused quite emphatically to do either of these things, or anything like them.

When the authorities of the present world demanded of him such 'signs from heaven', by which he might authenticate himself, he referred them to the sole sign which 'shall be given to an evil and adulterous generation', and which is accessible to everyone who 'has ears to hear', that is, the 'sign of Jonah'. This was the sign 'of repentance' (Matt. 12.39; 16.4). For Jesus this sign took the form of his fellowship with the 'tax collectors and sinners'. For where it was possible for such a thing to happen, the existing world of late Jewish piety in which one might not even approach a sinner to teach him the laws of God came to an end, and the kingdom of God as Jesus understood it was imminent. But where is this kingdom imminent? It is imminent in the sign – that is, in what happened through it. Thus it is to be found in what was quite without parallel in the world as it existed, that someone should draw into fellowship with himself, in the name of God, people who in the name of the prevailing piety of this world were excluded from the world as godless. In carrying out this sign, Jesus turned his back upon the thought of this world and upon the way in which it existed as the world, while at the same time he made himself one with those whom this world saw as excluded from it.

It is very important to realize how significant this sign is. This is only possible when one realizes that it was not the rejection merely of something that could be found within the world as it existed. Rather, it was the rejection of a whole world, of the very way in which it was the world. In this case, this meant in particular the rejection of the piety which was in accordance with the nature of this world and which maintained it. Of course,

Jesus charged only the guardians of this piety, the Pharisees and scribes, with putting the precepts of their world of piety in place of the commandments of God (Mark 7.1ff.), of thereby putting the world dominated by this piety in place of God, of shutting the kingdom of God against those who entrusted themselves to their guidance, and of not only not entering it themselves, but also of not allowing those who would enter to go in (Matt. 23.13). But we understand the all-embracing significance of these charges only when we realize that they are made not only against these particular men, but against the characteristic structure and constitution of the whole world which they represent, and under the rule of which they act and think as they do.

We have seen that the world which Jesus calls upon men to reject exists as the world in such a way as to be regarded as the final and all-embracing reality from which the men who live in it receive their life. Thus it is the power to which they are responsible, and the responsibility which they exercise towards it and the ordinance which prevails within it, is the only kind of piety possible in it. And therefore when Jesus turns from this world, the deepest meaning of this is that he denies as emphatically as possible any responsibility to it, and therefore to the piety which belongs to this world, and is required by it. In so doing, he condemns this world as a world which in its piety puts itself in the place of God. And by this condemnation he takes on, in the name of the same God, responsibility for the world's existing in a way which is in accordance with the dominion of this God over it. In the responsibility which is laid upon him in the face of the present world, which is expressed in his call to repentance, and which is given a visible sign in his fellowship with 'sinners', Jesus experiences the will of God as it is enjoined upon him.

Thus, before beginning his preaching, Jesus did not receive, either in the form of a special vocation imparted to him, or through the commandment of a generally valid law, which in fact could only be that of the present world, or through anything else of the kind, a commission which God, as it were, guaranteed him in advance, and upon which he could call for the authentication of his preaching. Rather, what his preaching says is always true of the will of God also applies to his own commission to proclaim the coming to an end of the present world and the imminence of the kingdom of God. In studying the preaching of Jesus, we saw that what it says about the will of God is not meant to be any kind of ethic which lays down generally valid commandments and directions for what man should do in the manifold situations of life. Such general commandments may exist, and may be necessary in their place. As Jesus says, in an immensely forceful epigram to the man who wanted to follow him but first asked for permission to bury his father, this is something that can be left to the dead, that is, to those who belong to the present world which is coming to an end. But it is not with this that Jesus is concerned. On the contrary: every word which Jesus says about the will of God is concerned with one thing only, the right attitude of man to God in accordance with his will. And even though it is not always explicitly stated, the most important thing, on which everything else depends, and from which everything else that he says follows and derives its meaning, is his call for repentance and a new mind, for the rejection of the present world and its thinking, and for a readiness, possible only in consequence of this rejection, for the coming kingdom of God.

Only when this is taken into account is it possible to understand what is demanded of man by the will of God as Jesus sees it, and what relationship man has to God in accordance with this will. For everything that Jesus says about God is determined by his purpose of setting free human thought from the domination which is exercised over it, with the force of a sentence of doom, by the world when it is thought of as the final and all-embracing reality, and which leads man to regard the ordinance of the world as God's will and to venerate it. Thus the first thing which must happen to man, and which he must learn, is to turn away from this thinking and from the world as it conceives of it. This is always a bitter experience for it means losing the life which he has gained, or hoped to gain, in fulfilling the ordinance of the present world, and which was believed to be the life which God has destined for man. Only when someone is ready to give up this life and the view of the world by which it is dominated can he receive the life which is destined for him by God in his kingdom. Thus the will of God demands of man both the abandonment of the life determined by the present world and its piety, and also the reception of the life given by God, which comes about in this abandonment.

How can we understand the interdependence of giving up and receiving, losing and finding which, according to Jesus, characterizes the carrying out of God's will? It will perhaps help to speak not of the demand made by the will of God but of its challenge to give up one's life and receive life by so doing. The difference between what I am required to do and what I am challenged to do is that in the second case the possibility of doing it is already there, whereas what is required of me I have first to achieve. Thus, the possibility of turning from the present world, which we are challenged to do by Jesus's call to repentance, is already present in the preaching of the coming kingdom of God. It is true that it is only possible to apprehend this reality by actually turning away from this world and thereby suffering the loss of the life lived by it. Thus, there is not first present a certainty of the coming kingdom of God such that it is possible to turn away from the world on the basis of this certainty. If this were so, then the concept of the kingdom of God would be parallel to that of the present world, and it would not in fact be possible to speak of turning away, and of the repentance, the change of heart, that happens thereby. We would still be in the position of the two disciples of Jesus who asked him to grant them to sit one at his right hand and one at his left in his glory (Mark 10.37). But, in fact, not merely the receiving of life, but also the abandonment of the old life, is in accordance with the will of God only when it takes place in faith. Thus man is challenged by the will of God, as Jesus understands it, to have faith. And the relationship to God which comes with God's will is such that in it man makes room in himself, in whatever he does, for this will and for what he is challenged by it to do. It is a relationship in which his action is such that both a change of mind with regard to the thought of the world dominated by its piety, and also a readiness for the coming kingdom of God, are exercised in faith.

But man's action cannot be like this if, in the present world, he acts on the basis of a commandment already laid down, which in accordance with the piety of this world he supposes to be the commandment of God, whereas in fact it is only that of the law by which this world maintains its present condition in being. Anyone who acts on this basis supposes that he knows with greater or lesser certainty, on the basis of the ordinance of this world which is expressed in the law, what the consequences of such action will be in the present world. The action he takes is, therefore, all that needs to be done, and there is no more room for the action of God. As Jesus says, expressing the finitude and vanity of this action, 'You have had your reward'. With action of this kind, man remains entangled in the present world, and is still relying on it, and since the prevailing piety puts this world and its ordinance in place of God, it is quite impossible for there to be room for God and the coming of his kingdom.

But if the sayings of Jesus which speak of the will of God are not meant as commandments which demand one or another particular kind of action, this is equally true of the sayings which speak of our attitude to our neighbour; though ever since they were uttered, down to the present day, they have been most obstinately regarded as commandments of this sort. These are the sayings which say, for example, that we should love our enemies, do good to those who hate us, bless those that curse us, etc.[1] The promise of divine reward with which all of these sayings conclude shows clearly enough that the purpose of all of them is an attitude in which man does not rely on his own action, but in which he is ready to allow God to act in him. Consequently, these sayings of Jesus concerning our attitude towards our neighbour are only understood aright when it is realized that the idea he expresses in them is the same as that which inspired the beatitudes of the poor, the hungry and the mourners. Just as Jesus says that because they possess nothing, or because they are hungry and mourn, they partake of the kingdom of God, he likewise says of those who in their behaviour towards their neighbours are not aiming, as is the rule in the present world, at what this world is able to give them, that they will receive 'a great reward' from God. Like the sayings about becoming like children in order to partake in the kingdom of God, and those about the tax collectors and harlots who enter the kingdom of God instead of the 'righteous', these sayings also make clear by the use of extreme examples what the action and behaviour of man must be like if he is to leave room for the will and action of God, and have a part in this way in the kingdom of God.

Besides these sayings, which use extreme examples in order to state what the will of God demands of man, there are others which seem to say the reverse, but in fact imply the same thing. These sayings affirm that what is done in accordance with the will of God is of itself nothing special, that is, not something 'pious' like the action required by the present world, dominated as it is by ritual and legal piety. Thus, for example, alms given in accordance with God's will are not any kind of 'pious work', which must be seen as such, but are neither more nor less than a gift to a human being in need of help. It must be like the actions of those righteous persons in the last judgment, for whom the kingdom is 'prepared from the foundation of the world' (Matt. 25.31ff.). As we have already seen, the same teaching is found in the parable of the Good Samaritan, who in contrast to the priest and the levite who 'saw and passed by' the man who had been robbed and was half dead, came up to him, saw him, and 'had compassion, and went to him and bound up his wounds, pouring on oil and wine; then he set him on his own beast and brought him to an inn, and took care of him' (Luke 10.25-37). The point of the story is that this man acted in direct response to the living event which he encountered, and not on the basis of a prescribed commandment of the law. For, according to the Jewish view of that time, as a Samaritan he knew nothing of the law of God. What he did, he did because, unlike the priest and the levite, he did not try to escape the situation into which he had unwittingly been led, but listened to what it required of him.

All these sayings clearly state that the will of God as Jesus understood it is not something which can be known only on the basis of a previously prescribed commandment of the law. For the will of God always demands more than such a commandment. It demands that we be open to whatever the living event, into which we may be drawn at any time, should demand of us. When someone is open in this way, it may be possible for him to do what is desired, without having previously been taught that it was something demanded by God. This is shown in an astonishing way in the examples of the righteous at the last judgment and the Good Samaritan. But in any case it is possible to recognize what is required as the will of God, and to put one's trust in this will, only when one dares to do what it demands.

. . .

We studied Jesus's understanding of the will of God to find out whether the fact that Jesus knew himself to be responsible for his preaching to God alone was in contradiction to our assertion that his existential life was historical, and so revealed history as the mode of human existential life. Would not this responsibility to God have lifted the existential life of Jesus out of and above history? But if Jesus understands the will of God in the way we have tried to set out; if he understands the preaching of the coming to an end of the present world and the coming of the kingdom of God, through which he takes upon himself responsibility for the present world and for the way in which it exists as the world, to be a commission laid upon him by God for which he is responsible to no one but God; and if, as we have seen, he refuses to claim as a possible authentication for his preaching any other 'sign' than that of repentance, then it is scarcely possible for his own knowledge of the divine will which commissioned him to carry out his preaching to be a knowledge of any different kind from that which he describes to others in his preaching.

But this means that Jesus experiences the will of God, as it applies to him, in the responsibility laid upon him, with regard to the condition of the present world, for the way in which it is the world. The situation of the Good Samaritan, who encountered the will of God without recognizing it in the sense of a previously laid down commandment, was determined by the half-dead man whom he 'saw and had compassion, and went to him'. So likewise, the situation of Jesus, in which he is brought face to face with the will of God, is determined by the crowd whom he saw and 'had compassion for them, because they were harassed and helpless, like sheep without a shepherd' (Matt. 9.36). Of course one can see at once that the situation of Jesus is different from that of the Samaritan. The latter appears in a parable which deals only with an episode in his life. Nor is it the intention of this parable to say everything that can be said about the will of God. Its sole purpose is to show that God's will is not comprised in a legal commandment, but is exercised by God through the living event which takes place within the world. But the series of events into which Jesus is drawn affects the condition of the whole present world in which he lives. The condition of this world does not merely bring upon certain individuals various kinds of harm and injury which can be alleviated by appropriate action. All who live in this world are 'harassed and helpless' as a result of the condition in which they find themselves, that is, as a result of the sentence of doom which prevails within this world because of the way in which it exists as the world. It is quite impossible for what happens in this situation to be merely an episode in the life of a person who sees that it has a significance which affects the whole world and determines the salvation or damnation of this world and the men who live in it. Because Jesus perceives this, he and his whole existence are drawn into this event. This means neither more nor less than that the salvation and damnation of the world, which is at stake in this event, is inextricably bound up with the salvation and damnation of his own existential life.

It is now possible to understand the full significance of the saying of Jesus concerning the 'only sign' which is to be given to this generation as an authentication for his preaching and its call to repentance. Its full meaning is only revealed when it is not regarded only as the 'sign', to which Jesus refers those who require an authentication – in the manner of the present world – of his right to preach. Rather, we must realize that it is also the 'sign' in which what is proclaimed in Jesus's preaching comes about for him personally – the coming to an end of the present world and the coming of the kingdom of God. In this way it is the authentication of the preaching which has been committed to him.

We have already said[2] that the sign he gave of a change of heart was his fellowship with the 'tax collectors and sinners', and with those others who were excluded from the present world. In order to understand what Jesus was doing with this 'sign', it is necessary to have some apprehension of the breath-taking daring, not to say arrogance, which was necessary for Jesus to do what he did in the world in which he was living: eating with such people and, in accordance with the significance which eating together had for the ancient world, and in particular for the Jews at that time, associating himself with them in a way that displayed, as nothing else could at that time, a complete lack of restraint and a complete commitment. For they were people who, for the sake of something as important as the continued existence of the world which excluded them, were 'outlaws' in the most acute and irrevocable sense, that of religion, and who threatened everyone who approached them with cultic and legal impurity. If we bear in mind that this is what was happening in this 'sign', we can understand that the issue was that which is set out in the preaching of Jesus: the coming to an end of the present world and the coming of the kingdom of God. This took place as a 'sign' in the sense of a visible demonstration, for those whose horrified eyes saw it happen. They could only understand what the sign referred to if they were capable of the change of heart appropriate to the transformation of the world which was here taking place. If they were not capable of this, then they could only see it as the sign of a threat to their world, which they had to resist with all their might. In the same way, to those who are excluded from this world it could occur in the first instance only as a 'sign'. But because they are excluded from the world, they have ears to hear the new thing which is seeking entry into the world. For Jesus, however, what he did when he 'ate with the tax collectors and sinners' took place with a seriousness which imposed a total obligation upon him. What he did, and what was to follow from it, was not to be taken away from him. For by so doing, and thereby preaching both to those who were ready to hear and to those who were not ready, that for which this was the only possible 'sign', the coming to an end of the present world and the coming of the kingdom of God, he took on responsibility for the way in which the present world exists as such, and this was the destiny to which he was called.

If there has ever been an event which did not take place within the framework of an eternal, self-contained and self-sustaining world, and for which no appeal was possible to the law which maintains the permanence of such a world throughout all ages, an event through which man was no longer completely enclosed within this world and was freed from the alternative of either adapting himself to the structure of this world and basing his life upon it, or rebelling against its law and succumbing to its implacable retribution, this event was that which took place when Jesus, because 'he had compassion on the crowds' (Matt. 9.36), gave the 'sign' of redemption which consisted in his eating with the 'tax collectors and sinners'. Here a man broke through the immovable structure of a self-contained world regarded as eternal and unchangeable. This was a world in which, as a result of the only kind of religion possible in it, God had been transformed into the god of this world. In fact the god of this world is nothing more than the law by which this world is preserved in its self-contained condition. Because Jesus called men away from the thinking that is based upon the godless alternative which represents the ultimate truth in the piety that prevails within this world, he came to perceive the complete liberty of the God who does not allow himself to be imprisoned either in this or any other existing world, and who is at work within the world with the complete freedom of his deity and subject to no worldly law.

And thus it was possible for Jesus to call for a repentance which was monstrous in the eyes of the present world and of the leaders whose task it was to preserve this world in being, because it overthrew the law which constituted and preserved the world. He did this with the 'sign' which is represented by his fellowship with those who are excluded from this world, and with sayings like the following (if we are to understand them, we must of course hear them as they were heard by those who sought to kill him because of them, because they were aware of the attack which these sayings made upon their world and its god): 'I have not come to call the righteous, but sinners', or 'The Sabbath was made for man', or else, 'You have heard that it was said to the men of old, "You shall not kill; and whoever kills shall be liable to judgment". But I say to you that everyone who is angry with his brother shall be liable to judgment.' This call to repentance calls men away from responsibility *to* the present world and the way in which it exists as the world, so that the world, too, in the responsibility of man for it, may be drawn *to* the freedom of the God who rules within it.

That God rules in the world in his perfect freedom means that he does not allow himself to be imprisoned by the law of the world within which Jewish piety saw him as included. And it cannot, therefore, be a law valid for all time, which lays down both the action of man and also of God with regard to the world and man. Instead, it means that he rules within the world in such a way that the life and activity of the world is directly open to him. This openness of the world, which is in accordance with the freedom of God's rule within it, does not mean that it is only open to a sphere beyond it, the sphere of God, from which God intervenes now and again in the sphere of the world. The kingdom of God proclaimed by Jesus is anything but such a kingdom outside or above the world. Rather, its place is in the midst of the world. That is why the parables of Jesus describe it in images which are all taken from the life and activities of the world. Moreover, the openness of the world means that the world and all that happens and is to happen in it is shown to be accessible to the responsibility which man has for it and for the way in which it is the world. This responsibility is in the first instance a responsibility to ensure that it does not become closed in itself once again, in such a way that God is no longer Lord in it through his free dominion, but instead becomes the law which the world believes it must fulfil in order to ensure its permanence. For as soon as man is no longer aware, in the responsibility which he has for the world, of the free dominion of God within the world — which is what makes him certain of his responsibility to God for this earthly world — the world once again becomes enclosed within itself, and the responsibility of man *for* it is transformed into a responsibility *to* it and to the powers of the world. These then become for him the true representatives of the world and its ordinance, which dominate its existence as a self-contained world, and to which he has, therefore, to adapt himself.

If responsibility *for* the world is changed into responsibility *to* it, and to the law which maintains it as it is, it becomes impossible to perceive the will of God as Jesus understands it. We said above[3] that the relationship to God which is in accordance with this will is such that in whatever man does he may not rely upon his own action, but must be ready to let God act in him. It is now possible for us to say more clearly what we meant by this. It is necessary, however, for the responsibility *to* God, to which man is called by his responsibility for the world, and the perception of God's free dominion in the world which comes about in this responsibility, to be taken in the original sense of the word, and understood strictly as a response which derives its meaning from the word to which it responds. But the word to which this responsibility to God is a response is the creative word of God, in which God promises himself to man as him who calls him into life. The answer which man gives to God by making himself responsible *to* him consequently means that he commits himself and his whole existence to the God who gives this existence to him by his word. And it is as a result of this reliance upon God, which affects man's whole existence, that man does not merely trust in his own action, but allows God to act in him.

Man exercises this responsibility for the world and for the way in which it exists as the world, and in it perceives the free rule of God in the world. He thereby becomes aware of himself as responding in this responsibility to God as he rules in the world, by being responsible *to* God for what he does in this responsibility. And in this responsibility the history which we said was made visible in Jesus, and in his preaching of the coming to an end of the present world and the coming of the kingdom of God, actually happened. Thus the fact that Jesus could not point to any authentication for his preaching in the present world, but was responsible solely to God, does not lift his existential life out of and above history. The reverse is true. It was through this responsibility *to* God, which is never possible except when it is also a responsibility *for* the world, that his existential life succeeded in being historical. For he did not encounter the God to whom he is responsible in a law which is understood as being in some way already laid down, and which in fact could only be the law of a world already existing, unchangeable in its form and self-contained. He encountered God in his free rule in the world, which man is able to perceive in his responsibility for the world.

NOTES

1. Cf. above, p. 111ff.
2. Cf. above, p. 144.
3. Cf. above, p. 109f.

13

TWO KINDS OF HISTORY

IT IS IMMEDIATELY obvious that history as it was manifested in Jesus and his personal history is not simply the same as that to which we are referring when we normally speak of history at the present day. In order to understand as clearly as possible the history which we encounter in Jesus, we must clearly distinguish it from what appears as history in modern historical scholarship.

These are two different kinds of history but they have nevertheless one point in common which permits us to call them both history in some sense. In both, the idea of the responsibility of man for the world and the form it takes is of decisive importance. For in both cases, it is through this idea that the existence of man and of the world becomes historical. We have already tried to show this with regard to the personal history of Jesus. Wilhelm Dilthey has shown that the idea of responsibility also played a decisive part in the transformation of the metaphysical thought of the Middle Ages, and the theology of history that corresponded to it, into the modern understanding of history. In many extensive studies he found that, according to the older conception, history is the realization of the eternal plan and will of God, 'as they are proclaimed in biblical revelation'. This kind of thinking sees 'mankind as a unity, as it were an individual, who must undergo a living development, but who on the whole receives the rules which govern this development like a pupil from a teacher who is working according to a plan'.[1] Modern historical thought, on the other hand, 'seeks the driving force of a historical process in mankind itself'.[2] Gerhard Krüger's comment on the Greek understanding of history is true of the older mode of thought; that it 'is a process within a fixed world, that is, a world understood metaphysically', whereas modern thought 'does the reverse and draws the world and man's whole attitude to it into history'.³ Thus the responsibility of man for the world, which has been reawakened in modern times, played an important part in depriving medieval historical thought of the dominating position which it had throughout the Middle Ages. This was already perceived two hundred years ago by Giambattista Vico, when he said that 'the historical and civil world was quite certainly made by men', and that 'its principles must be sought in the transformations of our human spirit'.⁴

There is a profound difference between these two kinds of history, that which was manifested in Jesus, and that of modern historical thought. The difference lies above all in the fact that virtually nothing remains in modern historical thought of responsibility *to* God, whereas for Jesus it is what principally determines responsibility for the world. This is true to such an extent that one can say that for him the whole meaning of this responsibility for the world lies in the fact that it makes possible responsibility to God. For it is clear from the preaching of Jesus, that the main concern of this responsibility is that the world should not again become enclosed within itself, but that God should be Lord of the world through his free rule within it, and should not be, as in the present world of Jewish piety, the law which maintains it in its unchanging existence. For otherwise man falls once again under the dominion of the present world, instead of perceiving God's free rule within it and being responsible to him and to no one else. When we say that virtually nothing remains in modern historical thought of responsibility to God, we are also saying that this mode of thought knows nothing of man's responsibility for the world. The same idea was expressed above in Dilthey's characterization of modern historical thought: that it 'seeks the driving force of a historical process in mankind itself'. But this is virtually to say no more, with regard to the present issues, than Wittram said of the 'revolutionary passion' of the Marxist view of history, that it is the consequence of the fact that 'man has discovered his power to transform the earth and at the same time, in the radical rejection of every concept of God, has understood himself as the substance of history, which constantly refers back to itself'.⁵ And Wittram, who himself was very close to being estranged from belief in God, says nevertheless in the concluding chapter of this same lecture on 'The Concern for History', that the theological statement that God rules over history, 'must not be allowed to replace the study of the method of scientific reason. Anyone who does this is abusing it.' In Wittram's view, when a historian 'turns to the things of the past, and inquires into it, he must do so with the intellectual tools and methods of modern historical scholarship. No one can go behind this apprehension.'[6] But as Ernst Troeltsch has shown, the method of modern historical scholarship is such that 'once it has come into contact with theology at a single point, it draws everything else into its consequences, and involves everything in an immense complex of relative effects and changes'. For

> through its criticism, analogy and correlation, it leads automatically, with an irresistible necessity, to the setting up of an interrelated structure of activities of the human mind, all influencing each other, none of which can at any point be isolated and absolute, but are everywhere connected and can therefore only be understood in the context of a whole which is as comprehensive as possible.[7]

All this means that the assumption on which the modern attitude to history is based is that man is responsible for the world and for what happens in it, that is, for history, while he completely ignores responsibility to God. But, as we saw, it is the latter which in the preaching of Jesus gives responsibility for the world its real significance. This is so not because this attitude to history denies belief in God on principle, but rather for what we must call purely methodological reasons. For, to use words we have quoted already, 'man has discovered his power to transform the earth' and 'has understood himself as the substance of history, which constantly refers back to itself'. Or again, in other words, there has taken place

> the definite establishment, as a result of the great discoveries of Copernicus, Kepler, and Galileo, and the theory which accompanied them of the construction of nature by *a priori* logical and mathematical elements of the conscious mind, of the sovereign consciousness of the human intellect and its world over material things.[8]

Finally, there came into being in the seventeenth and eighteenth centuries what Dilthey called 'the natural system of intellectual science', by which he meant 'the theories which go by the name of natural law, natural theology, natural religion etc.', 'theories of which the sovereign characteristic was the derivation of the phenomena of human society from the causality found in man himself'.[9] Once all this had come about, then, in so far as history could be studied and understood by scientific methods, it was regarded as produced by man, willingly or unwillingly.

Suppose we continue to affirm that the attitude to God of which Jesus's preaching speaks, and in which man experiences responsibility to God in his responsibility for the world, is a historical attitude, and that in it history is manifested not as taking place within the eternally enduring and unchanging and therefore wholly unhistorical framework of the present world, but as history in which both the existential life of man and the world itself has become historical. We then have, in this concept of history and in that of modern historical scholarship, two concepts of history which are both to be distinguished from what takes place within the framework of a world which endures and always remains the same, but which are nevertheless clearly distinct from each other. If this is so, then we are necessarily faced with the question of the relationship between these two concepts of history. Is one true and the other false? At first sight it seems that the difference between them is that in history as it appears in the preaching of Jesus, responsibility for the world is meaningful because it becomes possible through responsibility to God, whereas in history as it is understood by modern historical thought, there is no room for this responsibility to God, and it is concerned only with responsibility for the world.

But we should not be misled by this distinction into supposing that the former is true history and the latter false, and to suppose that they are mutually exclusive. Their relationship to each other would only be of this kind if modern historical thought excluded on principle belief in God and with it man's responsibility to him. But it does not do so. It excludes them only on methodological grounds. That is, it investigates history in so far as, in Dilthey's words, it 'seeks the driving force of a historical process in mankind itself'. Here, however, even responsibility for the world and what happens in it, as it is manifested in history understood in this way, is studied only as it takes effect in relation to the world. Modern historical scholarship can quite properly consider history using this methodology, because it is unquestionably experienced in this way. Thus anyone who sets out to study and understand history experienced in this way, cannot do so otherwise than by making use of the methods worked out by modern historical scholarship. Wittram has vividly described what happens when this historical method is used: 'Without some concrete starting and finishing point in the vast ruined expanse of historical tradition, and without experience of the certainty and uncertainty of historical statements with regard to this vast expanse of ruins' no one can 'pass through the numerous passport and customs offices of history'. If any attempt is made to look at history philosophically or theologically 'without experience of historical criticism', there is a danger of falling into 'speculation or tautology', instead of achieving a knowledge of history.[10]

However true this may be of history as it is studied and understood with the aid of modern historical scholarship, we must not forget that this method is restricted to the history that can be fitted to it – that is, as we have shown, in so far as it is dealing with history in which the driving forces are to be found in mankind itself. But if another kind of history exists where this is not the case; if – this is what is at issue here – Jesus is a 'historical figure', so that what took place in him and through him is an historical event; and if this is also true of his attitude to God, as it was manifested in what he preached, then although we speak of history here, we are not describing the history with which modern historical scholarship deals by means of its own methods. For what is called history in this new sense cannot be reduced to the statement, made in the terms of modern historical scholarship, that 'if the historical figure of Jesus had not existed', there would not have been any Christian faith or anything associated with it.[11] In this sense, the 'historical figure of Jesus' would mean nothing more than that on the basis of available literary documents one could prove with greater or lesser certainty the historical fact that at a particular time there existed a man Jesus of Nazareth, with whom certain events, which likewise could be ascertained with the aid of literary evidence, could be connected.

But if one takes seriously the faith which exists only because 'the historical figure of Jesus' existed, and if one understands him as this faith understands itself and its origin in the figure of Jesus, then to speak of 'the historical figure of Jesus' means something incomparably greater and essentially different. Consequently, one cannot avoid including Jesus's relationship to God in his historicity, in the way in which he understood it himself. But in this case the word history no longer means simply what is regarded as history by modern historical scholarship as long as it clings to its usual methods; and only when it does so can it remain what it is. For in relation to Jesus the word history means an event the driving impulses of which are not to be sought, at least not solely and not in the sense which is decisive for this event, in mankind in general as Dilthey was thinking of it. If the faith of Jesus which is expressed in his preaching is to be understood as he himself understood it, it is quite impossible to understand it as 'deriving the phenomena of human society from the causality found in man himself'.[12] For if there is anything which is characteristic and essential in the historical figure of Jesus it is that he understood himself as one whose thinking and action were determined by the will of God, and therefore as one who knew himself to be responsible to God for the world. As we have tried to show, historicity consists of this twofold responsibility. But this is not the same kind of historicity as is possessed by what is usually referred to as a 'historical fact'. If the attempt is made to see 'the historical figure of Jesus' as such a fact, it is seen without its own true historicity, and therefore as something different from what it is.

But what is the relationship of these two concepts of history to each other? We have already said that they are not mutually exclusive, so that one does not have to choose one or the other as the sole concept which does justice to the phenomena of history. For a long time the difficulty that arises here has been avoided by placing what happened through and in Jesus in some supra-historical sphere. It is clear from all we have said that this way out is now closed for the concept of the suprahistorical derives from intellectual assumptions which no longer exist, and together with which its significance has been lost. If it is still possible for us to understand Christian faith in any way at all, then the only way is by understanding Jesus as a true 'historical figure', yet in such a way that his own characteristic historicity is not lost.

The difference between history as it is manifested in the teaching of Jesus and history as it is studied and understood by modern historical scholarship has been defined so far by saying that in the former, man's responsibility for the world derives its meaning from the fact that through it his responsibility to God becomes possible. In history as it is understood by modern scholarship there is on the contrary no place for man's responsibility to God. Thus in it responsibility for the world has lost any connection with that to God, and consequently can only be understood in this context on the basis of man's relationship to the world. Consequently, these two concepts of history are distinguished by the different significance which each accords to responsibility for the world. No doubt it is the same world for which man is responsible in both cases but the responsibility he has to exercise is not the same in both cases.

We should first try to define more closely the responsibility for the world which is a constituent element in the history which originates in Jesus, and which, as we have said, is so closely linked with responsibility to God that without responsibility for the world it would be impossible for man to be responsible to God. For only as one who is responsible for the world, that is, for the way in which it exists as the world, can man do justice to responsibility to God. In order to make this intelligible, we must realize what it means to be responsible *to* someone. It does not merely mean that one has to give an account to oneself or to someone else about something. If one is responsible to someone in the full sense of the word, this does not mean merely that one is asked about something; the question is about oneself, and the only answer that can be given to it is oneself. True responsibility takes place between two people: a word is uttered by which one of them is called, and is called in the sense that he cannot answer this call with a thing, but solely with himself: he himself must come forward. What takes place in such a responsibility is exactly defined by the nature of the relationship between him who utters the call and him who must answer this call; or in other words, by what they both are in relationship to each other. Thus, for example, a son owes responsibility to his father as the son of the father. If we look closely at the word 'responsibility', and I believe we must, then we may say that in his responsibility to his father a son must give himself in response to the word of the father which calls him as a son. He then submits to the verdict of the father the decision whether he has fulfilled his sonship or not. In the most extreme case, this means that it depends upon the answer which the son is able to give to the father in this responsibility, whether the word of the father which calls him to this responsibility will be a blessing or a curse; that is, whether it renews and accords him this sonship once again, or finally denies it to him. Thus what is at issue in such a responsibility to someone is ability or inability to exist on the part of him who owes the responsibility, ability or inability to exist in the sense of the relationship he has to him to whom he knows he is called to be responsible.

But there is another factor in this responsibility which is of particular importance in our present context. This is that one must be independent in order to render responsibility in this very profound sense. That is, for someone to be able to give himself as a response, it must also be possible for him to deny himself to him who calls him to responsibility. But he could not do either if he did not have something with regard to which he can assert his independence, or, as we may also put it, his power over himself, making it possible for him to do one thing or the other as a result of his own decision. It is not by accident that we chose the son and the father as an example of the responsibility which one person must render to another. We could not have chosen a child; such a responsibility does not yet exist for a child, because it is not yet aware of a genuine independence towards its father. But the son is independent – I am thinking here of an adult son, such as Paul has in mind in Gal. 4.1ff., to whom the father hands over the inheritance to use himself at the appropriate time. Such an adult son is independent, because he is so with regard to what belongs to him as his own, and he is responsible for it. It is only because he is independent in this way that it is possible for him to be responsible to his father. What is at issue in this responsibility is whether he who is independent because he is an adult son remains in a state of sonship towards his father, or whether, like the Prodigal Son in the parable, he uses the independence which he has received with his inheritance to separate himself from his father. But that which belongs to man as his own, and in which man has received the independence with regard to God without which it would not be possible for him to be responsible to God, is the world in which he lives, and for which he is responsible – that is, for the way in which it exists for the world. Thus what is at issue in his responsibility to God is whether, in the independence bestowed upon him with this responsibility for the world, he gives himself as a response to the word of God which calls him, or uses his independence to refuse this response.

Jesus was speaking of this independence, for example, when he said that the sabbath was made for man, and not man for the sabbath (Mark 2.27), or that there is nothing outside a man which by going into him can defile him; but the things which come out of a man are what defile him (Mark 7.15). In so far as this is the significance of man's independence of the world, one can say of it that it is directly linked with his responsibility to God. For the latter completely excludes responsibility to the world. Consequently, in this independence man is responsible for seeing that he does not allow the world to become once again a self-sustaining and therefore self-contained universe, which he then venerates as a divine being in place of God, and that he does not allow himself to be caught up once again in this veneration, as happened in pre-Christian religion.

But this independence also signifies something else. We have already said that it consists in man's renouncing responsibility to the world and to its law because he knows that he is responsible to God; and we have already spoken of the first thing, man's independence with regard to the world. We have not yet said what it means to refuse responsibility to the law of the world. It would be possible to give the simple answer that both mean the same, for anyone who is free of responsibility to the world is by the same token free of responsibility to its law. But the question at once arises whether for man, once he is independent, any kind of law any longer exists. Or, as the question may also be phrased, where is man to look for guidance for his actions and behaviour in the world? When we consider how closely responsibility for the world is linked with responsibility to God, then the only possible answer can be that this guidance is to be sought solely in the will of God, to which man knows that he is responsible. But in giving this answer, we must not forget what we concluded about what is at issue in responsibility to God. Our most important discovery was that what mattered was not that something or other should be done, but whether or not man could continue to exist before God. The latter is infinitely more important. The essential thing is whether in this responsibility man gives himself to God in his existence as a response, or denies himself to him. Thus it is not possible to deduce directly from responsibility to God instructions for the various kinds of action required of man by his life in the world. Yet without such guidance he could not exercise the responsibility for the world which is accorded to him in his actions and behaviour, and unless he does this, it is clear from everything that we have said that he cannot be responsible to God.

Consequently, we must go on to ask where man, who knows himself to be responsible to God, and for whom there cannot therefore be any law which is available in a world to which he owes responsibility, can find such guidance. When we were discussing Jesus's understanding of the will of God we did in fact raise the question we are now asking. We found then that, as Jesus understood it, God asks two things of man. The first is that he calls him to a faith in which he becomes capable of turning away from responsibility to the world towards responsibility to God. Secondly, God requires of him that he be attentive to the demands made upon him by the living and concrete events which take place in the world and into which he is drawn at any time, for this is the only place in which he can find the guidance which he now needs. To make clear the significance of this second requirement, we referred to Jesus's saying concerning almsgiving. If this is in accordance with the will of God, it is not a pious work required by the law, but it is something that someone does because he has compassion on the needs of another as he encounters them. The same preaching is found in Jesus's parable of the Good Samaritan, who did not know the law, but who, by doing what the occasion demanded of him, fulfilled the will of God. We also recalled the actions of the righteous in the account of the last judgment, for the sake of which they are praised as those 'for whom the kingdom is prepared from the foundation of the world'.

In all these cases, there is no law already laid down which is regarded as the law of God, prescribing exactly what has to be done in a particular case. Rather, God's will is at work in the living events of the world in which man lives – and in this case, in an encounter with those who need his help. Someone who does not react to this event, like the priest and the levite in the parable of the Good Samaritan, who see the man who is in distress and pass him by, but who instead responds to the event like the Samaritan, has already received the guidance which he needs for his action in the world. This seems to be what Jesus means when, through the parable of the Good Samaritan, he changes the question asked by the 'lawyer', 'Who is my neighbour?' into a completely different question: 'Which of these three (the priest, the levite and the Samaritan), do you think, proved neighbour to the man who fell among the robbers?' The point seems to be that the lawyer had asked which of the many people one meets comes, according to the law, into the category of one's 'neighbour', in order to know in advance, on the basis of a law valid for every case, whether he had a duty to such a 'neighbour', and how he ought to behave towards him. But Jesus summarily sets this question aside and asks the questioner to decide himself, on the basis of his own observation, whether he ought to be a neighbour to someone he encounters and give him help.

For the man, then, who knows that he is responsible to God there is, because of the rejection of the present world that results from this responsibility, no law in it to which he can be responsible. It follows that the only kind of guidance which he needs for the action required of him in this world is that found in the decision which he must make himself on the basis of his own observation of what concrete events demand of him here and now. For this is the only way in which he can act in responsibility for the world and yet independently of it, and only in this way can he be responsible to God. Thus it is extraordinarily important to remember that such decisions, and the responsibility for the world associated with them, never affect either the whole of the world or the whole of man, but only individual and partial aspects. For the whole of man is involved, as we have seen, in the responsibility to God which can be exercised by faith alone. But the decisions which man has to make about his actions concern only what has to be decided here and now; for it is not possible for him to realize in his actions the decision affecting the whole of the world or of himself, but only to carry out certain individual actions. Consequently, the principles which it is necessary to seek for such cases cannot be generally valid principles into which particular occasions can be categorized, but can only be worked out by observing what any given moment demands of an individual. In short, they are principles which can be worked out only by the aid of reason.

However objectionable this conclusion about the principles of action may be to conventional theology, it is the factor which decides whether theological thinking achieves the change of mind with regard to what is valid in the present world by which the preaching of Jesus stands and falls. For as long as anyone believes that such guidance can be reliably sought only in a law already laid down, which is accepted as the law of God, he remains imprisoned in the thinking of this world, to which such a law belongs. And that means that anything which is done on the basis of principles understood in this way is done in responsibility to the world instead of responsibility for it. It may be supposed that such action can be associated with God if the guidance for it comes directly from God. But, in fact, the only way it can be associated with God is by anything that is done being done in responsibility to God and to him alone. Only in this way can it be done in accordance with the will of God, that is, in such a way that man does not rely upon what he does himself but is ready to let God act in him, by being responsible to him. In what takes place in this responsibility, the promise of the 'great reward', which Jesus gave concerning such action, is fulfilled.[13]

We have said that man must rely on reason for the guidance he seeks for his action, and with regard to this the following matters must be borne in mind. If responsibility to the world comes to an end in responsibility to God, and therefore the present world together with its laws ceases to be the object of religious veneration, then the reality of the world in which man lives and in which he has to act undergoes an extraordinarily profound transformation. It takes on a distinctive characteristic which we can describe by the word 'natural' in the sense which it has when we speak of something coming about 'quite naturally' or 'through natural means'.[14] An example of this transformation is the saying of Jesus: 'The sabbath was made for man, not man for the sabbath' (Mark 2.27). Here this day, which for

Jewish piety was 'holy', that is, set apart from all other days, with special laws describing what might be done or not done on it, became an 'ordinary' day, a day like all others. A decision about what was required or forbidden to be done on that day was no longer predetermined by commandments specifically associated with it. Instead, one had to decide on one's own account what might be done and what might not be done on it (Mark 3.4).

Thus, faced with this 'natural' world, man becomes aware of his independence in the sense that decisions about anything he has to do or not to do are assigned to himself and to his reason in its 'natural' capacity. The particular characteristic of this independence is that it makes it possible for man to maintain a distinctive neutrality towards the decision with which he is faced as an independent person through his responsibility to God: that is, the decision whether he has to give himself as a response to God or refuse to give himself. It is this neutrality which makes it possible for him to apprehend the concrete quality of the particular occasion which at any time demands a decision of him, and to perceive as a result what it is that it requires him to do, and so fulfil, as the independent person that he is before God, his responsibility to God. Thus it is the independence bestowed upon man by the 'naturalness' of the world which makes it possible for him to be responsible for the world both in the sense in which this implies responsibility to God, and also in the sense in which it refers solely to the world. And thus this independence is that of an adult son towards God, and is therefore the beginning of the history between man and God which takes place in the double responsibility to God and for the world, and in which the whole universe, or, in other words, the salvation of the world and of man is at stake. But where responsibility for the world is related only to the latter, the same independence is the beginning of the history between man and the world which is the theme of modern historical thought.

Man's independence of the world as well as his associated responsibility for it is a constituent element in both of the two forms of history of which we are speaking. It is of great importance to realize this in attempting to clarify the relationship between the two and to work out both the difference and the connection between them. Thus the difference cannot be that this independence is found only in one of them. It lies rather in the way in which this independence is understood in each. In the first case, it means that man is free from responsibility *to* the world in which he lives, so that in the independence which he so obtains it is possible for him to be responsible to God, instead of to the world, as is illustrated in Jesus's saying concerning the sabbath. In the second case, however, man's independence of the world is the prerequisite of an attitude to it which makes possible for him the relationship which is the main content of the history that takes place between him and the world.

This relationship is expressed above all in secular law and the civil and social institutions which man must constantly discover and work out anew for his life in the world in accordance with the various necessities produced by the constant change taking place in all the circumstances of the world. And similarly its most important expression is the greater and lesser works which are produced in the unceasing creative labour of the arts, science and technology. In these, man's relationship with the world is constantly realized anew. Thus the independence of the world which man has to realize, as well as the responsibility for it which this imposes upon him, is the prerequisite of the relationship to the world which man is seen to have by modern historical scholarship, and in which he is the object of the study carried out by its methods. At the same time, the limits of this kind of thought and of the reality which it sets out to understand, are laid down and it cannot overstep these limits without falsifying itself.

These limits are most clearly seen in what one can call the 'breaks in destiny' in history as it is here understood, for these show unmistakably that the full reality of the responsibility and independence of man cannot be understood by history carried out under the assumptions made by this kind of thought. For in the face of such 'breaks', which, whether they are great or small, are undoubtedly found in history, both the independence of man as it is here conceived, and the responsibility associated with it, are both at an end. The questions which history then asks of man, and which he cannot ignore, can no longer be answered by historical thought of this kind.

The limits inherent in this kind of thought are also shown in the tension which is produced by the fact that all it can ever understand is something partial, and yet part of a whole, that is, the whole of the events in the world. This concept of the whole world and the totality of the events taking place within it is something which is possible for historical reason to perceive of, and without it history would not exist in the sense in which modern historical scholarship understands it. For what makes a historian is the fact 'that he seeks to understand the whole complex of the history of mankind'. The individual 'does not have for him a value of his own, but only serves him as a source, that is, only as material of which he can make use to understand the whole historical complex'.[15] Without this totality there would not in fact be any parts, for they assume the existence of a totality. The events in which man is involved would then disintegrate into utter meaninglessness, or, as Karl Jaspers has described it, 'into the confusion of the fortuitous, into aimless coming and going, into apparent purpose leading nowhere'.[16] History would then cease to be history. And consequently it is in fact 'the urge of historical knowledge, which seeks its own ultimate meaning' to 'understand the unity of history, that is, to think of universal history as a whole'.[17]

But to say that reason is capable of conceiving the idea of the totality of the world and the events that take place within it does not mean that it is able to understand the totality of history, that which is called 'universal history'. Modern historical thought is able to have a concept of the totality of history and must think in these terms, in order for the history with which it is dealing to remain history even though it is still partial. At the same time it is impossible for it to comprehend this totality. This contradiction lays down the limits of the ability of modern historical scholarship to comprehend the reality of history. If it overlooks this, then it goes beyond the limits of the method by which it stands and falls. It may relapse into historical relativism, by making the particular parts of history which it is able to study into totalities, running parallel to each other but unconnected. If so, it has fallen prey to the 'anarchy of convictions' which Dilthey describes as the consequence of historical thought.[18] Or else, by supposing that it can in some way apprehend the whole of history, it may cease to be a science as it claims, and become a philosophical world view. This is probably one reason amongst others why, as Wittram points out, 'historical science, the more strictly it develops the method of factual investigation', renounces all syntheses of universal history, and why 'it has not been historians, but philosophers and sociologists who have been the first to make fresh attempts at such syntheses'.[19]

The most profound reason for this urge on the part of historical scholarship for unity, and for an understanding of the meaning of history, is presumably the fact that it is not the full reality of history which is apprehended by it, but only one aspect of it, that which is in accordance with its methods. When it forgets how for the sake of this method it has itself limited the reality of the history which it sets out to study, it tries to attain to the totality of history in the same way in which it applies its ideas to the temporal course of history, assuming in so doing that as the temporal course of history proceeds, the whole of history, and therefore its meaning, will be realized.

The history which began with Jesus and his preaching is concerned precisely with that which modern historical scholarship is seeking in its urge towards the totality and the meaning of history. This, however, must not be understood in a superficial sense, as though what is impossible for modern historical scholarship can be achieved by the aid of a theology of history. This would be an attempt by such a theology to fit what happened in Jesus into the course of history in such a way that in it the end of history was already anticipated, so that it was possible to have an understanding of history as a whole, and to give a valid answer to the question of the meaning of the course of universal history, an answer which would also include the conception of the meaning of the 'breaks in the destiny' of history.

In order to be able to express how the history which began with the preaching of Jesus is concerned with the totality and unity of history, we must once again ask what took place in this history. From what we have already learned of this kind of history, we may say that it is concerned with the totality of history because in it the way in which the totality of history constitutes the world is subject to a decision. Thus it is not concerned, at least not in the first instance, with the manifold variety of what man does and has to do in the world, but of the way in which the world exists as such and therefore with the nature of man's relationship to it. For this also decides his relationship to God. If his decision is for it to be the world in such a way that it is the final unchangeable reality for man, behind which his thoughts cannot go and which demands of him that he adapt himself to the eternal and unchangeable ordinance by which it is the world, a demand which, since his life comes from this ordinance, he must obey without reserve for the sake of his life, then he has decided implicitly against God. But if in this history he decides against the world being the world in this way, and for it merely being the historical world which exists at any present moment, man bearing responsibility for its permanence and order, then there is room for responsibility to God.

The relationship of man to the totality of the world, and therefore his relationship to God, is decided in the history which began with Jesus. This is perhaps seen most clearly in the distinctive nature of his preaching. One of its most remarkable features, to which we have already drawn attention, is that it contains virtually no instructions about what man has to do in the world. It is true that in the parables in particular, but elsewhere as well, Jesus speaks in an extraordinarily vivid way about things and situations in the world, and largely describes men as being occupied by such earthly affairs. It is not too much to say that in Jesus's preaching the life and endeavour of men in the world, and their tasks and involvements, are present in all their profusion and fullness, and in a reality which is very soberly regarded. But the interesting feature is that none of this is mentioned for its own sake. Realistic observation is never associated with advice about the kind of action which must be carried out in this world and its affairs. What is so vividly described always appears as a parable for something else, the relationship of man to God. This is particularly clear in the parable of the Unjust Steward (Luke 16.1ff.). The crafty and shameless deceit practised by this man is described extremely vividly, but in no way can it be regarded as guidance about the right way to behave. Characteristically, Jesus does not utter a single word of blame against it.

The narrator's intention is exclusively concerned with what the behaviour of this man represents in the parable, that is the concentrated vigilance which is required because of the imminent coming of the kingdom of God. One might perhaps suppose that a saying of Jesus, such as that anyone who seeks to follow him must be ready to renounce if necessary his own possessions, or leave his father and mother, was an instruction of this sort. But neither of these ostensibly ascetic sayings, which in fact were very early regarded by the church as such instructions, are meant to lay down a programme for human behaviour and action in the world, any more than the idea of the kingdom of God provides a pattern for the way in which men are to order the world. If we ignore this important characteristic of Jesus's preaching, that it says virtually nothing about what is to be done in the world, and set out to interpret his sayings as such instructions, we shall fail to appreciate what is at issue in his history, that is, the decision about man's attitude to the world as a whole, which is at the same time a decision about his attitude to God. Once this is understood, the lack of moral instruction, which the conventional understanding of his preaching almost always overlooks and regards as a scandalous thing to assert, is no longer surprising. It becomes clear that the lack of such instruction is emphatic evidence that Jesus is exclusively concerned with this twofold responsibility, to God and for the world, in which man's salvation is at stake. Since such instructions about human action in the world can never be concerned with anything but the multitude of different individual activities which exist in the world, and not with the world itself, and therefore neither with its salvation nor its damnation, they could serve not the slightest purpose.

But it is possible to say that Jesus's whole thinking and endeavour is directed, with a seriousness of purpose which concentrates on this above all else, towards man's relationship to the world as a whole. For if this is a right relationship, one in which man does not give to the world what is due to God, then his relationship to God will also be one which is in accordance with his true deity, and one through which alone man can attain to the life God has destined for him, by giving himself in responsibility to God to answer to this call, and so receiving the 'great reward' which is promised to such a response.

Here, of course, we must not forget that man encounters this call of God only in the world, in the rule of God within it, which is not subject to any law of the present world. And therefore the world inevitably forms part of man's relationship to God. This is so, first of all, in the negative sense that man must reject the form of the present world which is completely self-contained and constantly has a tendency to take the place of God. But it is also true in the positive sense that by rejecting the world as it exists as such in this idolatrous way, he recognizes it as that which God has given him for his own, for which he is responsible, and in responsibility for which he receives the independence which makes it possible for him to hear the call of God which is given to him, and to give himself to be God's in responsibility to him.

We have said that the difference between the two kinds of history, that which begins with Jesus, and the other, which is the theme of modern historical scholarship, is not that in one man is independent of the world because he is responsible for it, while in the other he is not. In both cases this independence is a constituent element of history. For it sets man free from his responsibility to the world, and only then is history of either kind possible. But the relationship to the world which this independence reveals is different in each case. The world is the same, but in each case is regarded differently. There is a saying of Jesus which expresses very clearly the difference between these two points of view. This is Jesus's saying about paying tribute to Caesar, in which he answers a question by which his opponents sought to face him with a fatal dilemma (Mark 12.13ff.). The question was: 'Is it lawful to pay taxes to Caesar, or not?' The assumption behind this question was the view which was held everywhere at that time, not only amongst Jews, but also amongst other nations, that the divine sphere and that of the state were not only closely linked, but were one and the same. If taxes were paid to Caesar, it meant, according to this view, not only that he was recognized politically, but that his claim to religious supremacy was admitted. Thus in the form in which Jesus's opponents posed the question to him, it implied an exceedingly cunning alternative: his answer must place him either on the side of Caesar or that of God. And concealed in this alternative was the question whether the money which Caesar demanded as tax belonged to God, and whether someone who sought to be obedient to God should have given this money to God and refused to pay tax to Caesar? If Jesus had answered the question, 'Is it lawful to pay taxes to Caesar?' by saying that it was lawful, then his recognition of the foreign rule of the Romans would have brought him into discredit amongst the Jewish people. For according to their piety everything that man possessed belonged to God. If he answered that it was not lawful, then he would have brought on himself the bitter enmity of the Roman rulers. Jesus answered the question by taking the coin with which the tax was paid and pointing to the fact that it bore Caesar's likeness and inscription, which made clear to whom it belonged. Thus by saying, 'Render to Caesar the things that are Caesar's, and to God the things that are God's' he abolished, in accordance with the transformation of the world which came about in his preaching, the unity between God and the world, religion and politics, which was the tacit assumption in the question which he was asked, and accorded to each what was due to it. But what is due to each is something basically different. What belongs to Caesar is the money, as can be seen from the likeness and the inscription; but what belongs to God is man. The money belongs to the world, and in the money the world is regarded in the way in which man is responsible for it and for the things in it, and has to administer it in accordance with the independence which he possesses with regard to it. But in so far as man belongs to God, the world is regarded from the point of view of man's responsibility to God for the way in which it exists as the world. Man does not belong to God through anything which he possesses in the world, and therefore not through money. Thus when Jesus's opponents asked him whether the money with which the imperial tax was paid belonged to God they were trying to force him into a false alternative which derived from the 'hypocritical' nature of their piety, for it is man himself who belongs to God. He cannot render to God what he owes him, as one who belongs to God, with anything that belongs to the world, but only with himself. And the only way in which he can do this is by his giving himself as a response to God, in responsibility to him.

As we have seen, a constituent factor of both kinds of history is man's responsibility for the world. And in both cases this responsibility implies man's independence of the world and the law which prevails within it. But although this independence is the same in both cases, it is understood in each case in a different way. In the history which is the theme of modern historical scholarship man's responsibility for the world takes into account the independence of man that goes with it only as an independence of the world, such as is evidenced, and constantly worked out anew, in the historical achievements which it studies. Thus in this independence the history which takes place between man and the world comes about. But in the history of Jesus this independence, and the responsibility for the world which comes with it, takes into account man's responsibility to God. And this is the starting-point of the history that takes place between God and man, in which the totality or the salvation of man and his world is at stake.

NOTES

1. Dilthey, *Gesammelte Schriften*, Vol. I, p. 348.
2. Dilthey, op. cit., p. 318.
3. Krüger, *Die Geschichte im Denken der Gegenwart*, p. 17.
4. Quoted in Karl Löwith, *Weltgeschichte und Heilsgeschichte*, Stuttgart, 1953, p. 113.
5. R. Wittram, *Das Interesse an der Geschichte*, Göttingen, 1958, p. 158.
6. Wittram, op. cit., p. 159.
7. Troeltsch, *Gesammelte Schriften*, Vol. II, p. 734.
8. Dilthey, *Gesammelte Schriften*, Vol. II, p. 260.
9. Dilthey, op. cit., Vol. I, p. 379 n. 1.
10. Wittram, op. cit., p. 159.
11. Op. cit., p. 148.
12. Cf. above, p. 158f.
13. Cf. above, p. 114.
14. Cf. my book, *Verhängnis und Hoffnung der Neuzeit*, 2nd ed., Stuttgart, 1958.
15. H. G. Gadamer, *Wahrheit und Methode*, 2nd ed., Tübingen, 1965, p. 185.
16. Jaspers, *Vom Ursprung und Ziel der Geschichte*, Munich, 1949, p. 335.
17. Op. cit., p. 319.
18. Dilthey, op. cit., Vol. V, p. 9.
19. Wittram, op. cit., p. 128.

14

THE WORLD OF EACH INDIVIDUAL MAN

WE MUST go on to say something about the difference between the two kinds of history of which we have spoken in the previous chapter, and about the different vision of the world in each. Modern historical thought sees the world as characterized by the great historical tasks of political and social institutions, of civilization, science and technology, which must be constantly worked out and created anew under the guidance of the responsibility which man has for the world. Consequently, the men who appear in history of this kind are those who are of particular importance for this world through their achievements and failures, and it is for this reason that history tells of them. In the world as it appears in the preaching of Jesus, the situation is quite different. The men who belong to this world are not the same as in the world of modern history, even if they are people who have an important place in that world. In the world of Jesus they never appeared as the 'historical figures' which they are in the other world. For in the world of Jesus it does not matter what importance a man has in the world of historical scholarship, or indeed whether he has a place in it at all, rather than simply disappearing into the 'unhistorical' mass. Although without these multitudes, of whom historical scholarship has virtually nothing to say, the history which is the object of such scholarship would be impossible, they appear in it at best only occasionally as a collective body. Only in relatively rare cases do they become the anonymous subject of historical events; usually they are only their objects.

We can perhaps call the world in which men come into association with Jesus, and in which they live out their history, the world of each individual man, by contrast to the world of historical scholarship, which is that of general phenomena. For the preaching of Jesus shows quite clearly that it is in this world that every individual must exercise a responsibility before God which no one can carry out for him. As we have seen, to exercise responsibility to God means to give oneself to him as a response to him. And thus what an individual is responsible for to God can only be that which directly concerns him and his existence: the world which according to Jesus's preaching is defined above all by a person's relationship to his 'neighbour'. One may say that it is reduced to this relationship, and to what takes place within it, to such an extent that everything else that may exist in the world is overshadowed as inessential. It does not matter how great or small any world defined in this way may be, and whether any attention is paid to it at all by any other world. Here the great are not greater than the less. The saying of Jesus that only those who repent and become like children will enter the kingdom of heaven (Matt. 18.3), applies to them. In the world of historical scholarship children are without any individual significance.

The standard by which this world of the individual, and the relevance of what takes place within it, is measured is consequently completely different from that by which one judges what has historical significance in the world which is the object of historical scholarship. Since man is responsible to God for what happens within his world as an individual, the only possible standard is what is acceptable to God. For it is only from God that this world and what takes place within it receives its meaning and significance. But the innermost significance of what takes place in this world is this: the standard of God, which applies here, cannot be compared with any standard which is applicable in a world which, however great or important it may be, has not become a person's own individual world. For it is God's reality and power, embracing great and small in the same way, which gives meaning and significance to everything upon which its light falls, whether it is the greatest or least thing in the other world of historical scholarship. That is why, if God's standard can be measured at all, it is not by what is great or greatest in the world, but by the least and most insignificant thing in it, which by the standards of world history would be wholly without importance.

In my view, Jesus had this in mind when he said of the least and most utterly unimportant thing which he could think of, the sparrows, of which 'two are sold for a penny', that 'no one of them will fall to the ground without your Father's will', and of the 'hairs of your head', that they are 'all numbered' (Matt. 10.29). Nothing that exists in the world of each individual man, when judged by God's standard, remains either great or small, as it was in that other world, but becomes what it has been made by God's being present to it in his reality and power. Thus, in so far as the world is the world of each individual man, the standard which applies in it lies in the fact that God is present in it and that only he can save it and make it whole. And neither the world itself nor anything that happens in it can be measured by the standard which we call historical in the conventional sense.

Perhaps no word characterizes the world which, in the history which began with him, Jesus revealed to man as the world of each individual, more than the word 'neighbour', in the sense in which he uses it for the relationship between men which is in accordance with the will of God, and which is therefore inextricably linked with his relationship to God, as the saying concerning the greatest commandment makes explicit. As we see from the parable of the last judgment (Matt. 25.31ff.), this relationship to one's neighbour can never be concerned merely with unusual matters, clearly distinguishable from normal behaviour. For those who are called to this judgment – according to the parable, 'all the nations' – will be judged there not according to the works which they may have carried out in exact accordance with the order of the ordinary world of history, and in order to maintain it. In a strange contradiction to what one must call the real concern of universal history, the final verdict which decides their salvation or damnation depends exclusively upon their attitude to their neighbour in the elementary needs of his everyday life.

Thus the word 'neighbour', understood as the characteristic of the world of each individual man, points in the first instance to the smallness, not to say the narrowness of this world, its historical insignificance in terms of academic historical scholarship. As the world of the individual it is not the whole world, the world of every man, or the world of humanity, but it is always the world of each single person. But it must not be understood as narrow in a merely spatial sense, but rather in a sense that the world which is defined by my neighbour and by his closeness to me, by comparison with which everything else that may exist in it apart from my neighbour becomes insignificant, can only be my own individual world. For here it is no longer the world in general, but the world which concerns and impinges on me, and on me alone. For in Jesus's preaching my 'neighbour' is the person who on any particular occasion is close to me in an exclusive sense, and towards whom I have to act in such a way that by comparison everything else with which I have to do, that is, everything in the world in general, and which is concerned with the order that prevails in it, fades into insignificance. This other world, which now becomes a matter of indifference, may include matters as important as the sacrificial cult in the world as it existed at the time of Jesus. Thus, for example, Jesus says: 'If you are offering your gift at the altar, and there remember that your brother has something against you, leave your gift there before the altar and go; first be reconciled to your brother, and then come and offer your gift' (Matt. 5.23f.). Thus through an encounter with my neighbour which is so close that there is no room in it for any of the other things which fill my life, the world is laid open in such a way that it no longer has any limit, because what now happens in it is of eternal significance. This eternal significance is the relationship to God which is revealed, for good or evil, in our relationship to our neighbour. This can be seen from the saying which in St Matthew follows that quoted above: 'Make friends quickly with your accuser, when you are going with him to court, lest your accuser hand you over to the judge, and the judge to the guard, and you be put in prison; truly, I say to you, you will never get out till you have paid the last penny' (Matt. 5.25f.). The significance of the encounter with one's neighbour which takes place in the world of each individual man can also be seen in the fact that Jesus promises the 'reward from heaven' to those who behave towards their neighbour in accordance with the will of God: 'Your reward will be great, and you will be sons of the Most High' (Luke 6.35). This saying clearly speaks of the will of God in two senses: first, in that it demands of man that he do something; and secondly, that in this same will, God has some purpose for man, and does something to him, that is gives him something. We have already asked[1] what this 'great reward' consists of, and what it is which God gives to those who behave towards their neighbours in the way he demands. We replied that this reward was liberation from the trust in the present world, and from the life of striving in accordance with its institutions, and the gift, given in this liberation, of the presence of the kingdom of God, and participation in it, and therefore of participation in a life which is lived for God.

If this is what takes place in the world of each individual man, then we may also express it by saying that the life which is given to man here is not determined, like life lived in accordance with the ordinance laid down in the present world, by the need to arrange things and relationships in accordance with the rule of 'like for like'. For as Jesus says, here one is not doing merely the good things from which one might expect, in accordance with the ordinance of the present world, to receive the same in return. Therefore one does not simply do good to those from whom one expects to be repaid in kind (Luke 6.32–34). Consequently, the life which is lived in the world of each individual man is not determined in the first instance principally by the things man needs, but is concerned, regardless of whatever else may take place in it, with man himself, both in the case of him who is my neighbour, and of me, who am his neighbour. Because this happens between men in the world of each as an individual, they are so close to each other in it that nothing can come between them to dominate their relationship to each other, as happens in the present world. Rather, each is directly concerned with the other; I am concerned for my neighbour's being human, by being human towards him. This is possible because life which is in accordance with the world of the individual person is nourished by the will of God which happens within it, is experienced in faith, and is therefore lived in the presence of God. Thus it is possible for the person who lives in this world to act in such a way as Jesus describes, for example, in the saying about almsgiving: his left hand does not know what his right is doing, so that room is left for the action of God.

Thus the characteristic way in which the world in which man lives is narrowed down when it is transformed into the world of each individual man, consists in its no longer being the multitude of things and relationships which has hitherto filled the world, and in which man is involved in accordance with the ordinance which prevails within it and makes it a world. As we have seen, this transformation takes place when someone who encounters a person becomes his neighbour, or he becomes that other person's neighbour. But this transformation can also come about when something or some happening in the world concerns a person and impinges upon a person with such force that as a result everything in the world, and particularly this present world with the ordinance which gives it its substance as the world, is forced into the background and becomes inessential by contrast to what is now happening to the person. This becoming inessential does not mean that the present world and the ordinance which prevails within it no longer exist. The world as it exists at present is always there as long as there is a world, and it can never be without the ordinance which guards it against becoming chaos. But certainly the significance which the present world has hitherto possessed undergoes an extraordinarily profound change.

To put it briefly, it is no longer the present world in the sense in which this term can be applied to the Jewish world in the time of Jesus, and one no longer encounters the will of God in the ordinance of this world and in the commandments prescribed in it. Rather, the will of God which applies to man can be perceived only in what happens in the world as it is now understood. This can never be laid down in advance. And in accordance with Jesus's preaching, this takes place in particular when someone comes so 'close' to me, that he is 'nearest' to me in a sense in which Jesus in most cases understands the term 'neighbour', or in the sense in which I become his nearest 'neighbour', as in Jesus's parable of the Good Samaritan. What happens here is that I am able to perceive the will of God directly, in the sense that it is I and none other that he has in mind here. As we have seen, Jesus expressed this in the parable by changing the question of the lawyer, which referred to such a commandment laid down in the present world: 'And who is my neighbour?', into a completely different question: who was the neighbour of him who had fallen amongst thieves? For only when the question of one's neighbour is posed in such a way does it point away from the general commandment and away from the present world in which such commandments are in force, and direct attention instead to the one real and living person who is close to me and with whom, therefore, I am directly concerned in the particular situation in which he finds himself. And so the question points to the decision which brings the person who asks the question unavoidably close to another human being, as a result of his own observation. If he follows what his observation demands of him, and remains as close as he has been brought to the person whose situation he has observed, then the world in which this takes place does not remain the same as it has been hitherto, the present world enclosed within itself. And it ceases to be sustained by the law that prevails within it, and by the commandments which those who live in it and trust in it and its law set out to fulfil in order to maintain their own position, or, as Jesus puts it, 'to save their life' (Mark 8.35), the life which they want to live on the basis of this world. When someone becomes a person's neighbour in this way, and draws so close to him, everything else is overshadowed. The world becomes for him, through this person, a world which concerns and impinges on him, and him alone, directly and inescapably. But this is the world in which God, who rules in the living events which take place in it, encounters him here and now, and gives him the life which he can live through the will of God.

When a man experiences something like what happened to the Good Samaritan, the world as it now appears to him ceases to be this present world. It is then no longer the world in which what and who he is, and what he has to do, is determined once for all by the ordinance that prevails within it, and which he fulfils in order to give significance to his existence. This ordinance becomes inessential, and what it has hitherto prescribed and laid down loses the validity which has more or less been taken for granted. All this – the transformation of the present world of each individual man – can, as we have already said, take place through anything that happens at all in the world in which man lives.

For some event in the life of a person to qualify for what is meant here, it is necessary, as I have already suggested, that it be an event which takes place in the world in which the person lives. That is, it must be something real in the sense of this world, as a person's thirst, hunger, estrangement, sickness or imprisonment are real – and these are the experiences which people are spoken of as taking account of, or not taking account of, in the parable of the last judgment. Only when a process is real in this sense is it possible for a person to feel himself concerned by it with such urgency that it affects him and no one else, and in such a way that it is the only event which concerns him here and now, by comparison with which everything else in the whole wide world becomes inessential. If someone undergoes this experience, then the world as it has seemed to him hitherto ceases to be this present and continuing world. We have already said that this can only come about through something which happens in the world in which the person concerned lives. But this must not be understood to mean that the impulse which produces the effect this event has here is derived from the significance which what happens in this event as such possesses in the present world. For the effect it has here is, in fact, that the world in which it takes place ceases to be this present and continuing world. This is a consequence of the oppressive and completely exclusive way in which such an event comes close to, concerns, and impinges upon, a single person, and on the characteristic narrowing down of the world which brings this about. There is no longer any place for it as the present world, or for anything which derives its meaning from the latter.

Consequently, however, what happens in this event as such also loses the significance which it possessed in the present world, regardless of whether this was great or small. All that remains of it is that it brings the person who experiences it face to face, in a completely new way, with the question of himself. Everything that happens in the present world derives its meaning from the ordinance which maintains this world in being, and man, too, derives the meaning of his existence from it, so long as he lives not only in it, but by it. But all this becomes inessential when the world in which he lives is no longer the present world, and is reduced to this one event and what follows from it. Thus if man allows this event to concern him and impinge upon him as closely as it comes upon him here, it becomes impossible for him to assert himself in the face of it as him who he is in the present world. All that someone on whom such an event impinges can do is to realize that it is he who himself is called upon to be present and ready. If this is the situation in which man finds himself in the world which is his own as an individual, then this is the world in which he encounters his destiny, and must face the decision either of committing himself to it and so gaining the life which is destined for him in it, or of refusing it and so losing this life.

We use the word 'destiny' to describe not merely any casual event in a person's life, but something in which he comes to realize that it concerns his life as a whole. If something like this happens to him, he is faced with the question of the meaning of his life, and therefore also that of the meaning of the world in which he lives. He must ask whether this world and the life he lives in it has a meaning or not. Anyone who pays serious attention to this question cannot give any partial answer to it, but can answer it only with his life itself, and with his life as a whole. That the question posed to man by the event in which he encounters his destiny can be answered by him only with his life as a whole, and therefore only by the person himself to whom the question is posed, is shown by the fact that we speak only of two possibilities with regard to destiny: that of submitting to it or rejecting it. It is in this way, too, that destiny is distinguished from what we may call the vicissitudes or strokes of fate. The difference between the two is clear when we consider that one can speak of many vicissitudes of fate which a person experiences in his life, whereas a man has only one destiny. If we call strokes of fate the events in a person's life in which he perceives in the good or evil, the fortune or misfortune which they bring him, that his life and what happens in it is not completely under his own control, we may perhaps say that to a more or less minor degree his destiny is made known in them. For though we have said that a man always has only a single destiny, this does not mean that he encounters it only once in his life. In various ways, such as in the strokes of fate he encounters, he can come face with it on numerous occasions. Perhaps one may also say that the relationship of destiny and the vicissitudes of fate to one another is that in destiny the numerous things which occur in the strokes of fate which occur in life are drawn together, and that these numerous and varied vicissitudes derive from man's one destiny, and the way in which he encounters in them the more profound and ultimately unified significance which they possess in the context of his life. The decision with which man is faced by his destiny, wherever he encounters it, is that of gaining the life which is prepared for him in his destiny by submitting to it, or of losing it by refusing his destiny. Since it is in the nature of human life that it cannot be lived without decisions, and above all, cannot be lived without the decision which man's destiny demands of him, one can say that as sure as men are men, they all experience it. But just as it is true of death that although it comes to all men alike, each must die it as his own death, and his alone, so it is true of destiny that it comes to every man as something irreplaceably his own. To say that destiny always comes to man's life as a whole is also to say that it can only be sent to him from where his life originates. As we have said above, it is prepared for man by God.

The German word for 'destiny' derives from a root which originally means 'to set to work'; and in the context in which we are speaking of destiny here, it means the way in which God 'puts to work' man's life. In our account of the way in which the relationship of man to God and to the world is understood in the preaching of Jesus, we have already discussed at length the way in which God does this, and were, therefore, in fact discussing the destiny he has prepared for man, although we did not use this word. We saw that as Jesus understood this relationship, it depends upon a twofold responsibility on the part of man, a responsibility to God and a responsibility for the world, and that the first is not possible without the second. For it is only in the independence of the world which man possesses as one responsible for it that it becomes possible for him to give himself in response to God, with his whole existence, as one whom God has called to responsibility to him. And only in this way can he live his life through God in the freedom for God which is made possible for him by this responsibility alone. As we have already seen, this possibility of freedom for God would be unreal if man did not at the same time retain the possibility of refusing himself to God instead of responding with himself to his call. But if he chooses to refuse himself, then his independence and responsibility with regard to the world undergo a profound and fateful transformation. They cease to derive their meaning from man's relationship to God, and derive it instead solely from his relationship to the world. The responsibility which he had for the world as one who has been made independent of it ceases to take into account anything but the world and the life that is lived by it. And in the same way, the independence he has of the world comes to mean only his self-assertion, and is no longer the responsibility to God in which as an independent person he gives himself as a response to God. Now destiny is the way in which God 'sets to work' man's life by giving him the world as his own, so that he may be responsible for it, independent of it, and therefore able to give himself in freedom to be God's own. This means that the consequence of the choice to refuse this destiny, and the fateful transformation which results from it, can only be that although he gains life as it can be lived through the world alone, by so doing he loses the life which God has prepared for him in the destiny he has prepared for him, and which is therefore the only life that can be lived through God.

When we were discussing how the relationship of man to the world is regarded by modern historical scholarship, our attention was drawn to the limits of the sphere of history with which this deals.[2] We can now go on to say that the destiny which is characteristic of man as such, and which each individual has therefore to experience for himself as his own, is excluded here from the reality of history. Consequently, the history of man is considered here only in respect of the significance of his relationship to the world through his outstanding achievements, and to the position he obtains in the ordered structure of this world as understood by this historical thinking. That is, it is regarded from the point of view of man's raising himself by his achievements from amongst the mass of other men, who remain unimportant to history and are not considered by it; although there is no doubt that without the mass of people of whom history makes no mention these achievements could not have the significance which they must have to be historical in the sense of this kind of historical thought. But there is another point which is of great importance in our present context. It can hardly be denied that every individual, regardless of whether he belongs to the unhistorical mass in the sense of academic history, or to those whose historical importance is known and recounted by historical scholarship, has a history of his own in the encounter with the destiny of which we have spoken, which all men encounter, and which faces them with the decision that is inseparable from this destiny, whatever choice in fact may be made. Although this history remains inaccessible to the methods of modern historical thought, the meaning of each individual's life is as much at stake in this personal history as anywhere else, and so, too, in the meaning of the world, in so far as he lives in it.

Thus a limit is placed by man's destiny on the reality of history, as modern historical scholarship understands it. And this limit is the same as that imposed by the dilemma, as we found it, into which this mode of thought was irresistibly forced by the question of the totality and the meaning of the history which it tries to comprehend. For as we have seen,[3] it cannot avoid posing this question if it is to remain historical, that is, if the event with which it is dealing is not to be fragmented into numerous single pieces, each of which may be 'histories' in themselves, mutually independent and parallel, but never able to become 'history'. For that is always the history of the world, if only in the sense of an inquiry into it. But modern historical scholarship can no more answer this question than it can avoid it.

Thus the totality of history or, as the historian expresses it, the idea of universal history, which seeks to deal with the totality and the meaningful unity of history, is 'at once a certainty and an impossibility' for this kind of historical thought.[4] It is this dilemma which lays down the limit of its comprehension of the reality of history. If it nevertheless purports to apprehend the totality of history, it is going beyond its limits and abandoning the method by which it has hitherto been guided. It then ceases to be historical and falls victim to the temptation to create a world view by which to attempt to apprehend this totality. But the kind of totality it envisages could never be other than one which man had to realize himself, through a responsibility for the world in this sense, and in accordance with the prescribed actions which one would hope to find in the world and in the attitudes which fulfil them. These prescriptions would be interpreted on the basis of the world view which was chosen. There would be a belief that in these prescriptions and in what they demand of man, the key was to be found to history and to the goal which reveals its meaning. But then the world would become, as in the pre-Christian era, the final and all-embracing reality in which alone a man can find the meaning of his life.

It would no longer be such a reality in the religious sense, where it was regarded as an eternal and unchangeable ordinance, whole and entire in itself, in the wholeness of which man can only participate by adapting himself to it in accordance with its laws. According to that view he was held captive in the self-contained structure of the world by his responsibility *to* the world and its eternal ordinance. If historical scholarship goes beyond its brief, he is seen as held captive by his responsibility *for* the world, which no longer knows or desires to know anything of responsibility *to* God. Instead, the responsibility of which it is aware is no longer concerned with detailed individual matters, but applies to the world as a whole, so that it has become a responsibility for the salvation of the world.

If we are not to misrepresent modern historical scholarship, we must state explicitly that as long as it does not succumb to this temptation to form a philosophical world view, man's responsibility for the world is limited exclusively to the world, and therefore the ignoring of the responsibility to God is of purely methodological significance. That is, in this way historical thought remains within the limits of its methodological procedure, which is a scientific one, and only makes statements about the reality of the history which it is investigating in so far as it is accessible to it on the basis of this method. But this methodology must not forget that the significance which responsibility for the world contains derives from the fact that it is related to responsibility to God. For if it becomes a fundamental principle through the influence of a philosophical world view, and man's responsibility for the world derives its meaning purely from his independence of the world, then it is being used to deny God. When this happens, the inevitable consequence is that man regards himself as the wholly autonomous lord of the world and its history, upon whose actions alone the salvation of the world, and his own salvation, depend. It is the conviction of the most important and influential of the modern doctrines of salvation, based upon philosophical and historical world views, that this is in fact the case. They see the inescapable task which results from man's domination of the world in this sense as that which Proudhon, one of the first to propound such a historical doctrine of salvation, described as '*défatalisation* of providence'.[5] According to Löwith, the meaning of this assertion is that 'man and human righteousness must take upon themselves the guidance of all human affairs. Man will replace God, and faith in human progress will replace faith in providence'.[6] The more forcefully and comprehensively man's responsibility – for the world as it is understood here – is affirmed by the discovery of his power 'to transform the earth', and especially by the reshaping of all political and social ordinances, the more the world which we have called the world of each individual man, and the history which takes place in this world, is excluded from the picture of the world which man alone is responsible for saving and making whole. A mode of historical thought which believes that it controls the salvation of the world, whatever form this may take, can only regard as absurd the assertion that this world of each individual man, and the destiny which he encounters within it, is for man the one thing that is essential and that by comparison with it everything else, including the world history in which historical thought assumes that the salvation of the world is realized, becomes inessential. At best it will be regarded as something which belongs to an old-fashioned and individualistic petit-bourgeois concern for history, which is incapable of conceiving the idea that man is in any sense in control of the totality of the world and its history, and which is therefore hopelessly excluded from real history as historical thought, now become a world view, conceives of it and believes it controls it. It is wholly in accordance with this that historical philosophers of this kind, as Löwith notes, deal 'with collectives, but not individuals'. As Comte, one of the greatest amongst them, says, what is at issue here is the history of humanity and not man.[7] It is obvious that this faith in humanity, and what it is regarded as capable of, is held at the expense of the real man, who is always, albeit not exclusively, the individual. He cannot be more thoroughly deprived of his humanity than when he is deprived both of his own individual world, his destiny and his own individual history. The history of mankind, conceived of without these, cannot restore them to him.

As we have already said, in the light of the destiny of man, the limit of the reality of history as conceived by modern historical thought is seen to be defined in exactly the same way as in the dilemma to which we were led by the question of the totality of history. But where man's destiny is concerned, this limit is seen from the other side; the reality which historical thought does not apprehend and cannot apprehend is revealed in it. This is the reality which is concerned with the totality of history. It was immediately clear that the question of the totality and the meaning of history is posed differently here than by historical scholarship. The latter conducts its inquiry in terms of the temporal course of history, and in the expectation of a consummation of history at the end of its temporal course. That is, it thinks of a 'potentiality of universal history' from which the meaning of human life and existence might be known. But as we have seen, if the question is posed in these terms, it becomes impossible to answer because the anticipation of the final course of history which it requires is impossible for the human mind. It is of course possible for the mind to apprehend the partial unities of history, and what is commonly known as their meaning. And man, too, can be understood in the same way, as he exists in each separate epoch of history, and as he participates in the realization of their 'meaning'. But the final word concerning the totality and the unity of history seems likely to be the comment of Karl Jaspers, that it is a 'coming into being of unities', and as such 'an enthusiastic seeking of unity', and therefore it is likewise 'again, a passionate destroying of unities'. Anything more than this goes beyond the limits of history and is discussing its 'overcoming', in which it 'disappears into the eternal present'.[8]

But the question of the totality of history is quite different when it is posed from the point of view of what we have called the world of each individual man, which is revealed to man in the preaching of Jesus. The totality of history, as it is conceived in the inquiry carried out by historical scholarship into the 'potentiality of universal history', can be called a quantitive totality, because any knowledge of it would assume the consummation of its temporal course (though this can never be apprehended). But what is sought in the kind of history which we are discussing now can be called a qualitative totality. That is, it is thought of as a totality here in the sense of the salvation and wholeness of man and his world, for the decision of each man in his own individual world is concerned with this. This salvation is the life which God 'sets into motion' in the destiny determined by him for man in the world of each individual. As we have seen, this happens when man, who is responsible for the world, gives himself as a response to God in responsibility to him.

We do well here to remind ourselves of what we have already said in another context about the meaning of being responsible to someone.[9] We made it clear that such a responsibility assumes a word which calls someone in the sense that he cannot respond to it in the right way, that is, in the way which is in accordance with the word that calls him, by any partial and individual action, but solely by giving himself. We also recognized that what takes place in such a responsibility is exactly defined by the relationship which exists between him who calls and him who is called. In each case any relationship in which responsibility in this sense is possible affects the existence of him who is called, as it is determined by him who calls and his word. Thus what is at issue is the being which he who is called receives from him who calls him in his relationship with the latter. We gave as an example of this the responsibility of a son to his father. If we apply this to the relationship between God and man, we can say that the life that someone receives by giving himself to God in response to him, when he is called by God to be responsible to him, is his salvation. This means that he can then be in the sight of God what he is through and according to the will of God. For man experiences his salvation by being able to dare to be himself by responding to the word of God. And it is this salvation which is decided in the world of each individual man.

NOTES

1. Cf. above, p. 114.
2. Cf. above, pp. 169f.
3. Cf. above, pp. 170f.
4. Wittram, *Das Interesse an der Geschichte*, p. 136.
5. Quoted in K. Löwith, *Weltgeschichte und Heilsgeschehen*, Stuttgart, 1953.
6. Löwith, loc. cit.
7. Löwith, op. cit., p. 85.
8. Jaspers, *Vom Ursprung und Ziel der Geschichte*, pp. 327, 339.
9. Cf. above, pp. 162.

15

THE WORLD OF JESUS AS AN INDIVIDUAL

IN HIS preaching Jesus showed to man that the world in which he is faced with the decision whether to gain or lose the life which is determined for him by God in his destiny, is his own world as an individual. In this world, as we saw, the issue concerns what Jesus called the kingdom of God, the coming of which he proclaimed at the same time as the coming to an end of the present world in which he lived. Thus the world of each individual man is not the kingdom of God already. But if the decision which must be taken in this world, and which can be seen in this world to be inevitable and necessary, is made in such a way that in it man gains the life determined for him in his destiny, then man's own world as an individual becomes the kingdom of God. When Jesus spoke of the kingdom of God he was thinking of something which is in irreconcilable opposition to the world in which the Jews of his time lived. In this kingdom, 'No one can serve two masters; for either he will hate the one and love the other, or he will be devoted to the one and despise the other' (Matt. 6.24). It is a hopeless misunderstanding of the idea of the kingdom of God to think of the world which Jesus directly contrasts with the kingdom of God in the sense of the conventional language of religious edification. It does not simply mean everything contrary to the piety which is expressed in religious language. It is the world which is turned by the prevailing piety into a substantial and enduring world in the sense that it becomes its God, who reveals himself in the enduring substance of this world, and whom it is capable of serving only by maintaining the enduring substance of this world with the aid of the ordinances and laws which apply in it.

In the previous chapters we made clear that the relationship of man to a world which is maintained in its enduring substance by the piety prevailing in it can only be that of responsibility to it and to the law which applies in it. But this responsibility to the world makes responsibility to God impossible, for even if a piety sustained by such a responsibility supposes that it is serving God, in fact it is only serving the world which is dominated by it. Its true and only purpose is to maintain that world in being. Thus the kingdom of God which Jesus proclaims is in such irreconcilable opposition to this world and to the piety that belongs to it, that with the coming of this kingdom the end of this world begins.

We have seen that this preaching cannot simply be understood as though it were a doctrine. However, it was characteristic of it that, immediately it was proclaimed, what it proclaimed, the kingdom of God, was present in its coming, and at the same time the coming to an end of the present world, to which it is in opposition, came about. We expressed this by saying that this preaching was a historical act of inestimable significance because, immediately it took place, the relationship of man to God and to the world was fundamentally transformed. And since in this preaching Jesus revealed to man the world of each individual man, one cannot understand the true significance of this revelation if it is understood to mean that in his preaching Jesus gave man only some form of advice or guidance, and left it to man to bring his own world as an individual to realization by his own actions.

The question here is one which is of decisive importance for christology, that is, for the way in which we speak about what happened in the appearance of Jesus in the world. Through this question, what is said of Jesus becomes christological in the sense that the primitive Christian kerygma is undoubtedly christological. It certainly is so when, for example, Paul says: 'Christ is the end of the law, but every one who has faith may be justified' (Rom. 10.4). The law of which Paul is speaking here is the law of the world dominated by Jewish piety, in which righteousness and, as this piety taught, the righteousness which is acceptable to God, exists only on the basis of works which are done in fulfilment of this law. That Christ is the end of this law means that with him it loses its validity, so that he is also the end of the world, or more precisely, the end of its existence as it is constituted by the law. And Christ is the end of the law by making room amongst men for the righteousness which is in fact acceptable to God, and of which this piety knows nothing (Rom. 10.3). By doing this, the world's existence as such is no longer based on the righteousness required by the law of the Jewish world, but in the 'righteousness of God through faith in Jesus Christ for all who believe' (Rom. 3.22). When Paul also says that this Christ has been made our righteousness by God (I Cor. 1.30), and that participation in this righteousness is only given through faith in Christ, he means that what happened through Christ was not merely the beginning of something which, once the first impulse has been given, continues to happen of its own accord. What happens afterwards is still bound up with it. For someone to partake in this righteousness and in its law in the world is only possible through his having faith in the man through whom alone he can receive the righteousness which God gives him. For this is the man who, in Paul's words, has been made this righteousness before God.

Of course it is true – and it is well to be clear about this – that some of the effects of Jesus's preaching owe their immediate origin to his preaching, but continue to be effective of themselves once they have been set in motion. This is true, for example, of man's responsibility for the world, in so far as the significance of this lies in the fact that man's independence of the world, which makes it possible, continues to be worked out in the further course of history. One may say that these effects of Jesus's preaching continually manifest themselves within the history of human ideas.[1] Such effects have at best only an indirect connection with the christological significance which is ascribed to what happened in and through Jesus, and the latter is not visible in them.

In this sense, one might also say of the world which we have called the world of each man as an individual that it is one of the effects of Jesus's preaching in the history of ideas. This, admittedly, is true only if we disregard everything which we looked upon as its real significance; that is, everything which we said about its relationship to God. If that is ignored, then it is easy to see that all that remains of Jesus's preaching is, or leads to, what can be called the inner life of man as it has come to be conceived of in the modern period. We mean by this the peculiar reality of which man became conscious when he began to pay particular attention to his emotional life and, as it were, to cultivate it. But this inner life draws its nourishment from itself, and indeed its significance is only that which it has in itself, and to this extent it belongs to history as modern historical thought conceives of it, a history whose 'motives are to be sought in man'. It is impossible to deny that as a result of this concept the reality of history, as historical scholarship now understands it, has been much enriched and rendered more profound. But it is wrong to be led by this into attempting to use an idea of history which has been enriched and made more profound in this way to locate the historical reality of Jesus in his personality.[2]

We are asking how Jesus revealed to men the world of each individual man, if he did not do so simply by teaching them about it. In order to answer this question, let us look at the way in which the world was for Jesus himself 'his world as an individual'. Only if this is what the world was for him could he draw those who listened to his preaching and believed in it into this world. We have seen that the world of each individual man is the place in which the salvation of man and his world is at issue. This is so in the sense that in his own world as an individual man encounters the destiny which is determined for him by God. Whether he consents to this destiny or refuses to submit himself to it is what decides whether he wins or loses the life which God has prepared for him in it. Thus if we are asking how the world is the 'world of Jesus as an individual', then we must first ask how he encounters the destiny prepared for him by God in the world in which he lived.

If we look at what happened to Jesus in the world to which he belonged, we find a single man who became aware, in the condition of this world, of the call which God intended for him. He became aware of it in the responsibility which was laid upon him, in the face of the condition of the world, for the idolatrous way in which it existed as the world. This, of course, was the natural corollary of a piety which claimed to be devoted to the service of God, but which in fact existed to maintain the world in its present condition, and therefore made it impossible for those who lived in this world and trusted in it really to serve God. Jesus's response to the call of God which came to him was his message of the coming to an end of the present world and the coming of the kingdom of God. As a 'sign', visible to all, of the change of outlook and turning away from this world which his message demanded of those who lived in it, he became the 'friend of tax collectors and sinners' (Luke 7.34), that is, of those who in the name of the piety prevailing in this world were excluded from it, and therefore had to be scrupulously avoided by anyone who belonged to it and sought to share in its permanent and enduring condition. We have already referred to the fact that the situation of the Good Samaritan, as Jesus described it in the parable, was very similar to his own. Just as the Samaritan became the neighbour of the man who had fallen amongst thieves, so Jesus became the neighbour of those who were taken captive by the idolatrous way in which the present world exists as such, and were separated from God. It is true that by comparison with the situation in which Jesus found himself as a result of his apprehension of the situation of the world in which he lived, what he told in the parable represents only a single episode, albeit a very important one, in the life of the Samaritan. For the person to whom he became a neighbour was only an individual in need on a single occasion. Jesus, on the other hand, shared the life of men as a whole in the present world. The need he observed was consequently not merely an external need, nor was it caused by some chance and limited circumstance. Its basis lay in the situation of a whole world, and therefore affected all who lived in that world, and as a result the only way in which help was possible was by a change in the condition of the world and therefore in the relationship of men to it. Thus the need which Jesus observed was the need of all who live in the world, the need which had come upon the world for these people. And by being their neighbour, Jesus became the neighbour of the whole world in which they lived.

Jesus became the neighbour of the present world by realizing the idolatrous way in which it existed as the world; it is this which happened in the world to which he belonged, and through which it became his own individual world. For in the sense in which the word 'neighbour' is understood in the preaching of Jesus, it expresses the closeness, the immediate concern or contact, through which the world in which a person lives turns into the world which is his own as an individual. This happens when everything else which might otherwise exist for him in the world becomes inessential by comparison with what concerns him here, and he is called to exist for this alone. Thus we can only say that the word 'neighbour' refers to representation in the sense that one can take the place of another and make his need his own. But such a representative function assumes that a person is dependent upon the help which his neighbour can bring him. Although much that we read in the New Testament tradition about the help which Jesus gave to those he encountered may be legendary, we can say that Jesus helped those whom he encountered and who were in need whenever it was possible for him. We must nevertheless add that to give help in this way, regardless of the degree to which individual incidents may be historically certain or probable, was not his true work. We have already pointed out that the thought of Jesus was almost exclusively concerned with the relation of man to God. This was his calling; it was here that he became a neighbour for here the need of man as he knew it was greatest. Here he found men in the utmost and most hopeless desolation, and therefore most urgently in need of help.

In our discussion of the ritual and legal piety of the Jewish world at the time of Jesus we mentioned this need, and the fact that the preaching of Jesus can only be understood in its proper sense if it is seen in the light of the irreconcilable conflict which existed between it and the piety of his time. Jesus showed how bitter and profound this conflict was when he said that he had 'not come to bring peace, but a sword' (Matt. 10.34; cf. Luke 12.49). The worst and most evil thing about this need is that it was not evident. For this piety had so penetrated the world and the people who lived and thought in it that they were quite unable to recognize it as the desperate need which, in fact, it was. Consequently, it prevailed in that world with the irresistible force which we described by saying that only a sentence of doom can prevail in this way. The characteristic power of a sentence of doom is that as long as it is in force, those to whom it applies are unable to see it for what it is. For as long as it prevails everything in the sphere which it affects comes under its spell. Any attempt to escape the evil which it brings with it, of which any particular evil phenomenon is a symptom, likewise comes under this spell and, instead of helping, only leads into a fresh and probably worse confusion. Jesus saw the dominance of this piety over those who were his compatriots as the cause of their profoundest need and suffering, a cause which they were themselves unable to recognize; and it was this very piety which formed the sentence of doom. Thus the sentence of doom which lay upon the world in which Jesus lived with these men was the need in which he becomes their neighbour.

We have spoken of this piety as a sentence of doom, because what happens in it is of the nature of such a sentence. It contains a confused mixture of right and wrong, truth and lies, which can only be separated by great difficulty, if at all. This piety represents such an inextricable confusion, to the utmost degree imaginable, because in it divine righteousness and human unrighteousness are indistinguishably confused and intermingled. Because it is such an inextricable confusion, it possesses the power of dominating irresistibly all the life in the world in which it prevails, and of making it the closed world of which we have spoken. This piety, which dominated the world of Judaism as it was at the time of Jesus, was a perversion of the faith of the Old Testament prophets. In their faith the knowledge of God had come to the point of realizing that God does not belong to any individual person or object which exists in the world, but is Lord of heaven and earth, and man can only affirm this truly when he belongs to God in his whole existence. Thus they knew that this God could not be satisfied by the fulfilment of cultic laws. In Isaiah this God says:

> What to me is the multitude of your sacrifices? Bring no more vain offerings; incense is an abomination to me. New moon and sabbath and the calling of assemblies I cannot endure. Wash yourselves, make yourselves clean; remove the evil of your doings from before my eyes; cease to do evil, learn to do good; seek justice; plead for the widow' (Isa. 1.11ff.).

To this God, and to no one and nothing else belong 'the greatness, and the power, and the glory, and the victory, and the majesty; for all that is in the earth is thine' (I Chron. 29.11).

This is the righteousness and truth of God, and it was not unknown to devout men at the time of Jesus. Nevertheless, they did not conceive of it in the pure form in which the great prophets of the early days had venerated and proclaimed it. They still knew that righteousness and truth are God's alone, and that only when they are preserved as such in purity can they remain what they are. But the men of later times were anxious for the life which they led in the world and became concerned to maintain and preserve it against this almighty God, though for him a man cannot 'hide himself in secret places so that I cannot see him' (Jer. 23.24). From then on, they were no longer content for righteousness and truth to belong to God alone, and they believed that in order to be able to endure before him, it was necessary to participate in his righteousness and truth in such a way that they were realized in their actions and behaviour. Consequently, the will of God which is revealed in his righteousness as such, and which could not be realized otherwise than in an obedience which man could not exercise through any particular object or action, but only in his whole self, was changed into a multitude of commandments, corresponding to the thousands of different situations in the world. But the only possible purpose of such commandments is to aid men in the individual situations and circumstances of their life in the world to obey a law which is not aimed at the will of God. For God's will is concerned with one thing alone, that man himself and all that he possesses should belong to God. Instead it becomes the law of this world, constituted for piety in an increasingly incalculable multitude of commandments, the real object of which is the law itself. Thus the meaning of all these commandments is that under their guidance man gains his life in the world which they preserve in being. Not only, then, are the righteousness and truth which are God's alone perverted into the unrighteousness and untruth of man whose piety, instead of being directed towards God and life lived through him, is intended to obtain life in and through the world. It is they, too, which give this piety the passion that forces it to cling to the perversion of righteousness and truth by which it has transformed them into an unrighteousness on the part of man which cannot be corrected, and an untruth which can no longer be enlightened.

This sentence of doom passed upon the present world is the need in which Jesus saw men and in which he became their neighbour, in such a way as to embrace the whole world in which they lived. In saying this, we are at once forced to ask how this was possible, and indeed whether it is possible at all for man to be neighbour to the whole world, or whether the claim which this implies is not a blasphemous presumption. The religious authorities of the Jewish world of his time certainly believed that they found this presumption in his preaching and in his attitude to their world. This does not mean that the idea that someone could be the helper and saviour of their whole people was altogether foreign to them. On the contrary: they looked forward with passionate impatience to the appearance of the Messiah whom God had promised to their people. But the one thing that was impossible for them to believe was that this Messiah could be someone who was bitterly opposed to their piety and to the world which it maintained in being. The only way it was possible for them to conceive of the Messiah was as someone who was ready and able to show himself, in accordance with what was valid and accepted in their world, to be him who was promised in holy scripture, and who would bring about the victory of their piety over all the nations and forces which were opposing it. Only if this was the case did it seem certain to them that someone who came forward with a claim similar to that of the promised Messiah would not be acting on his own blasphemous and arrogantly assumed authority. This was the view of the devout and those who held positions of responsibility, and thus, when they saw and listened to Jesus, they could only think, 'This man is blaspheming' (Matt. 9.3).

In fact Jesus was blaspheming the God of their piety by what he said about it in his preaching, and in particular because it was impossible for him to authenticate himself and his preaching by the authorities on which their piety was based, and so, as they were bound to think, presumed to be able through his own authority to do what would have been possible for the promised Messiah only through the power bestowed upon him by God, exceeding all human capabilities, and authenticated by unambiguous 'signs from heaven'. Thus the blasphemy of which they accused Jesus was that he put himself in the place of God and claimed to be capable of what God alone could do. But we come here to the question which we are forced to ask: whether it was not in fact a blasphemous *hybris* for Jesus to claim in his preaching that he could be the helper and neighbour not only of particular individuals belonging to his own people, but to the whole Jewish people in their state of need, where, if anyone could help them, it could only be God.

We consider it necessary to discuss this question because only when it is answered is it possible to continue our argument to the point where we are speaking not merely of the way in which the preaching of Jesus is teaching and doctrine, but also of its christological significance and the historical significance which goes with it. As we have said, we see this christological significance in the fact that the event which Jesus preached continually comes about anew through him; and this is so because it was brought about by God through him; and in this event God became one with Jesus and Jesus with him. It is impossible for our argument to proceed to this profound level, where we are able to conceive of the unity of God and the man Jesus, unless we are prepared to consider the idea that in his preaching Jesus may have been guilty of blasphemous *hybris*.

Of course this would not be so, and the charge of the authorities of the Jewish religion at the time that 'this man is blaspheming' would itself have been no more than a blasphemous incomprehension, if Jesus were to be thought of as the heavenly son of God, who, if he wished, could appeal to his Father, 'and he will at once send me more than twelve legions of angels' (Matt. 26.53). But in this case, Jesus would not have been the neighbour, in the sense which the word has in his preaching, of those who, while they were unaware of it, lay under the sentence of doom which had been passed upon the idolatrous way in which the present world exists. That is, he would not really have been someone who could genuinely stand in their place and take their need upon himself as his own. As the Messiah – as Jewish piety conceived of him – he would from the first have been exalted above this state of need by the heavenly power which he would have possessed. In spite of Jesus's preaching, messianic ideas were still present in the earliest Christian congregation, as can be seen from the case of the disciples who sought from him positions of prominence in his kingdom. Jesus's answer to them was 'You do not know what you are asking. Are you able to drink the cup that I drink, or to be baptized with the baptism with which I am baptized?' (Mark 10.35ff.).

Though the account of the temptations in the form in which we find it in the gospels of Matthew and Luke may be a legend which 'reflects upon the way in which Jesus is the Messiah',³ the idea that underlies it is wholly in accord with Jesus's own view of his destiny. The idea is that the will and the promise of God was given to him, Jesus, in the same way as to all other men. And when he revealed to his disciples the possibility of his suffering, we can tell from the anger with which he rejected Peter's unwillingness to see him suffer, 'Get behind me, Satan! For you are not on the side of God, but of men' (Mark 8.32f.), that he was powerfully moved by what was in Peter's mind. One may perhaps even say that it came to him as a temptation. But he rejected any exceptional position with regard to God such as would have been natural to the Messiah as Judaism conceived of him. This can also be seen from the saying to the disciples, which he knew included himself as much as anyone else: 'Whoever would be great among you must be your servant, and whoever would be first among you must be slave of all' (Mark 10.43f.).

If Jesus brought help in their need to those who lived in the same world as him, and to whom he was a neighbour, he did not do it in the way which was expected of the Messiah for whom Jewish piety was hoping. The distinguishing mark of what such a Messiah would do was that he could appeal concerning his actions to what was 'written' about them in the holy scriptures, which would mean that they would be accepted without question as 'signs from heaven'. The miracles which the devil demands of Jesus in the story of the temptation are of this kind. Thus in the second temptation he demands that he cast himself down from the pinnacle of the temple, as a proof that he is the son of God in the sense of the Jewish messianic hope. As a basis for this demand the devil appeals to a psalm verse which was understood as a messianic promise: 'He will give his angels charge of you. On their hands they will bear you up, lest you dash your foot against a stone' (Ps. 91.11f.). But Jesus rejects this because it would mean that he was acting against the saying, 'You shall not put the Lord your God to the test' (Deut. 6.16). This means no less than that he rejects any special status for himself before God, and that the same unconditional obedience of faith is required of him as of any other human being. And therefore in the answers he gives to the devil he dissociates the sayings which the devil uses to tempt him, and which in each case are words of holy scripture, from the miracles which would authenticate him as the Messiah, and understands them in the sense in which they apply to every human being. The way in which Jesus brings help to those who are in need, as their neighbour, is wholly in accord with what we said of his preaching about the relationship between men which he describes in the word 'neighbour': that it is a relationship in which one takes the place of another, by letting the situation of the other become his own.

Jesus did not do this as the piety of the present world expected of the Messiah; he did not come forward as one who was equipped with the possession of supernatural power. He rejected expectations of this kind so persistently that the idea came to be present in the tradition that he intended to keep his messianity a secret. But in reality all he sought to be was one who was in no such way distinct from those for whom he desired to exist, and were the lowest and least in the present world. He had fellowship with them, and saw the kingdom of God which he preached as already present in them. When he came into the house of the tax collector Zacchaeus in order to rest there he said, 'Today salvation has come to this house' (Luke 19.1ff.). This is the point at which the piety of this world rises against him in passionate opposition. It was impossible for Jesus to authenticate himself as the expected Messiah before those in authority over this piety. Again, he put himself on the same level as other men, and indeed as the meanest and most despised amongst them. Yet he claimed to be proclaiming the coming of the kingdom of God with authority, that is, in the name of God. For the piety of this world this could only be an unparalleled blasphemy.

Was not this claim exactly what we said should never happen – and not only as far as this world's piety is concerned? For man is here laying claim to the righteousness and truth of God for what he, man, is doing. This was the origin of the inexplicable confusion that prevailed in the world as the sentence of doom upon it. Of course it is possible to argue that the righteousness and truth of God to which Jesus was laying claim, in his irreconcilable opposition to the authorities of this world, were not the same as in their piety. They were not perverted into the righteousness and truth which the world claims for itself. But because the righteousness and truth of God, to which Jesus laid claim, were different from the righteousness and truth which are claimed by the present world, were they then what they were in the prophets, the pure righteousness and truth of God, which only continue to be God's as long as they are never anything else? It is true that man can participate in them. He has to, for they are the only source of his life. But how else can he participate in them, except by responding to them with the obedience which is not achieved in single individual acts, but only by giving himself? And the law of this obedience is that only he who loses his life gains it.

Jesus proclaimed the coming of the kingdom of God in this obedience. And this is the claim he made for himself when he called upon God alone to authenticate this proclamation. But he did so in the very world over which a sentence of doom reigned, through its confusion about its claim to the righteousness and truth of God. Thus he was inevitably bound to bring this sentence of doom upon himself as the result of his preaching. This is what happened when, because of his preaching, the representatives of this world accused him of blasphemy. There is no need to stress how serious an accusation this was in the eyes of those who made it, and what weight it carried in the world in which it was uttered. But we must consider what weight it carried with Jesus himself, or, in other words, at what point it found its mark in him. This is the touchstone of whether he was in truth the one who, in an obedience in accordance with the righteousness and truth of God, was able to be the neighbour of those who under the spell of this sentence of doom accused him of blasphemy and rejected him because of it; and was able to save them by taking on himself the sentence of doom passed upon them and their world, thereby averting it.

The characteristic power of a sentence of doom, which is so difficult to escape once one falls under its domination, is due to the confusion of righteousness and unrighteousness, and truth and lie, which take place in it. It can only be averted if this confusion is resolved, and righteousness once again becomes righteousness alone, and is effective as such. When this happens, unrighteousness is once again laid bare and revealed for what it is, and is no longer able to pass itself off as righteousness, as it did under the domination of the sentence of doom. In the world in which Jesus proclaimed his message of the coming to an end of the present world and the coming of the kingdom of God, the very essence of the confusion, by which the sentence of doom dominates the world, lies in the righteousness and truth of God – that is, in the form in which they have been perverted by those who live and trust in this world into a pretended righteousness and truth which serve to uphold this world. The sentence of doom which draws its power from this perversion can therefore be averted only by the liberation of God's righteousness and truth from this perversion. But they are the righteousness and truth of God only when they remain God's; so it is God alone who can set them free and restore them as his own righteousness and truth. If a human being claimed this ability for himself, the result would be no more than what happened previously: the fateful perversion would merely be repeated. And if it were really the case that by calling upon God as the sole possible authentication for his preaching Jesus had claimed to be averting the sentence of doom by his own power, then the charge of blasphemy made by his opponents would be justified. This would be so not because of the righteousness to which the representatives of this world believed they could lay claim by divine authority. On the contrary, his own blasphemous arrogance would have been even worse than this. No man by his own power can free the righteousness and truth of God from the abuse to which the sentence of doom has subjected them. The only way this is possible is by God himself displaying them for what they are and bringing them back into force – as his righteousness and truth and his alone.

But if it is true that Jesus called on God alone, was not he, too, claiming to possess the righteousness and truth of God by using them as the basis of his claim to be the one who was bringing salvation to a lost world? One cannot but admit that this is the case. Once again, then, we must ask whether he had the right to do this, and what this right consisted of. Now it is not the case that man cannot in any way participate in the righteousness and truth of God. We have already said that he is meant to do so. If this is so, everything depends on the way a person proposes to derive his life from them.

He may do so, as we have seen, in two completely different

The World of Jesus as an Individual 207

and mutually exclusive ways. One is that which prevailed in the piety of late Judaism. It was supposed that a person had to assist the righteousness and truth of God by his own actions, and bring them to realization in the world in which he lived in order to maintain it in being. This necessarily brought about the perversion we have described. Righteousness and truth no longer remain God's, but are turned into the righteousness and truth of the present world. The life that is derived from them is life lived not through God, but through the world. And although responsibility to them was put forward as responsibility to God it was in fact rendered not to him but to the world. For it was supposed that the world had to be preserved through a righteousness that had been transformed into the world's righteousness. The other way in which one can set out to live by the righteousness and truth of God is that which we encounter in the preaching of Jesus. This means opening oneself without reserve to God and to his righteousness and truth. The only possible principle is found in the saying: 'Why do you call me good? No one is good but God alone' (Mark 10.18). And at best, when one has done 'all that is commanded', one can say no more than that 'We are unworthy servants; we have only done what was our duty' (Luke 17.10). Since Jesus's words do not apply only to those to whom they were addressed, but to himself as well, we can say that this is the way in which Jesus understood his participation in the righteousness and truth of God, when he called upon them as the sole authentication for his preaching.

Which of the two a person has chosen can be seen unmistakably from his attitude to the evil that follows from the misuse of the righteousness and truth of God. His opinion may be that this evil affects those who are guilty of this misuse, but not himself. He is not guilty, having done for his part everything possible, in the name of the righteousness he holds in such high regard, to avert the evil from the world. This seems to have been the view of those who, according to Jesus, believed that: 'Those eighteen upon whom the tower in Siloam fell and killed them – were worse offenders than all the others who lived in Jerusalem.' But Jesus said to them, 'I tell you, No; but unless you repent you will all likewise perish' (Luke 13.4f.). I have deliberately spoken here of evil, and not of a sentence of doom, because for anyone who holds this view it is not possible to speak of a sentence of doom in any real sense. For once one recognizes that one is living in a world that is subject to a sentence of doom, it is no longer possible to set oneself apart from it.

There are two things to say about Jesus's claim to participate in the righteousness and truth of God in the face of the sentence of doom which he recognized had been passed upon the world. The first thing concerns the way in which he apprehended the sentence of doom, or rather apprehended the righteousness and truth of God which had been perverted into the unrighteousness and untruth of the present world, so bringing a sentence of doom upon the world and those who lived in it. Jesus saw that this perversion, and the confusion of righteousness and unrighteousness, truth and lie, which it brought about, was the cause of the sentence of doom. He thereby also recognized that it is through his righteousness and truth that God exercises his judgment upon the world in the form of the sentence of doom. For it is indeed possible for men to pervert God's righteousness into their own pretended righteousness by taking possession of it themselves, and to entangle it so deeply with what is really their own unrighteousness that they can no longer resolve the confusion.

But this does not mean at all that God's righteousness and truth cease to be his. Rather, because they have been perverted in the world and must remain perverted in it as long as it endures as what it is, they bring evil on it. Because within the world in which they have once been perverted they cannot be disentangled, and because in consequence this inextricable confusion has become a sentence of doom upon the world, the righteousness and truth of God bring about what is now their unceasing work, the sentence of doom. That is, they carry out God's judgment upon this world. This is what is meant when the preaching of Jesus proclaims the coming to an end of this world, and it is what he realized when he became aware of the responsibility laid upon him in the face of the condition of this world, for the way in which it exists as such.

Something else must be said about the way Jesus encountered the sentence of doom which he recognized as that of the world in which he lived. We have seen that anyone who has recognized that he lives in a world which is subject to a sentence of doom cannot set himself apart from it, as though it did not affect him.

The World of Jesus as an Individual

He has only two choices: either to despair, or to submit to the sentence of doom. Jesus chose the second alternative. He was able to choose it only because he recognized that this sentence of doom was the judgment exercised by the righteousness and truth of God upon the world, which endures by the very fact that in it the righteousness and truth of God are perverted into its own supposed righteousness and truth, and therefore into its unrighteousness and untruth. Thus for Jesus to submit to the sentence of doom meant that he subjected himself, as one who belonged to this world, to God's judgment, which is carried out through this sentence of doom. It is this that Jesus did by turning towards those who like him lived in this world, and became their neighbour. And thus the responsibility for the way the world exists as such, which was laid upon him when he became aware of the sentence of doom, also became a responsibility for the men who lived in it.

In our present context, we can perhaps best express what he experienced with the aid of the concept of the world of each individual, which we have already used. As we have already said, the characteristic feature of the world experienced in this sense is the unavoidable closeness and immediacy of one's neighbour. And the characteristic feature of the world of Jesus as an individual is that he is the neighbour not of a particular person whom he occasionally finds in a state of need, but of men as a whole, who are living under the sentence of doom which has been passed upon their world. If the attitude of Jesus to the sentence of doom is that which we have described, then the idea that he made himself the neighbour of men by an authority arrogated to himself becomes meaningless. For if ever a fate was visited upon a person, of which it is simply impossible to say that he chose it of his own authority, this is what happened here. This destiny came upon him, because, recognizing the ungodly way in which the present world exists as such, he fulfilled the commandment which in his interpretation (he is not alone in this) was equal to the first and greatest commandment, that of love of God (cf. Luke 10.25): 'You shall love your neighbour as yourself.' Thus what he experienced here was the will of God. What he did to fulfil it was not something he planned himself, and was not therefore arrogated to himself by his own authority.

He did it in obedience to the will of God, which applied to him as to everyone else. It is true that the situation in which he experienced the will of God was not the same as that of others. This we have seen from the difference between his situation and that of the Samaritan who was faced with the man who had fallen among thieves. The basis of this distinction lies in the difference in what each of them observed in the living events of the world which surrounded them. The Samaritan observed that the half dead man with whom he came into contact needed his help. Therefore 'he went to him' and by making the need of this man his own, helped him, and therefore fulfilled the commandment of God which is equal to the greatest commandment. What Jesus observed was the evil situation of the present world, which Jesus called the 'hypocrisy' of the piety that dominates the present world, or as we can now put it, the conversion of the righteousness and truth of God into the unrighteousness and untruth of man, a perversion in which men are so imprisoned by the constraining power of the sentence of doom which consists of this perversion, that it has an irresistible determining effect upon their thought and action. In the first instance the same can be said of Jesus as of the Samaritan in the parable: he remains faithful to what he observes, and like the Samaritan 'goes to' and helps this world, by making what concerns it, the sentence of doom which holds it prisoner, his own as its neighbour. Thus he does the same as the Samaritan: he fulfils the commandment, by fulfilling which the first and greatest commandment is also carried out.

But here the difference between the situations in which the two men find themselves becomes apparent. We have already said that what happened to the Samaritan was, of course, an extraordinarily significant episode. But once it comes to an end, i.e. once the Samaritan had done his duty to the person whose neighbour he had become, and when they both went the way on which each had set out before they met, then it would once again be the present world which surrounded them and made the rules by which they lived. But it is probable that the episode would also continue to be significant for the rest of their lives, not only for the Samaritan but perhaps also for the man who received his help – at least in so far as the present world, which for once had been transformed into the world of each of them as

The World of Jesus as an Individual

an individual, could no longer remain a world closed upon itself as it would have been previously. For Jesus the case is fundamentally different. This is not only because he became the neighbour of the whole world by becoming aware of the sentence of doom which lay upon it, and because his concern was with the necessity for a change in the condition of the world and therefore the attitude of the men who lived in it. As long as the world remained the present world, maintained in being by the piety that prevailed within it, and as long as those for whom it had been transformed into their own individual world were not finally liberated from the danger of falling once again under its power, Jesus had to remain the neighbour of this world. Thus being its neighbour could never be for him a single episode in his life, however significant. Instead, being the neighbour of the whole world determined his whole existential life. We cannot say of him what we said of the Samaritan, that when the episode that provided the situation in which he found himself came to an end, he would once again live by the rule of the present world. Rather, the world in which Jesus lived remained his own world as an individual, the world that it had become by his observation of the idolatrous way in which the present world existed as such. It was this, and the need which it represented for those who live in this world, which concerned him exclusively in the way which something can concern a person only in his own world as an individual – to the extent that in his world as an individual it is by this alone that everything else is decided. We can say of this need that it consists of men having incurred their fate as a result of the sentence of doom dominating the world in which they live; and because he had become their neighbour, it became Jesus's own destiny.

It is this which concerns him above all else. This is most clearly seen in the circumstance to which we have often pointed as the key to the understanding of his preaching. His preaching is concerned almost exclusively with the salvation of the world, the basis of which lies in man's attitude to God. Associated with this is the remarkable characteristic of this preaching to which we have already drawn attention, that it contains scarcely a single piece of guidance as to how things and affairs in the world are to be administered. Of course the attempt was soon made to interpret Jesus's sayings as if they gave such guidance. It is easy to understand how this happened. The congregations which quickly formed needed such instructions for many reasons, and naturally sought them in the preaching of Jesus. If no conclusions are drawn from the absence of such instructions, and the not immediately unreasonable view is also held that they must exist in his preaching, it is very easy to fail to understand the only thing that Jesus intended to say. This is, that there is nothing on which the salvation of the world and that of man can be based except upon God and man's relationship to him, and that the latter in its turn can only be based upon God. Once it is understood this is what Jesus intends to say, then the assertion that instructions about other matters are lacking in his preaching will no longer be surprising. It will be seen that the very lack of these things points most emphatically to Jesus's exclusive concern with the salvation of the world, which is based on man's attitude to God. For since instructions of this kind can of their nature be only concerned with the multitude of individual objects and affairs that exist in the world, and never with the world itself, i.e. with the way in which it exists as the world, and with its salvation or damnation, they cannot be of the least use. As Jesus says, it is as though one were to sew a patch of new cloth on to an old garment. The only result is that the patch tears away from it, the new from the old, and a worse tear is made. Or it is as if one were to put new wine into old wine skins. The wine will burst the skins, and be lost, and the skins with it (Mark 2.21ff.). But if man's relationship to God is right, and is in accordance with the nature of God, i.e. if man is saved, then and only then will his world be saved. This is what is meant when Jesus says that sound trees cannot bear evil fruit, just as a bad tree cannot bear good fruit (Matt. 7.18). It is also what is meant by the statement about the eye which is the lamp of the body. 'If your eye is sound, your whole body will be full of light; but if your eye is not sound, your whole body will be full of darkness. If then the light in you is darkness, how great is the darkness!' (Matt. 6.22f.).

This realization on the part of Jesus that the salvation of the world and that of man can have no basis other than in God and man's attitude to him, is like every such realization on his part; it is true not only for those to whom he imparts it, but equally for himself. We must go so far as to say that this realization, like the others, can be understood in its full sense only when it is taken as applying first and foremost to Jesus himself. If this were not so, and it only applied to others, it could only be another doctrine teaching that the salvation of the world is dependent upon that of man, whose world it is. Its only effect upon those who heard it could then be to cast them into the most hopeless despair. For this realization would imply that they were inextricably entangled in the sentence of doom which lies upon the world in which they live, and that they are therefore like the rotten tree which can only bring forth rotten fruit, and like the body which must necessarily remain in darkness, because its eye is not sound, and that they would be as incapable of setting themselves free from this entanglement as, by being anxious, 'of adding one cubit to his span of life' (Matt. 6.27), or of making 'one hair white or black' (Matt. 5.36). The sayings could only mean more than this, if the realization which they contained were true not only of those who heard them but also of Jesus himself. Whether this was the case depends upon how closely he was linked with the world which he realized exists as such in an idolatrous way. We can say at least that in such sayings as we have just quoted, which state that the salvation of the world depends upon the men who live in it, nothing was further from his mind than to abandon to the sentence of doom which lies upon the present world those who were subject to it. For he knew that he was associated with them in being subject to it also. In this he was their neighbour.

NOTES

1. Cf. my book *Verhängnis und Hoffnung der Neuzeit*, 2nd ed., Stuttgart, 1958.
2. Cf. chapter 3, above.
3. Bultmann, *Theologie des Neuen Testaments*, p. 28, tr. *The Theology of the New Testament*, p. 28.

16

JESUS'S UNITY WITH THE WORLD

WHEN WE were discussing what it means to be called by God to be responsible to him, we saw that it means something different, and something more, than being called to account by somebody. Such a responsibility calls into question the existence of the person who is responsible. If he has to exercise his responsibility towards God then he is called by God to give himself to him as a response. But the independence, without which this responsibility to God would be impossible, implies the independence of man towards the world, for which he is responsible. That is, he is responsible for seeing that he does not lapse into existing in the world in such a way that it is confused with God and relied upon in the way which is due to God. If man is able to give himself as a response to God, and in this responsibility to God can exercise the responsibility for the world which is in accordance with it, then two things happen to him. Firstly, the word which calls him to responsibility demands of him the abandonment of his existence as he has previously lived it in responsibility to the present world, and therefore in reliance upon it and upon the ordinance which prevails within it. If he trusts this word and dares to do what it demands of him, then he possesses his existence in a new way. He is able to live in the world, trusting in God, recognizing it as God's creature in the responsibility for it which he exercises through trust in God.

This means the same as Jesus's saying that whoever loses his life finds it. It is perhaps scarcely necessary to say that this finding is not something that automatically follows the losing of one's life, although the way the saying is formulated may suggest this. Like all Jesus's sayings, it refers to something which takes place between God and man, and consequently its meaning only becomes clear when it is understood as spoken in faith. What it speaks of takes place only in faith. This is true both of the losing of life and the finding of life. Moreover, the fact that it takes place in faith also means that it takes place in the power of God, and therefore with a logical consistency which seen from outside seems to be automatic. The reason for this is in fact that both the losing and the finding of life take place in the same faith. This is faith in God, about whom Jesus says in the parable of the Pharisee and the tax collector, that in his sight the tax collector was justified for no other reason than that he dared, in contrast to the Pharisee who affirmed his own piety and was therefore hopelessly enclosed within himself, to confess his sin, to abandon himself, and to commend himself without reserve to the grace of God (Luke 18.9–14). Thus his abandonment of himself and his call for the grace of God both took place in the same faith in the power of God which both released him who had hitherto been enclosed within himself from this constraint, and set him free for the life which he could now live in the sight of God.

The giving up of one's life, which is required by the word which calls us to be responsible to God, takes place in the same faith and in the same power of God as the reception of new life. This does not mean that it is made any easier, as if the life which is found in this way were already present, or were easily accessible. For anything that took place under such an assumption would not really be the losing of life, nor would it imply a real faith, 'the conviction of things not seen' (Heb. 11.1). What would be happening would be merely the exchange of one thing for another, each of which had a value equivalent to that of the other, so that one could be fair exchange for the other. But what is meant to be 'lost' here, life lived in responsibility to the present world and in reliance upon its ordinance, is of no value at all in the sight of the faith in which this 'losing' takes place and therefore cannot possibly be regarded as something of an equivalent value which can be exchanged for the life which is to be gained and which is to be lived in responsibility to God. One might suppose that the two parables of the 'treasure in the field' and the 'pearl of great price' (Mark 13.44–46) were suggesting that the losing of life through which Jesus says life will be 'found' were to be understood as referring to an exchange of this kind. Both do in fact speak of a purchase, and therefore of an exchange. The parables tell of two men, one of whom finds a hidden treasure in a field that does not belong to him and another who finds a pearl of great price, and who 'sell all that they have' in order to possess something of equivalent value which enables them to purchase the field and the pearl, the great value of which is unknown to their previous owners. But to think of an exchange is to miss the point which Jesus is making in these parables. The idea that man should ever possess something which can be exchanged, as of equivalent value, for what is to be sought from God, is quite impossible for Jesus.

We said earlier that the losing of life in which, according to Jesus's sayings, life is found, is of such a kind as takes place in the experience of God's judgment.[1] When we now say that it takes place in faith and through the power of God, we mean the same. For this losing of life is such that in it nothing remains to the person who loses his life which can be offered in exchange for something of equivalent value. And only if the loss is of this kind is it possible to find in it the life which Jesus has in mind here. Unless it is a loss of this kind, there is no place in it for the power of God, which alone is able to create the life to be found in it, nor for the faith without which the life bestowed by the power of God cannot be received and lived. This is as much as to say that the power of God which becomes effective in this losing of life is experienced as the utterly annihilating power of the judgment of God, and that the faith without which it is not possible to lose life in this way is faith in this judgment. We can express this by saying that the losing of life which man experiences when he has to give himself to God as a response, in the responsibility to him to which God calls him, takes place in the confession of guilt which he has to make to God, and for which he is completely incapable of making recompense. Only this confession of guilt brings to light the reality, which man cannot escape, of his obligation to lose the life which he supposed he could live through the present world and the ordinance which prevails in it, and to abandon it.

We shall now apply Jesus's saying concerning the losing of life to himself. As we have seen, this is the only way in which its full meaning, which includes the gaining of life that takes place in the losing of life, becomes apparent. We must say that this losing of life took place in Jesus when he became the neighbour of the present world by taking upon himself the sentence of doom that hangs over it as his own, in order to avert it. As we have already said, a sentence of doom can only be averted when it is revealed as such. That is, the inextricable confusion of right and wrong, truth and lie, must first be resolved, and each clearly recognized for what it is, righteousness as righteousness, and unrighteousness as unrighteousness. This is the only way in which the sentence of doom can be deprived of its power to lead men inescapably and irresistibly into error, a power which persists as long as the deceptive confusion which is its essence remains hidden. Two things are necessary for the removal of this confusion. First of all, the sentence of doom which came about through unrighteousness taking possession of righteousness for its own ends must have worked itself out to the bitter end in the evil which results from it for the world and those who live in it. This is the only way the unrighteousness can become known and be recognized for what it is. But this would not in itself signify the averting of the sentence of doom. It would merely be its consummation. If nothing more happened, it would mean that it had brought to ruin and destroyed those whom it had affected. For a sentence of doom to be averted, something else must take place – the confession by those affected by it that they have used righteousness in the service of unrighteousness, and through their own guilt called forth the sentence of doom and given it its irresistible destructive force. Furthermore, in spite of the evil that has come upon them on the basis of righteousness, they must maintain their faith in this righteousness, or rather, come to believe in it for the first time in its true sense. But without this faith, such a confession is impossible.

It is this, we suggest, which had to take place in the attitude of Jesus to the world if he was to be the person who not only recognized the sentence of doom which lies upon the present world, but averted it and deprived it of its power. If we are to say this, we must take note of the fact that he recognized it not merely as one person affected by the sentence of doom, like everyone else who lives in the world – which of course he did, for he was one of those who belong to this world – but also received a responsibility for the way in which the present world exists as the world, by recognizing the sentence of doom as the consequence of the idolatrous way in which the world exists as such. Jesus himself put this as follows: 'Whoever would be great among you must be your servant, and whoever would be first among you must be slave of all' (Mark 10.43f.). It is not sufficient to understand this saying only in the sense that it 'demands a renunciation of one's own claims'.² Its full significance is only realized when it is considered in relation to the whole substance of Jesus's preaching and to what took place through this preaching. It must be related to what it means to be the neighbour of the men who live under the spell of the sentence of doom which prevails in the present world. For Jesus's recognition of the way in which the present world exists as such, and the responsibility for this which followed from his recognition, required of Jesus that he be man's neighbour in this sense. If the saying of Jesus that whoever seeks to be first must be the servant of all is understood in this context, then it points towards the destiny that was laid down for Jesus and to which he had to commit himself as the task and significance of his life. It is then impossible not to see that the saying signifies that no other service can lead into such depths as the service of one whose destiny, as laid down by God, is to be, in responsibility to God, the first among the brethren who with him are responsible for this world, and that none of them will be the last as much as he who is the first. It is this very responsibility to God which leads him into the ultimate depths, of which no one else has fully been able to conceive, and in which the sentence of doom which is laid upon this world works itself out in him as it has done in no one else. If he is the 'slave of all' he takes on himself not merely the evil which affects him as it does everyone else who lives in this world, but *in* this evil, the evil which affects the whole world and all men who like him live in it. Thus the fate which is destined to be his is that of all who live in the world, the fate brought about by their reliance on the present world and the ordinance which maintains it in being.

Consequently, it is Jesus's destiny that the first thing necessary for a sentence of doom to be not merely known for what it is, but also averted, must take place in him. The evil which it brings with it must be worked out in him to its very end. This means for Jesus that the life which he loses as the first amongst his brethren must be as it were not merely his private life, but that of the present world. In the destiny laid down for him, he is so closely associated with this world as its neighbour that its life becomes his own. Consequently, he can give himself to God as a response, in responsibility to him, only as one who is responsible for the life of the world. Thus the true mystery of his life, which is the hidden basis of his destiny, is to be sought in this connection with the present world. This does not mean that this mystery is Jesus's relationship to the world, however close this may be, and however much it determines his whole existence. Rather, it is his relationship to God. But this mystery becomes effective as the hidden basis of his destiny, and must therefore be sought solely in his relationship to the world in which he lives, and in which he has taken over responsibility for the way it exists as the world.

We have already discussed this relationship to the world and what takes place in it as fully as is possible on the basis of Jesus's own preaching as we find it in the synoptic gospels. We were guided by the questions which arose from our understanding of the apostolic kerygma. The assumption of everything in the kerygma is that Jesus of Nazareth, whom it preaches as the Christ, took on himself responsibility for the world in his responsibility to God. This affects the understanding of the question, so urgently posed in present-day theology, of the relationship between Jesus's own preaching and the apostolic kerygma. Was it the primitive Christian congregation which first came to realize that man, instead of being responsible *to* the world and to the forces of the law which constitute it, bears responsibility *for* it, that is, for the way in which it exists as the world? Did it then go on to proclaim in its kerygma as Lord of the world the Christ who was crucified for the sake of the sin of men and for the sake of their righteousness? And was it therefore the primitive Christian congregation which first brought about the consequent change in the attitude of man both to the world and to God? Or was it Jesus whose destiny was this realization, and who was therefore the first to proclaim it?

We can sum up the most important conclusions which we have reached so far in our study of Jesus's preaching with this question in mind, and with regard to his relationship to the world, in the following two statements. First, it was Jesus who first recognized man's responsibility for the way in which the world exists as such. Secondly, it was he who took this responsibility upon himself, as imposed upon him by this very recognition and by the preaching which resulted from it. Since this responsibility is concerned with the way the world exists as such, then, regardless of any question or detail that may remain unanswered, it always affects the world as a whole, and therefore the way in which it exists as such. Thus the meaning of the responsibility that Jesus took upon himself is that the world is no longer, as before, to be venerated as a world enclosed in itself, and enduring by its own power on the basis of what is supposed to be its eternal ordinance, to which man has to adapt himself as one responsible to the world, which he believes provides him with guidance for his individual actions, and which he fulfils in the hope of participating in the eternal permanence of the world. Jesus recognized in his responsibility for the way in which the world exists as such that by existing in the way it does, the present world has shut God out, because the only piety which can possibly prevail in it can never be directed towards anything except the permanence which derives its basis from the world itself. Consequently, his call is to turn away from this piety, and towards the God who is Lord of the world in the sense that he rules within it with the freedom of his deity, which is subject to no law of the present world. The world can only truly exist as such on the basis of his lordship over it. And it is man's responsibility *to* this Lord of the world which gives meaning to his responsibility *for* the world, and which alone makes it possible for it to be exercised properly, and prevent the world from being thought of as before, when God was confused with it and the creator exchanged for the creature. On the other hand, only through this responsibility for the world is it possible for man to be responsible to God as the Lord who rules in the world with the freedom of his deity. It is only in this responsibility that he is capable of receiving the free rule of God within the world, and of giving himself in response to God in this twofold responsibility, to God and for the world, as one who receives his life from the word of God which has called him.

We have already said that in this twofold responsibility a history takes place which came into being with Jesus. This is the history which takes place between God and man with regard to the world. We have said *with regard to* the world, and not *in* it, intentionally. We are seeking here to express the fact that in this history the world is no longer the unhistorical and unchangeable framework for the change which forms the essential content of the only history which is possible within it. Instead, the world here is drawn into what happens in history, and by participating in it in this way has become historical itself. And in this history Jesus's own existence also becomes historical. A primary sign of this is that it is no longer possible for him to authenticate his preaching in the sight of the authorities of the present world. For he encounters the God to whom alone he knows he is responsible in his preaching, not in the already prescribed law of the present world, but in the living events within the world, as he observes it in his responsibility for the way in which it exists as such.

In enquiring into Jesus's relationship to the world as expressed in his preaching, we found that this responsibility for the world brought to light something else which gave this relationship its outstanding characteristic. Hitherto we have expressed this by saying that he took this responsibility upon himself as something imposed upon him by his recognition of the idolatrous way in which the world exists as such, and the proclamation of this fact. But there is something we must add. We have already seen that the relationship of Jesus to the world which results from his responsibility for it is not concerned with individual actions which are possible in it, and which man has to carry out, but with the fact that in this responsibility the way in which the world exists as such is at stake, so that his attitude is therefore concerned with the world in its totality. This is also the interpretation we placed upon the remarkable and distinctive characteristic of the preaching of Jesus, that it lacks guidance for what man has to do in the world, and instead is almost exclusively concerned with his relationship to God, because it is upon this alone that the salvation and damnation of the world depends. Similarly, from Jesus's point of view, it is the totality of his existence which is involved in this way in his relationship to the world. This again we have expressed by saying that Jesus's relationship to the world, as determined by the responsibility laid upon him for the way in which it exists as such, is his destiny. That is, it is the event on which the decision about the totality of his own existence, its salvation or damnation, in fact depends.

He encounters this event in the form of the sentence of doom to which the present world is subject as a result of the way in which it is the world, and to which, as a result of the responsibility he has accepted for the world, he has become subject. We have finally arrived at what is decisive for a full understanding of his attitude to the world. That is, the essential thing is that he has become one with the world. We can now see that it is this alone in which the true mystery of his life must be sought, and which is the hidden basis of the destiny that has been laid down for him.

We have already said that the true mystery of his life is his attitude to God. We can perhaps see what is meant by saying that this is the hidden basis of his destiny if we first ask how Jesus's preaching is distinguished from the message of the Old Testament prophets, and in particular from that of John the Baptist, whose preaching was a renewal of that of the prophets. It is true that one cannot simply speak of a difference here. Jesus gave his approval to the Baptist, when, as cannot be doubted, he let himself be baptized by him (Matt. 3.13). In the Gospel of Mark, the baptism of John was called a 'baptism of repentance' (Mark 1.4). The 'repentance' which it called for and which was sealed by it was understood by the Baptist as a 'repentance' from the prevailing piety, which he too condemned as hypocritical. This can be seen by his saying to the authorities who administered it:

> You brood of vipers! Who warned you to flee from the wrath to come? Bear fruit that befits repentance, and do not presume to say to yourselves, 'We have Abraham as our father'; for I tell you, God is able from these stones to raise up children to Abraham. Even now the axe is laid to the root of the trees; every tree therefore that does not bear good fruit is cut down and thrown into the fire.

According to John, his baptism was a preparation for the imminent judgment which was to be carried out by the Messiah, whom he preached as 'he who is coming', whose 'winnowing fork is in his hand, and he will clear his threshing-floor and gather his wheat into the granary, but the chaff he will burn with unquenchable fire' (Matt. 3.7ff.). Jesus repeatedly gave acknowledgement to the Baptist on later occasions. For example, he said:

> What did you go out into the wilderness to behold? A reed shaken by the wind? Why then did you go out? To see a man clothed in soft raiment? Behold, those who wear soft raiment are in kings' houses. Why then did you go out? To see a prophet? Yes, I tell you, and more than a prophet. This is he of whom it is written, 'Behold, I send my messenger before thy face, who shall prepare thy way before thee'. Truly, I say to you, among those born of women there has risen no one greater than John the Baptist; yet he who is least in the kingdom of heaven is greater than he (Matt. 11.7–11).

It is true that in Matthew the message of the Baptist is summed up in the same words as that of Jesus; 'Repent, for the kingdom of heaven is at hand' (Matt. 3.2; 4.17). They nevertheless differ from those of Jesus, in that the Baptist is speaking of a change which is indeed imminent, but which is nevertheless still in the future, and it will happen principally in the form of a judgment. The coming Messiah will appear as the judge of the world. It is as such that he already carries the winnowing fork with which he will separate the wheat from the chaff. But the change which Jesus proclaims takes place in the immediate present through his preaching itself; it is this preaching which *is* the change. And although Jesus speaks of judgment, we must not overlook the fact that in his preaching it is salvation which is dominant. When the Baptist sent to him with the question whether he is 'he who is to come' or whether they are to look for another, the answer Jesus gave does not contain a single word about judgment, but only words of salvation – although he is quoting the words of the prophets. Moreover, in these words he is not making promises for the future, which is how they are usually understood, but is speaking of what is directly fulfilled in his preaching (Matt. 11.5; Luke 11.20). This salvation, which is fulfilled in the present, is what he is referring to when he says in interpreting a passage from Isaiah, 'Today this scripture has been fulfilled in your hearing' (Luke 4.16–21). When he was asked why his disciples did not fast like those of the Baptist and the prophets, he compared the time which had begun with his preaching to a wedding: 'Can the wedding guests fast while the bridegroom is with them?' (Mark 2.18f.).

The difference between the Baptist and Jesus can also be seen in the fundamentally different attitude they adopted in accordance with what they had to preach, both to him whose commission they were carrying out and also to their hearers. The attitude of the Baptist was entirely determined by the judgment which he proclaimed as imminent. He stood before his hearers in the name of the coming judge of the world: he had to proclaim him in the definite and urgent certainty of the judgment which he was to carry out in the immediate future. It was not his task to say anything about salvation; the judgment had to take place first. Only the sentence passed in this judgment would decide who received salvation. This is the essence of the Baptist's attitude both to him in whose name he spoke, and also to his hearers. Any other connection he may have had with the latter was of no significance for his message. But the relationship of Jesus both to him at whose command he preached, and also to his hearers, was quite different. We have already described his attitude to his hearers as that of a neighbour who took upon himself as his own the sentence of doom to which they were inescapably subject in their lives. To this we must add that he desired to be their neighbour not merely as one who proclaimed salvation for them in the future, but as one who brought it to them in the present through and in his preaching. But he did not bring it like the Baptist, who also awaited salvation from him whom he proclaimed as coming to bring judgment, and who would bestow salvation only after he had carried out the judgment, not as the Baptist was now doing with water, but baptizing with holy spirit and with fire. We have already said that Jesus, too, spoke of the judgment. His woes, apart from other similar sayings about the pride of the Pharisees, reproaching them as 'hypocrites', who in their blindness presume to be the leaders of their people, are no less terrible than the Baptist's threats of judgment (Matt. 23). But without any risk of underestimating the seriousness with which the preaching of Jesus proclaims the judgment which threatens the present world, and in which it comes to an end, one may say that this preaching, as befits him to whom Jesus knew he was responsible, is not the proclamation of judgment, but of the salvation which has come with this

Jesus's Unity with the World

preaching. And if the words in which the gospel of Matthew sums up both the message of the Baptist and that of Jesus are to be understood, when the Baptist uses them, to mean that repentance must first be carried out for participation in the coming kingdom of God to be possible, when Jesus uses them they state that it is the preaching of the kingdom of God, and participation in it, which makes repentance possible.

Thus Jesus is not preaching the beginning of the rule of the judge of the world, but the incomprehensible joy of God at everyone who because of the message of the kingdom of God brought by Jesus turns away from the present world. Jesus dares to speak of this joy of God in such a way that he compares it with the exuberant joy of a shepherd who has lost one of his hundred sheep, and a woman who has lost one of her ten silver pieces, and whose joy at finding what they have lost is so great that they call their friends and neighbours together to rejoice with them over this one thing that they have found again. Even closer to God's joy over one person who repents is that of a father as Jesus describes him in the parable of the Prodigal Son. At the conclusion of this parable, the father says to the son who remained at home, and was angry about his father's joy at the return of the Prodigal, who had wasted his father's property on harlots, and for whom the father killed the fatted calf in joy: 'It was fitting to make merry and be glad, for this your brother was dead, and is alive; he was lost and is found' (Luke 15). It is surely possible to hear in these words Jesus's justification for his preaching being not a proclamation of judgment but of salvation. He proclaims that in heaven there is more joy over a sinner who turns away from the present world than over ninety-nine just persons who do not need repentance. And thus Jesus's preaching, and therefore his relationship to the men to whom he utters it, is in its innermost significance determined not as in the case of the Baptist by the anger of the judge of the world who has already laid his axe to the roots of the tree, but by the joy of God over one person who repents. Jesus is saying that his task is to proclaim salvation, when he says to his disciples: 'Many prophets and kings desired to see what you see, and did not see it, and to hear what you hear, and did not hear it' (Luke 10.23).

Finally, the difference between the attitude of the Baptist to men, and that of Jesus, can be seen in the way they address sinners. The Baptist regarded those who came to him to be baptized as sinners in the sense that such people as the tax collectors and soldiers have particular sins to confess. He was then able to give them particular advice about the kind of action which would enable them to show themselves worthy, at the judgment, of forgiveness for the sins they have committed (Luke 3.10ff.). But it is characteristic of Jesus that nothing like this ever appears in the New Testament accounts of his dealings with people. Of course this does not mean that those who came to him had no sins to confess, or that he did not regard such things as sins. He knew perfectly well what men are like – that they are 'evil', even though there is no one amongst them who, 'if his son asks for bread, will give him a stone' (Matt. 7.11). Each of them would have had plenty to confess on his own account. But this is not what Jesus speaks to them about, and it is clear that it does not occur to them that this is what he has to speak to them about. But although he admittedly regards them as sinners, he has in mind something quite different from individual sins. One may perhaps say that he saw something like a general subjection to sin at work in them. Sometimes, as when a sign which would be unambiguous to the present world is demanded of him as an authentication of his preaching, he speaks of an 'evil and adulterous generation' (Matt. 16.4), which will never be given such a sign. This may be regarded as a general subjection to sin, with which Jesus finds himself faced in such people. But it must not be understood in the sense of a doctrine of 'original sin', applicable to the whole of mankind. Jesus gives no indication of any such doctrine. But it is possible to speak of a general subjection to sin of the present world, and regard it as a consequence of the sentence of doom passed upon the world, the sentence under which men live in it. The sin of which Jesus is aware in men would then be the power under which they live in this world, and by which their whole existence is dominated in its every expression. To call this sin means that the person who is dominated by it is responsible for it. The domination of this sin is irresistible, and it can even be recognized as sin as long as it dominates. But it is nevertheless justifiable to call it sin because it only came into being, and remains in force, with the consent of those who live under it. That is, as we have said, they place their trust in this world and its ordinance, and suppose that by their religious practice they can possess the righteousness and truth of God, in order to maintain the continued existence of this world in its idolatrous state. In religious piety of this kind they are like the blind who are led by the blind (Matt. 15.14; 23.17, 26). And those whom they allow to lead them in fact shut the gate of the kingdom of heaven with their religious practice, cannot enter it themselves and do not allow those who would enter to go in (Matt. 23.13).

If this is so, it explains why Jesus does not speak to those who come to him about any individual 'sins' they may have to confess. For they are the consequence of something worse, and the attack must be made on the latter, if men are to be helped. This ultimate cause is of course their domination by the present world and its ordinance as a result of placing their trust in it, and directing their whole endeavour towards it. Consequently, they are firmly set on the wide and easy way that leads to destruction, and are far away from the narrow way that leads to life (Matt. 7.13f.). This is how Jesus regards these people. They pass their whole existence dominated by a destructive force, from which they cannot set themselves free because it is impossible for them to recognize it for what it is. As the force which maintains the present world in its existence as such, it does not merely promise them life, but can give it to them as a reward which exactly corresponds to what is in reality a destructive force. He who receives it has 'had it'. This is roughly the meaning of the term Luther uses to render the Greek word, which is literally translated 'receives', but means here a receiving in which one is 'done with' something, or, to use an even more explicit term, is 'paid off'. For this reward does not reach beyond the world which gives it. The 'treasures' which are laid up in this way are of the same transitory kind as those which 'moth and rust consume and thieves break in and steal'. But those who seek the reward that this world can give have nevertheless set their heart on these empty treasures and are thereby blind to the true treasures which God alone can give (Matt. 6.19ff.).

Thus for Jesus those who put their trust in this world are like those who are cast into the worst imprisonment imaginable. For as long as they remain imprisoned in it, they are not even aware of what it is. The force which keeps them captive Jesus calls

Satan. 'Satan' here is simply the enemy (Luke 10.19), the enemy of God and of men. He compares him to the 'strong man, fully armed', who 'guards his own palace' (Luke 11.21). His 'palace' is 'all the kingdoms of the world', which are vulnerable to his power and which he can give to whom he will (Luke 4.5ff.). And he gives them to whoever will worship him (Luke 4.1ff.), until the end of his life (Luke 22.53). It is he whose power constantly threatens men. Thus one of the few petitions in Jesus's prayer reads, 'Deliver us from the evil one' (Matt. 6.13). One may assume that the parables of the building of the tower and the planning of a war, which say that one must just 'sit down and count the cost, whether he has enough to complete it' (Luke 14.28–33) also apply to the struggle with this 'evil one'.

Because Jesus regards those to whom he knows he is sent as imprisoned in this sense, his attitude to them was fundamentally different from that of the Baptist to those who came to him. The Baptist's work was done when he had proclaimed the demand on which the sentence passed in the coming judgment would be based, and when he had baptized those who were ready to confess their sins, as an affirmation of their readiness to repent. He could do nothing more, and had nothing more to do. He had to leave everything else to 'him who was to come', who would pass the final judgment. In the view of the Baptist, 'he who was to come' was he through whom God would set up his rule upon earth, and was therefore the 'mightier' one, for whom the Baptist did not consider himself worthy to perform even the very least service (Matt. 3.11). In respect of the Baptist or even of the 'mightier' one who was to follow him and fulfil what he had begun, it would be quite impossible to speak of that which makes Jesus's preaching what it is. We are referring in particular to what we have described as being the neighbour of the men who live in the present world, and to his accompanying responsibility for the idolatrous way in which this world exists as such. What for the Baptist lay in the future, and did not belong to his task, but would be done by 'him who was to come' was for Jesus immediately present. It is present, of course, in a way quite different from that which the Baptist expected of him who should follow him. What the Baptist hoped for must be borne in mind in understanding what Jesus meant when he was asked whether he was 'he who was to come', and concluded his reply with the words, 'And blessed is he who takes no offence at me' (Matt. 11.1ff.).

This is in any case a disconcerting statement. In his answer Jesus affirmed that the saving acts which were expected of the Messiah in the prophetic tradition were now happening through him. But his answer contains not the slightest reference to the judgment which according to John was to be the real work of 'him who was to come'. This is all the more remarkable in that Isaiah's prophecy of the Messiah's saving acts (Isa. 35.4ff.), which Jesus explicitly echoes, begins: 'Behold, your God will come with vengeance, with the recompense of God. He will come and save you.' Instead, Jesus says in his answer: 'The poor have good news preached to them.' It is true that this saying, like the other miracles mentioned, formed part of the messianic expectation. But the final saying gives a completely new significance to everything that precedes it: 'And blessed is he who takes no offence at me.' This statement implies two things. First, that Jesus is saying of himself that the expected salvation is present in him, that is, in his preaching. Here, then, he is answering the Baptist's question in the affirmative. On the other hand, however, he warns that he, Jesus, and his appearance and ministry, are such that belief in him will be refused. For that is what 'to take offence' means here.[3] In so far as Jesus's saying implies this, it is a negative answer to the Baptist. But apart from this, it is not a saying which any prophet could have uttered, either in the first or in the second sense. For no prophet could have linked the promised salvation with his own person. Nor could he here even have suggested the possibility that faith might have been refused to him whom he promised was to come as Messiah. How could that be so of him in whom, in accordance with the promises of scripture, God himself was to set up his kingdom on earth in unveiled power and majesty, which would be conclusively manifest to the whole world? This was so impossible that it was wholly contrary to the thought of this world, that anyone to whom this could happen could be 'he who was to come'. But in saying that offence may be taken at him, Jesus is saying that it is by this very impossibility that he should be recognized for what he is. Moreover, in this saying he gives the Baptist his real answer to the question whether he was the one who was expected. His answer was: Yes, I am 'he who is to come', but not as you expect him.

We have seen time and again that the situation of Jesus with regard to the present world is decisively determined by the impossibility of authenticating his preaching in the eyes of those who have authority in the world. The claim he made in his preaching was that in this preaching the salvation the prophets promised for the future was now taking place in the present, but he could appeal only to God, and to no one and nothing else, to substantiate this claim. It was therefore inevitable that he should draw upon himself the charge of blasphemy, the most serious charge possible in the present world and one which, once the opposition of the authorities to him had gone beyond the stage of discussion, would finally lead to his death. We have already said that this was not because the idea of such a salvation, which would be inaugurated by the coming of the heavenly Messiah in human form, was alien to the thought of the present world, or regarded by it as blasphemous. On the contrary, this hope was one of the mainsprings of the prevailing piety, which conceived of it in numerous different ways. But it was taken for granted that for such a Messiah to be recognized, he had to be in accordance with the ordinance of the present world, as it is maintained in being by its piety, and would help this world to achieve perfection and victory through a manifestation, visible and recognizable to the whole world, of the power and glory of God. It was this assumption which Jesus failed to fulfil.

If Jesus's answer to the Baptist is understood, as it must be, against the background of his whole preaching, then the penultimate saying in it, 'The poor have good news preached to them' can surely be regarded as the summary and culmination of all that is previously said about the messianic saving acts. And 'the poor' can likewise be understood not in the literal sense of the world but as typifying all to whom salvation is proclaimed and made a reality. The word would then refer to all those imprisoned under the sentence of doom which lies upon the world, whose neighbour Jesus had become: 'the crowds' on whom he had compassion, because they were harassed and helpless, like sheep without a shepherd' (Matt. 9.36). If the saying about 'offence', with which Jesus concluded his answer to the Baptist, is taken together with the first part, which speaks of the saving

Jesus's Unity with the World

acts, it is highly improbable that faith in him would be refused because of the latter. Thus the reason for this refusal can only be that he who was to bring salvation was not going to do so in the unmistakable glory which the piety of the present world understood as the glory of God, but was himself one of the 'poor', the blind, lame, lepers, deaf and dead, for whom the good news was meant. Thus the meaning of these sayings is that whoever he was, the present world would refuse to believe in him, because it could not see in him anything of the visible glory of God which it looked for in 'him who was to come'. Instead it was obvious to all that he was 'a friend of tax collectors and sinners' (Matt. 11.19). He said of himself that he 'came not to call the righteous, but sinners' (Mark 2.17). This is of course in direct contradiction to what the Baptist expected of 'him who was to come', who would 'clear his threshing-floor and gather his wheat into the granary, but the chaff he will burn with unquenchable fire' (Matt. 3.12).

We have already said of this fellowship with 'tax collectors and sinners'[4] that he saw it as the 'sign' of what was taking place in his preaching, the change from the rule of this world over man to God's rule over them. This 'sign', which Jesus gives is the only possible one that can be given to the 'evil and adulterous generation' of the present world (Matt. 12.39), because it requires that it should turn away from its 'adulterous ways'. The word 'adulterous' is here, as often in biblical usage, to be understood in the derivative sense of abandoning God. Here it stands for the abandonment of God which has come about because these men, instead of trusting in God, have put their trust in the present world and its ordinance. The turning away which the sign requires of them does not concern merely single specific actions in their lives, but the abandonment of the piety which is in accordance with the present world as it is. For it is this piety which maintains the present world in its present being, as the world from which men derive their life by trusting in it and its ordinance, and so cut themselves off irrevocably from God. Jesus's saying concerning 'the sign of Jonah', the only sign which will be given to 'an evil and adulterous generation', is described as a 'riddle'.[5] So it is. It is a riddle in the same sense as the parables in which Jesus speaks of the coming kingdom of God. The difference is only that in the 'sign' given by Jesus's fellowship with sinners and tax collectors, the substance to which it points is already present.

The substance of this sign is the kingdom of God, in which those can partake who, like the tax collectors and sinners, no longer partake in the present world. The sign points to what is already present in it, but remains only a sign, in that this fellowship with tax collectors and sinners is not the *whole* matter. That is, because this fellowship is meant to be a sign to the men of the present world of the gospel preached by Jesus, it is not to be restricted to the tax collectors and sinners, but is meant for all who live in this world.

The parables of Jesus are also enigmas. The way in which they are riddles differs from that of the 'sign' of which we have been speaking in that Jesus uses them to speak about the substance of his gospel. He speaks about it in parables because he wishes to point to the mystery he is speaking of without unveiling it. For it is a mystery which only reveals itself to him who recognizes it for himself, and remains hidden to those who do not. This is the meaning of the repeated exhortation, 'He who has ears to hear, let him hear' (Mark 4.9). Anyone who seeks to speak of some matter with the aid of a parable, does so by taking a familiar reality from more or less everyday life, which in itself has nothing to do with what the parable signifies. But he tells it in such a way as to pick a particular feature of it, and points out the similarity between this and what the parable is intended to describe. Thus, for example, Jesus says that the kingdom of God is

> like a grain of mustard seed, which, when sown upon the ground, is the smallest of all the seeds upon the earth; yet when it is sown it grows up and becomes the greatest of all shrubs, and puts forth large branches, so that the birds of the air can make nests in its shade (Mark 4.30–32).

Jesus compares the kingdom of God with a mustard seed because it can be said of it that in its way it is both the smallest and the greatest of all. To understand this parable we must forget about the idea of development and growth, the idea that the kingdom of God is like a mustard seed because it grows from a tiny beginning to something great. This idea is as remote to Jesus, as a man of the ancient world, as it is familiar to us. Moreover, the idea that Jesus has in mind is not that something can become great, but rather that something as great as the kingdom of God can be so small. For the kingdom of God *is* great, and it can never be small and great in the same way as something which is originally small but becomes great later. And so the mystery of the kingdom of God of which Jesus is speaking in this parable, and which, since it is God's kingdom, comprehends the whole world, is that when it appears in the world it is small and insignificant, so much so that when he proclaims it his preaching cannot be authenticated by anything in this world.

Everything Jesus spoke of is a mystery in the sense that what in its nature should be 'uttered in the light . . . and proclaimed upon the housetops' is told by Jesus in the dark and 'whispered' (Matt. 10.27). He always had this characteristic concealment when he described the nature of God's dealings with men, through which he effects men's salvation. The reason for this concealment is the irreconcilable opposition between the present world and the God whom Jesus proclaimed, an opposition which we have seen to be so deep that it was impossible for Jesus to authenticate his preaching in the eyes of the world. If this is so, God's actions and, in particular, the way in which he effects the salvation of men and of our world, can only be flatly contradictory to the salvation expected in the thinking of the present world. For what this present world looks forward to as its salvation can only be what is in accordance with the ordinance of the present world and maintains and perfects it in its present mode of existence. By contrast, the action of God which Jesus proclaims will practically always take place in opposition to this ordinance and the salvation expected through it. Perhaps Jesus's bluntest expression of this is in the saying we have quoted that those who are last in the present world will be first under the rule of God (Matt. 20.16). The same is implied when the good news Jesus preached is said to be above all for the poor, the little ones, those who are nothing and possess nothing in this world, and for those who are excluded from it without question, the tax collectors and prostitutes, promising them that they, and not those who are well thought of in this world for their piety, will have a place in the kingdom of God. Thus this kingdom is not so constituted that it could be in accordance with the current expectation of this world concerning what 'he who was to come' would bring. Consequently, Jesus's answer to the question when the kingdom of God would come, was that its coming was not such as could be observed, and that it would not be possible to say, '"Lo, here it is!" or "There!" for behold, the kingdom of God is in the midst of you' (Luke 17.20f.). It was in the midst of them, for example, when Jesus invited himself to be the guest of the tax collector Zacchaeus, which, at least in the view of the devout persons who witnessed this, was for someone acquainted with the law anything but the appearance of God, and in fact a monstrous blasphemy.

NOTES

1. Cf. above, pp. 114f.
2. Bultmann, *Jesus*, Tübingen, tr. *Jesus and the Word*, p. 109.
3. Cf. W. Bauer, *Wörterbuch zum Neuen Testament*, art. σκανδαλίζω
4. Cf. above, p. 114
5. Schniewind, *Das Evangelium nach Matthäus*, Göttingen, 1937, p. 157.

17

JESUS'S UNITY WITH GOD

WHILE HE constantly and repeatedly refers in his preaching to the concealment characteristic of the revelation and action of God towards man, Jesus is also concerned with something else. He seeks at the same time to show, as unmistakably as possible, that when it is a question of God and his dealings with man, it is really God and he alone who is to be understood as acting. This is the purpose of the warning that devout acts should not be carried out before men, in order to be seen by them. For they then remain without God and have no reward with the Father in heaven (Matt. 6.1). But what brought such total condemnation on this world, and made its piety hypocritical, was the very fact that although God was constantly and everywhere spoken of in the world of Judaism at the time of Jesus, the piety that prevailed here had in reality only this world in mind. For it was taken for granted that one could do what this piety required, trusting in the present world and fulfilling its ordinance, and could thereby expect what it had to give. But in reality this meant relying on one's own acts and the reward that this world offered them. Jesus, however, constantly emphasizes that in the revelation of God and the setting up of his kingdom on earth, when, as Jesus prayed, his name would be hallowed, his kingdom come and his will be done on earth as it is in heaven (Matt. 6.10), this is done by God himself, and he alone acts.

Jesus makes this clear by describing the situation of the men whom God shows himself to be acting in as the God who in reality he is. He gives a particularly impressive account of the state of such men and their relationship to God in the saying, 'Ask and it will be given you; seek, and you will find; knock, and it will be opened to you. For every one who asks receives and he who seeks finds, and to him who knocks it will be opened' (Matt. 7.7f.). It is not difficult to see that this saying does not refer to occasional asking, seeking and knocking, in request for one particular thing. The kind of truth it refers to is only verified when everything is at issue. One cannot overemphasize the importance of what is omitted from this saying. There is not a single mention of what is to be asked for or sought, or where to knock. This clearly is not an exhortation to ask, seek and knock, as is usually the case, for particular objects or on particular occasions. Its meaning derives exclusively from the person to whom these actions are addressed, and in whom it expresses the assurance that he is one who of his nature, gives, lets find, and opens to those who ask of him, seek, or knock. In such a petition, which is possible and derives it meaning solely from him towards whom it is directed, he who asks becomes in the sight of him who asks nothing more, in his whole being, than a petitioner. Jesus unquestionably considered the petition he called for as directed to God.

Thus anyone who asks in this way becomes in his whole being a petitioner in the sight of God, who alone can make such a request possible and from whom alone it derives its meaning. And therefore in this petition everything that he possesses and can achieve of himself necessarily becomes unreal. In Paul's words, one can say that he has it as though he has it not (I Cor. 7.29ff.).

We may add that such a petition, and the possibility of making it, comes only to one for whom the world in which he has lived hitherto ceases to be the world as it is, and becomes his own individual world, in which everything that hitherto formed his world disappears before the fate which he encounters in it. We have already said that this strange transformation of the world in which a person lives can come about for him when something that happens in the world in which he lives so oppresses him that everything else falls into insignificance in comparison with it.[1] This comes about when what happens is something through which by its nature the existence of this person is called into question to such a degree that there is no longer any possibility in this world of taking things for granted as he habitually did in the past. The more this possibility of taking things for granted is brought into question, the more the particular cause falls into the background by comparison with the person's whole existence, which is now at stake. This is so, for example, in the stories of Jesus's miracles. It is clear that the decisive thing in them, that which heals and brings the turning-point with it, is faith. This can be seen from the saying of Jesus which frequently occurs in this context: 'Your faith has saved you' (cf. Matt. 9.22; 15.28).

It is already clear that what we have said about petition also applies *mutatis mutandis* to faith as Jesus understands it. For he spoke of faith in the same absolute sense as of asking. Just as he did not say what one should ask for, so the faith which he recognizes as such is not associated with the normally accepted conceptions of faith. For this reason he could speak of faith in people who it can be assumed did not hold these conceptions. Thus, for example, he says to the Syrophoenician woman, 'O woman, great is your faith! Be it done for you as you desire' (Matt. 15.22ff.), and to the Roman Centurion, 'Not even in Israel have I found such faith' (Matt. 8.5ff.). Thus whereas it is wrong to think of faith as the belief which Jesus regards as correct, it is, like the 'asking' discussed above, the concrete reason which brings people to him. Here, too, the distinctive characteristic of faith, as Jesus described is, is that the concrete reason touches the very existence within the present world of the person concerned, in a way which goes far beyond the immediate circumstances. This existence is called into question, and the person is thereby faced with his destiny, and the decision he must make.

In the context in which we use the word destiny, we refer as before[2] to the way in which God 'puts to work' human life. Man encounters this destiny when an event in his life is such as to oblige him to decide to participate in it or refuse any part in it. We tried to show that God's way of 'putting to work' human life is to enable man to give himself, with his independence of the world and consequent responsibility for the pattern of this life, in response to God's call to be responsible to him. He thereby lives by the word with which God calls him into being. In this way he is faced with the decision whether to submit to the fate and double responsibility God has destined for him, or to refuse to do so. This is a decision which cannot be made through any particular act, but only with the whole of one's existence. For the gaining or losing of one's life is at stake, for it is with one's whole life that one's fate in this sense is concerned. Man gains his life if he participates in his destiny and is enabled to give himself in response to God, as one responsible to him for the world. He loses it, when he refuses this destiny.

Thus the asking, seeking and knocking, which concern not particular individual matters, but the whole of human existence, given to man with his destiny, takes place in his encounter with the destiny which God has given to man as such. This encounter, of course, includes the decision with which it faces man, and in which the gaining and losing of his life is at stake. The faith of which Jesus speaks is likewise possible only in this encounter. It is only possible to understand the certainty with which Jesus affirms that this petition will be answered, and that all things are possible for this faith, if we realize that they take place within this encounter. He can say this of the petition uttered in this encounter, because what man's destiny demands of him in order to be fulfilled in him is that he should abandon the multitude of concerns which he has hitherto sought to possess and so gain the life the world gives, and that he should become one who asks, who is ready to receive salvation from him who has determined this destiny for him. Because the petition is of this kind, Jesus has no need to state explicitly what it asks for or to whom it is addressed. For if man has any knowledge at all of his destiny and of him who gives him it, he knows it in this petition, and there alone.

The same is true on the whole of faith. There is, however, a difference which must be noted. This concerns not so much the matter with which this petition or faith is concerned, but rather with what might be called the different perspective in which it is regarded in each case. Even where it is not explicitly stated, what happens in fact is always thought of as what is 'possible with God' (Mark 10.27). Thus we must say that everything faith can do is possible only because it is possible for God, but impossible for men. This is what Jesus means by dramatic statements such as: 'If you have faith as a grain of mustard seed, you will say to this mountain "Move hence to yonder place", and it will move; and nothing will be impossible to you' (Matt. 17.20). It is hardly possible to take this statement as a challenge to prove faith with the help of a mountain. Those who heard

Jesus knew that it was God alone 'who by his strength has established the mountains', and 'stills the roaring of the seas, the roaring of their waves' (Ps. 65.6f.) and that this is something which would happen at the end of time, as it had at the beginning of time. Nevertheless, Jesus chooses this familiar expression to illustrate the 'all things' (Mark 9.23) that are possible to faith, and strengthens it by bringing in the comparison with the grain of mustard seed. The latter expression does not mean a small measure of faith, but the complete insignificance of faith, by comparison with what it can achieve, but can only achieve because it is possible for God.

If this faith, then, partakes of the power of God, and can therefore do what is possible for God alone, this emphasizes that this faith is faith in God and has its significance from him and him alone; and the emphasis is far greater than if the point had been made explicitly. In all these sayings about faith, Jesus only once uses the expression 'faith in God' and in fact in some manuscripts the words 'in God' are missing (Mark 11.22). For the same reasons, one obviously cannot take 'all things', which Jesus says are possible to faith, to mean anything that one may fancy. The saying concerns the believer, and only refers to what comes within the sphere of faith and is at issue in it. 'All things' means everything that God intends for man. In a word it refers to the destiny which God sends him, that he may submit to it and so gain the life destined for him in it. Thus we can say the same of faith as we did of the petition for which Jesus called and which he promised would be answered. If man knows of his destiny at all and of him who prepared it for him, he knows only through faith, in which he submits to his destiny and receives it from him who has prepared it for him. The petition can only be made with the certainty that is proper to it if, in an encounter with his destiny, the whole existence of man becomes that of a petitioner. And faith can only exist when a person believes, that is, when he allows God to be so powerful in his destiny that he gains his life from God.

We have often remarked that most of Jesus's sayings can be understood in their full sense only if we remember that they are not only aimed at those to whom he uttered them, but also apply to himself. This is particularly so of these sayings about petition and faith. It may seem strange, in this case, that Jesus said nothing about his own faith. This is nowhere mentioned in the gospels, nor is there any explicit reference elsewhere to Jesus's faith. This does not seem to justify the conclusion that when Jesus spoke of faith, what he said applied only to those who were listening to his preaching. This would only have been possible if he had understood the faith he was speaking of exclusively as faith in himself. Elsewhere in the New Testament faith quite often means faith in Jesus. But in the sayings which the synoptic gospels record as his own, this is only once the case. In Matthew 18.6, Jesus speaks of the 'stumbling block' prepared for 'these little ones who believe *in me*'. In the parallel passages, Mark 9.42 and Luke 17.1f., this addition is lacking, so that one can probably assume that the latter gave the original form in which the saying was handed down. Apart from this one exception, the synoptic gospels have maintained the original form of Jesus's sayings about faith and have not introduced the idea of faith in him. This fact is all the more surprising, in that this usage was widespread at an early stage, and had already found its way into these gospels in another context. But the evidence makes it highly probable that Jesus did not understand the faith for which he called as faith in his own person. In the sayings in which Jesus speaks of faith, it is always faith in God. One must, however, add that this expression also occurs only once in Jesus's sayings in Mark 11.22, where again it is very likely that it is the addition of a redactor.

But even if we must say that, according to the New Testament, Jesus never explicitly spoke of his own faith, it is evident that his proclamation of the coming kingdom of God would have been impossible if he had not had faith in God. To deny that he did have faith in God, would be to say that his preaching was inspired in some extraordinary way, or according to the ideas of the traditional christology of the church, that as a result of his identity of substance with the triune God, Jesus was equipped with a knowledge of the past and the future which did not require faith.[3] We have already noted that the characteristic feature of Jesus's situation in the world in which he lived was that the only way he had to authenticate himself and his preaching in the eyes of the authorities of this world was to appeal solely and directly to God, and to no one and nothing else. But this means that he and his preaching could be based only on his own faith.

If faith, then, is of such fundamental importance for Jesus, it seems even more remarkable that he never spoke of faith as his own faith. We must, therefore, look again at the nature of this faith, or, in other words, explain what it means for Jesus to base his preaching on it; that is, what this faith does for him. We have already seen that the faith we are discussing here is such that 'for him who believes, all things are possible'. But we noted at the same time that 'all things' here does not mean anything one pleases. Thus it is not the case that everything man desires as a non-believer is made possible for him as a believer. Rather, a complete new reality is opened to the believer, the reality of God. That which is made possible for the believer belongs to this reality. For since the believer relies on God for his whole existence, what is possible for him is that which he receives from God, and which affects his whole existence. What he receives from God is consequently not merely a matter of specific individual items, but his existence, which he receives in all the specific things he needs in the world, as an existence given to him by God. Consequently, faith is not merely given to the believer as a true conception of life, so that the believer now knows how he must live his life, as a life given to him by God. For the 'all things' which faith makes possible for the believer is this very life itself. Faith does this by showing the believer this destiny prepared for him by God, to which he submits and so gains the life prepared for him in it; and also, and not least, by making it possible for him to submit to this destiny, and so receive his life.

Just as it is of the nature of faith, that in it the believer partakes of the power of God which gives him his life, so it is equally essential for the believer to realize that without this participation man is lost. Here, too, it is important that to be lost, in the sense in which faith becomes aware of it here, should, like the 'all things' which are possible to the believer, be defined from its association with faith and therefore with God. What is lost is not a series of particular things in the world, but the life that is lost when the destiny prepared by God is refused. Thus it is of decisive importance that this realization should come with faith. For only when the believer dares to abandon himself to the utmost depths of man's lost condition in the sight of God, is faith capable of attaining to the certainty that all things are possible to it by the power of God, and of becoming what faith is. The nature of this faith is not fully understood if it is seen as having to do only with the salvation of man, but not with his damnation.

'All things' are possible, then, to the faith on which Jesus bases his preaching; the meaning of 'all things' is derived from the life which is received in faith from the power of God. This explains why, although Jesus did not speak explicitly of this faith as his own, he proclaimed the coming of the kingdom of God in and through this faith. We must first note that there are two different ways in which faith can be brought to utterance. The first is that which Jesus used when he called on his hearers to have faith, and told them what faith could do. We have sought to show what he was doing and saying in our discussion of his sayings concerning faith. In this respect he does not in fact speak explicitly of faith as though he shared it. I have already said that it does not seem proper to conclude from this that one cannot speak of Jesus's faith at all. Rather, we must ask whether it is ever possible to speak of a faith such as we have described as one's own. This, as we have seen, is because the nature of this faith is such that in it the believer submits to the destiny prepared for him by God and so receives the life destined for him in it. But this means – and this is the other way in which faith can come to utterance – that in faith the turning of the believer's whole existence to God takes place. It is this which happens in his confession of faith in God, and in the acceptance in faith of what God gives him in it.

How this takes place is most clearly described in the words of the father of the epileptic boy: 'I believe; help my unbelief' (Mark 9.24), and in Jesus's parable of the Pharisee and the tax collector, where the faith of the tax collector is expressed in his confession of faith: 'God, be merciful to me a sinner' (Luke 18.9ff.). When Jesus then says of the tax collector, 'I tell you, this man went down to his house justified rather than the other', he means that in this very faith which came to utterance in the tax collector's confession, and which had the same God and the 'all things' which are possible for faith as its aims, the grace of God is directly imparted to the believer.

This is also the only way in which Jesus's faith can come to utterance. Thus, if Jesus does not speak explicitly of his own faith, we must nevertheless say that by proclaiming the coming of the kingdom of God without any possibility of authenticating it in the present world, he spoke from his faith. It would be more in accordance with the nature of the faith that is at work in Jesus's preaching to say that in this preaching his faith speaks from him in such a way that it brings with it the event that is appropriate to it and it alone. This is a better way to put it, because if this faith is the kind for which 'all things are possible', 'all things' must be what he proclaimed in his preaching, the coming of the kingdom of God, of which he himself said that it took place directly in his preaching (Luke 4.21).

We said that most of Jesus's sayings can be understood in their full sense only when they are regarded as sayings applicable not only to those to whom they are addressed, but also and in the same measure to himself. If this is so, both his sayings about faith, like the sayings, scarcely different in their significance, concerning asking, seeking, and knocking, take on their full meaning only when we look at what they have to say, albeit indirectly, about Jesus's own faith, and his own petition, which is virtually identical with his faith. We have already said that both the faith and the petition, which Jesus's sayings speak of and call for, are understood in an absolute sense. He did not say what should be asked for or what could guarantee the certainty that the petition would be answered. Likewise, in the case of faith, there is no reference to previous correct belief which would be the content of faith, and could serve to guarantee its truth. He assumes concrete motives which lead to this petition and this faith, as is particularly evident in the stories of healings. But, at the same time, it is characteristic of the petition and the faith which are spoken of that the absolute way in which they are understood here ignores the immediate cause and the concrete motive given them by the specific reason which originally called them forth. All that remains of the immediate cause is the disaster, the calling into question, into which they have brought the existence of the person they affected. Thus the petition and faith brought about by these immediate causes find their real concrete context in the destiny which appears in this calling into question, and therefore in the existence of the petitioner and believer as it is determined by this destiny.

In order to understand the particular sense of Jesus's sayings about petition and faith as they apply to his own human destiny, we must seek for the concrete cause which led to his own petition and faith. As we have already seen, its cause is his awareness of the sentence of doom which, as a result of the idolatrous nature of the world, dominates everything. We have seen that, in this awareness, Jesus is called upon to redeem the world from existing as the world in this way in order to avert the sentence of doom and to help it to obtain salvation. This means that in the distress brought on the world by this sentence of doom he becomes its neighbour, and that, as a result, the way it is the world lies upon him as his own distress. If this is the immediate cause of Jesus's faith and petition, it is clear that it is a cause quite different from those in the instances discussed above. There the immediate cause, with the concrete circumstances that originally called forth faith and petition, had to be distinguished from the significance which faith and petition took on only when they were directed towards him who was asked and believed in. We can begin by saying that the immediate cause of Jesus's petition of faith is distinctive in that it does not permit this distinction between itself and the true significance of the faith and petition it calls faith; it is not overshadowed by the latter. We may express this in positive terms by saying that from the very first Jesus's petition and faith are directed solely towards that which provides their real significance. They have absolutely nothing to do with any partial or occasional needs which may exist in the world and give rise elsewhere to petition and faith. As we can see from almost every word in his preaching, his sole motive was always the sentence of doom upon the present world. Only in this light can we measure the full significance of the fact that his preaching contains none of the guidance which is necessary for man's life in the world and that his thought is almost exclusively concerned with man's relationship to God. The reason for this exclusiveness is that Jesus's thinking is constantly oppressed by this sentence of doom and the hopelessness of the world held under its domination.

But it would be a serious misunderstanding to regard this as making faith and petition impossible for Jesus. As we have said, the reverse is the case; although the oppressive tension is never relaxed in the slightest. For it is this oppression, with all its inevitabilities, which is the direct cause of his petition and faith.

We have said that it was of the essence of this faith that in it the believer partakes of the power of God, to whom all things are possible; and that, likewise, this faith does not exist without the recognition that everything that lacks this participation is lost. For just as this realization first made possible that of the power of God, only through that realization, and the unqualified abandonment of himself to it by the believer, can faith attain to the certainty that 'all things' are possible to it, by the power of God alone.[4]

How can we say, as we must, of the faith of Jesus that in it there took place a self-abandonment to the realization that man is utterly lost? And how did this take place in him? Let us recall what we said about Jesus's relationship to the present world. We sought to show[5] that for a full understanding of this relationship everything depended upon the realization that this relationship, which came into being through Jesus's taking on himself responsibility for the way the present world, subject to a sentence of doom, exists as the world, entails his complete unity with this world. The reason why it is so important to realize this is that it is in this unity with the present world that Jesus meets the destiny prepared for him. We understood destiny[6] in this context as the way in which God 'sets in motion' the life of man as such. He 'sets it in motion' by giving man life by preparing a destiny for him. Thus it is, above all, man as such who has a destiny. This all men meet, and it is determined for them. We also said that this destiny is like death, which comes upon all men, but which each must die as his own death, and his alone. Thus the death that each must die is only distinct from all other deaths, because each must die it as the death which is his own, which he cannot exchange and which no one can die for him. The particular value of the death of any individual results solely from the different life that he has passed through. The same is true of destiny. Each meets his destiny as his own, and he must meet it himself; no one can meet it for him; yet here, too, his destiny is different from that of others only in respect of the different vicissitudes of fate which he meets.

We considered above the particular cause which motivated Jesus's own faith and petition. We must now ask how the destiny of Jesus is distinct from that of other men. For if destiny is the way in which God 'sets in motion' human life, and if Jesus is a man like other men, his destiny must, of course, also be the same as that of other men. We said that the only thing that distinguishes one man's destiny from another's is the circumstances in which he meets it. He meets it in what we called the different vicissitudes of fate, by which we meant the many and various events or circumstances which man encounters in such a way as to call into question, to a greater or lesser degree, his understanding of himself, which he has taken for granted and with the aid of which he has led his life for greater or lesser periods in his own familiar little world.[7] When we look for such vicissitudes of fate in the life of Jesus, we do not find many of them recounted in the synoptic gospels. Nevertheless, one may accept that they occurred in Jesus's life as in anyone else's. At least Jesus always knew that they occurred in the lives of those to whom he was speaking. For what else can he have in mind in his sayings about being anxious?

> Therefore I tell you, do not be anxious about your life, what you shall eat or what you shall drink, nor about your body, what you shall put on. . . . Therefore do not be anxious, saying 'What shall we eat?' or 'What shall we drink?' or 'What shall we wear?' For the Gentiles seek all these things; and your heavenly Father knows that you need them all. But seek first his kingdom and his righteousness, and all these things shall be yours as well. Therefore do not be anxious about tomorrow, for tomorrow will be anxious for itself. Let the day's own trouble be sufficient for the day (Matt. 6.25–34).

What Jesus intends in these words is that men must not be halted by the vicissitudes of fate, and become entangled by the calling into question of this world which comes about through these vicissitudes, so that they are all that there is, with their trouble repeated from day to day. For just as the life that is lived in this world is more than food, and the body more than clothing, so the life that is announced in the calling into question of the present world is more than the life that this world can give, and its loss cannot be made good by gaining the whole world. 'For what can a man give in return for his life?' (Mark 8.36f.).

The reason why the New Testament tradition tells little or nothing about such vicissitudes in the life of Jesus is presumably that Jesus's life was wholly determined by a single stroke of fate, his perception of the idolatrous nature of the way in which the present world exists as such. Jesus saw that in all reality it was the world, the world in which he lived, and with which, as its neighbour, he was united in responsibility for the way it was the world. For anyone who realized this, nothing that he encountered in such vicissitudes of fate as came upon other men could have any distinctive individual significance for him. The many and various circumstances and events which brought good and evil, happiness and unhappiness to men, were far overshadowed by the one thing that was always present in them. Not only was it senseless to be anxious about tomorrow; it was impossible. Before the one 'trouble' which was sufficient for every day in the life of Jesus, and which he felt as his own, this anxiousness for oneself became as nothing. For this 'trouble' (the Greek word translated here is *kakia*, which can be used as a synonym of *kakon*, evil), is the evil of the world. Jesus speaks of seeking the kingdom of God and its righteousness as of something which sets man free altogether from being anxious for himself, and this saying of Jesus must also be taken to apply not only to those to whom it was uttered but equally to himself. We must therefore not forget that this seeking for the kingdom of God had its origin in that 'trouble', which really is sufficient for every day, the evil of the world, with which Jesus had been united, so that its evil became his own.

We may say that here, in the origin of Jesus's own seeking for the kingdom of God, or, to say the same thing in other words, his preaching of the kingdom of God, we have found the true immediate motivation for the petition and faith which is his own. And this, too, is the reason why a total self-abandonment to the realization that the present world is absolutely lost, a realization gained in the perception of the idolatrous way it exists as the world, is of the essence of this petition and faith. This understanding also makes it possible for us to understand the profound significance of the concealment which marks God's dealings with men, and to which Jesus constantly refers in his preaching. This concealment is not something which belongs only to the beginning of God's dealings, and then gives way to an open revelation which is never veiled again. It is a constant characteristic of God's dealings with men. Thus Jesus can say that the only 'sign' of what his preaching proclaimed, and what took place in it, is his fellowship with the 'tax collectors and sinners'. But if there are any people who, according to the piety which dominated the world in which Jesus lived, are completely excluded from the promised kingdom of God, these are they. Thus if Jesus's fellowship with them is the 'sign' of what he proclaims in his gospel, then it is a sign, albeit a very paradoxical sign, of the concealment in which alone this kingdom of God is to be found. It is the same concealment or, as the synoptic gospels put it, the same mystery or riddle, of which his parables speak, and which, as he said himself, belongs to the kingdom of God (Matt. 13.11 and parallels). And it is to these that the following saying refers: 'With many such parables he spoke the word to them, as they were able to hear it; he did not speak to them without a parable' (Mark 4.34; Matt. 13.34).

We said at the beginning of the chapter that one important reason for Jesus's repeated reference to the concealment in which God comes to man's aid is that it makes clear more than anything else that real piety is concerned with what God does to man, and not with the supposedly pious activity of man, as in the prevailing piety of the present world. For God acts in man, when man can no longer help himself by his own action – that is, when he is in distress. God in fact helps man in his distress, or perhaps more accurately, through it. This does not mean that as a result of God's help the distress is no longer there, but rather that the distress itself is the help that God brings. This is the concealment in which he acts. In other words, whenever the world in which man lives is called into question for him, that is, whenever he suffers distress which he cannot overcome himself, and is brought by it into the situations where he must ask for help, God is close to him with his help. We sought to show, by Jesus's sayings, 'Every one who asks, receives' (Matt. 7.8) and 'Your faith has made you well' (Matt. 9.22), how it comes about that God is close with his help to those who ask and believe. This help does not merely consist of what man considers necessary to avert his distress. It is really the help of God, the help which God himself is for the whole man. As we said, this cannot happen without a profound change both in the petition and in the distress which originally oppressed the petitioner. It frequently happens that instead of being removed or relieved, it became more severe and oppressive than before. It then affects not merely isolated aspects, greater or lesser, of the petitioner's life, but his whole existence with which he has to exercise his responsibility in response to God. It may be that before this happens the distress which was the original cause of his petition is removed. But if man is content with this, he has evidently missed the true help of God. Was this not true of the nine lepers, who failed to do what the tenth did – and he was a Samaritan?

> Then one of them, when he saw that he was healed, turned back, praising God with a loud voice; and he fell on his face at Jesus' feet, giving him thanks. . . . Then said Jesus, 'Were not ten cleansed? Where are the nine? Was no one found to return and give praise to God except this foreigner?' And he said to him, 'Rise and go your way; your faith has made you well.' (Luke 17.12–19).

If it is faith which helps when man can no longer help himself, it is faith which brings about what happens here in man. The effect of faith on the man who believes is that he partakes of the power of God, through which, according to Jesus, all things are possible to him. But this participation is possible only in the shattering realization of his own impotence and nothingness before him who helps him in faith. Thus the concealment in which God deals with a man is this: whatever may happen to him with regard to the distress which originally brought him to petition and faith, God leads him into the depths, in which he must undergo this realization. Jesus says the same in the central saying of his message, that whoever loses his life, gains it.

If we realize that God acts in man in this kind of concealment, and not otherwise, it becomes clear that a piety guided by this realization – the only piety appropriate to the God whom Jesus proclaims – cannot have as its primary aim the pious activity of man, nor can it rely on such activity. Instead, it must principally be directed towards the action of God, and not in spite of, but within the concealment in which God's action comes from man in his distress – that is where man in very truth needs God, and God alone. This is basically what we were saying when we described how we were trying to understand what takes place in the petition and faith which Jesus calls for, and which we saw were also the petition and faith of Jesus himself, and were the basis of his preaching of the coming kingdom of God.

We have already noted that Jesus's own petition and faith were distinguished by being from the very first directed towards their real significance. We are not concerned, as are other men, with the occasional and partial forms of distress which constantly occur in the world, but solely with the distress which is represented by the idolatrous way in which the present world exists as such. It is characteristic of this distress that it does not merely affect the present world. As long as men remain subject to the sentence of doom which is the consequence of its idolatrous nature, it affects the world as a whole. For as long as this sentence of doom is not averted and deprived of its force, the whole world, and not merely its present condition, is forsaken by God. Only when this is understood is it possible to appreciate the full significance of the fact we have often mentioned, that Jesus's preaching contains virtually nothing of the guidance which is so necessary for the many and various concerns of man in the circumstances and situations he encounters in the world, and that his thinking is concerned almost exclusively with the relationship of man to God and God to man. If this is so, it also becomes clear that the perception of the abandonment of the present world by God, made manifest in the idolatrous way in which this world exists, is the one stroke of fate which brings about his unity with the world, or, in other words, makes him its neighbour. It is so powerful that it overshadows all the other experiences of his life. And in this stroke of fate he encounters his destiny, which takes its particular form from it.

We can see what is distinctive in his destiny by looking at the significance of this fact – that in the life of Jesus there were not numerous vicissitudes of fate, as in the lives of other men, but only this one. We have seen that the significance of vicissitudes of fate in the life of a man is that through these events his easy and conventional understanding of his life, as he lives it in accordance with the rules and experience of the historical world that exists at the present moment, is called into question. As a result, every time this happens, the person concerned then becomes aware of his own world as an individual and the destiny he encounters in it. What happens is, as it were, a very significant and more or less fruitful episode in the history of the individual human being.

We saw this in considering Jesus's story of the Good Samaritan.[8] As long as such an episode lasts, the historical world that exists at its present moment, and in which the person normally lives, loses the significance it automatically has for him, and so do the rules and the ordinances through which it is such a world for him. In its place, the other world which we called his own world as an individual, is manifested and becomes real to him. But when this episode comes to an end, he is guided once again by the rules and commandments of the historical world that exists at the present moment and the numerous vicissitudes of fate, from which no human life is free, take on the significance they have in that world. Thus we can say that in such a life there is an alternation and competition between two ways in which a world exists as such – as the historical world that exists at the present moment and a person's own, individual world.

All that we have hitherto said about Jesus suggests that this alternation was scarcely present in his life. For this alternation is possible only because of the multitude and variety, and the episodic character, of these vicissitudes of fate. But in the life of Jesus there was only one such stroke of fate, which determined his life from beginning to end, and which so completely dominated the other events of his life that they had no significance of their own by comparison with what happened as a result of this one single stroke of fate. So this alternation between the two worlds was not possible in his life. This does not, of course, mean that the whole of his life was lived in only one of them. On the contrary, throughout his life he lived in both. For Jesus only one stroke of fate was decisive, his perception of the idolatrous way in which the present world exists as such. And it was in this stroke of fate that he encountered his destiny and gave it the form which was peculiarly his, that of responsibility for this world. In this way he became the neighbour of the present world, which is in distress because of the sentence of doom imposed upon it, by accepting in his own life as an individual the destiny prepared for him. United with the present world as its neighbour, and deriving the power to be united with it from his own individual world, he lived his whole life, from beginning to end, in these two worlds, without any alternation between the two. We saw that the concealment in which God brings help to man consists in his helping him through the distress in which man finds himself. We may now add that this distress is nowhere so profound as in what took place in the life of Jesus, both in the fate that overtook him and in the destiny he encountered in this stroke of fate. Nor is there any other distress greater than that which Jesus had to suffer here. For as much as it was his own, it was also that of the whole world.

In what Jesus says about the concealment in which God acts in man, he repeatedly emphasizes that in the kind of religious devotion for which he is calling – the relationship of man to God which is the basis of man's valuation and that of his world – everything depends upon the action of God. The same is true here as of all his words; they yield their full meaning only when they are applied to himself. Thus, if we take his insistence on the specific action of God as it applies to him, then our statement that the concealment in God's action in man is nowhere so profound as in what took place in Jesus, must signify that in this concealment God acts in him in a way more far-reaching than in anyone else. We may also add that this concealment of God's action reaches the profundity it does in the life of Jesus, above all in the fate that overtook him and the destiny he encountered in it, and it becomes clear that it is this stroke of fate, and this destiny, which provide the clue to his experience of God's action in him and the unity with God contained in this. We may here recall what we said at the beginning of this chapter when we tried to understand what Jesus meant when he said that he who asks receives, and that all things are possible to him who believes. We saw that in both petition and faith, as Jesus understands them here, 'all things' signifies the life man receives when he submits to the destiny God has prepared for him. But that 'all things' are at stake here clearly means that he who asks and believes is of himself wholly powerless in this respect, and nothing that he is capable of by his own strength can help him to achieve what he is asking for and believes in. Anyone whose petition and faith have brought him to this point must be unmistakably aware that it is God alone who can give and bring help in this matter.

Thus if we ask how Jesus experienced God's action in him in the fate that overtook him and the destiny he encountered in it, we must reply that he experienced it in the petition and faith which were aroused in him through them. Here what Jesus meant in his sayings, 'Everyone who asks receives' and, 'All things are possible to him who believes', comes true in him. But what is received in this petition is what is given by God alone, and what is possible for this faith is possible through God alone. Thus everything that happened when Jesus asked and believed, in the fate that overtook him and the destiny he encountered in it, was the work of God and of God alone. And since this faith and destiny determined his whole life from beginning to end, it was in this life and in what took place in it that God revealed himself in his action in man as he has never done elsewhere. In the life of Jesus, this fate and destiny form the very event on which the world and its salvation depend, to a degree that can scarcely have occurred in anyone else. And in the same way the action of God as revealed in the life of Jesus affected not only his life but thereby affected the salvation of the world and of those who live in it.

NOTES

1. Cf. above, pp. 181f.
2. Cf. above, p. 186.
3. Cf. G. Ebeling, *Wort und Glaube*, p. 240 n. 92; tr. 'Jesus and Faith', in *Word and Faith*, p. 234 n. 1.
4. Cf. above, p. 241.
5. Cf. above, pp. 221f.
6. Cf. above, p. 186.
7. Cf. above, p. 185.
8. Cf. above, p. 197.

18

FAITH IN JESUS AND HIS RULE OVER THE WORLD

EVEN IF the saying recorded at the end of the Gospel of Matthew, 'All authority in heaven and on earth has been given to me' (Matt. 28.18), does not come from Jesus himself, but from the church, and testifies to the church's belief in him and his work, we may nevertheless say that it is wholly in accord with his own consciousness that what happened to him was the fulfilment of the salvation promised of old by his nation's prophets. When he was given the book of the prophet Isaiah to read and expound in the synagogue at Nazareth, he came to the passage:

> The spirit of the Lord is upon me, because he has anointed me to preach good news to the poor. He has sent me to proclaim release to the captives and recovering of sight to the blind, to set at liberty those who are oppressed, to proclaim the acceptable year of the Lord.

His comment, as surprising as it was decisive, was: 'Today this scripture has been fulfilled in your hearing' (Luke 4.16ff.). On another occasion he said to his hearers:

> Blessed are the eyes which see what you see! For I tell you that many prophets and kings desired to see what you see, and did not see it, and to hear what you hear, and did not hear it (Luke 10.23f.).

Without the certainty that the salvation Jesus preaches is directly present in his preaching, it would lose its true meaning and the complete and world-embracing unity that can be summed up in the saying: 'Repent, for the kingdom of heaven is at hand' (Matt. 4.17). But we must also recall that he warns against a too ready acceptance of his message. We tried to show how scandalous the saying was with which he answered the Baptist's question, whether he was 'he who was coming': 'Blessed is he who takes no offence at me'.[1] The intention of his message is never to corroborate those who suppose that salvation can be possessed or found through trusting in the present world. The same will happen to them as to those for whom

> a man once gave a great banquet, and invited many; and at the time for the banquet he sent his servant to say to those who had been invited, 'Come; for all is now ready'. But they all alike began to make excuses. The first said to him, 'I have bought a field, and I must go out and see it; I pray you, have me excused'. And another said, 'I have bought five yoke of oxen, and I go to examine them; I pray you, have me excused'. And another said, 'I have married a wife, and therefore I cannot come'. So the servant came and reported this to his master. Then the householder in anger said to his servant, 'Go out quickly to the streets and lanes of the city, and bring in the poor and maimed and blind and lame'. And the servant said, 'Sir, what you commanded has been done, and still there is room'. And the master said to the servant, 'Go out to the highways and hedges, and compel people to come in, that my house may be filled. For I tell you, none of those men who were invited shall taste my banquet' (Luke 14.16ff.).

The salvation Jesus preaches, and which is immediately present in his preaching, is that of the whole world. But as such it is also, in the strictest sense, his own salvation. That is, as the salvation of the world it is intimately linked with what was the real heart of the life and history of Jesus, the stroke of fate which influenced his whole life, and consisted of his perception of the idolatrous way in which the world exists as such, and the destiny which was prepared for him, which he encountered in this perception, and which laid upon him the responsibility for the way in which the world exists as such.

Just as the salvation with which his life and history is concerned is his own, so equally it is that of the world. Because this is so, without knowledge of his life and history there is no knowledge of the salvation with which they are concerned and, without participation in Jesus's fate and destiny, no participation in this salvation. In Jesus's preaching this is expressed very clearly in the sayings which state that whoever will share in the kingdom of God must 'follow' him. It is important to be clear what this following consists of. However different the situations in which men are called to follow him, in every case they include the 'repentance' without which no one can be 'fit' for the kingdom of God. For only someone who, in accordance with this 'repentance', abandons his trust in the present world and the life that it promises to those who submit to its ordinance, is ready to receive life as it is lived in the kingdom of God. We have seen what happens when someone undergoes such 'repentance'. The present world ceases to be for him that which, with the commandments it brings with it, has provided the basis for the life he has lived hitherto, and so he encounters what we have called the destiny of his life.[2] It is to this encounter that Jesus calls those who wish to follow him. It is only in this encounter that they become able to understand that they have to follow Jesus in his destiny itself. This is what Jesus means when he says that 'A disciple is not above his teacher, but everyone when he is fully taught will be like his teacher' (Luke 6.40). For only someone who follows him in his destiny can share in the life gained by submitting to his destiny.

We have seen that the form in which a man meets this destiny always comes from the stroke of fate in which he meets it, and therefore Jesus calls those who wish to follow him from situations that are different in each case. Thus, he said to one who said he was ready to follow him but asked to say farewell first to his family, 'No one who puts his hand to the plough and looks back is fit for the kingdom of God' (Luke 9.57ff.). To another he said: 'Foxes have holes, and birds of the air have nests; but the Son of man has nowhere to lay his head' (Matt. 8.20). When someone asked him what he should do to inherit eternal life, and answered, when he was told to observe the commandments, that he had kept them all from his youth up, Jesus said to him: 'You lack one thing; go, sell what you have, and give to the poor, and you will have treasure in heaven; and come, follow me' (Mark 10.17ff.). Elsewhere we read: 'If anyone comes to me and does not hate his own father and mother and wife and children and brothers and sisters, yea, and even his own life, he cannot be my disciple' (Luke 14.25f.). But whenever anyone comes to make

Faith in Jesus and His Rule over the World

the resolve which his destiny requires, he must do as the man who was going to build a tower:

> Which of you . . . does not first sit down and count the cost, whether he has enough to complete it? Otherwise, when he has laid a foundation, and is not able to finish, all who see it begin to mock him, saying, 'This man began to build, and was not able to finish' (Luke 14.28f.).

However certain Jesus was that salvation is present in his preaching, it is clear from what he said about following him that he did not think participation in this salvation came simply from belief in what God had done in him, from belief that God gave him what he had prayed for and made possible what he believed, that his own salvation should be that of the world; nor simply from calling him 'Lord, Lord'. And it follows that no one can participate in this salvation without doing 'the will of my Father who is in heaven' (Matt. 7.21). For although Jesus makes following him an absolute condition of salvation, he does not suppose that it is he who is giving salvation. It becomes present by what happens in him. But to share in it is possible solely through what God does in him and through him, and what God wishes to be done by those for whom this salvation is given. In everything he says about following him, Jesus gives way to what God does. When someone who sought to follow him addressed him as 'Good Teacher', Jesus replied: 'Why do you call me good? No one is good but God alone' (Mark 10.17f.). And when two disciples asked him to let them sit one on his right hand and the other on his left, he drew their attention to the severe burden he had to bear, and then pointed away from himself to God; it was not for him to give a place at his right hand or at his left, but only as prepared by God (Mark 10.35ff.).

Thus what God has done in and for the world through Jesus has not to be sought from him, but from God alone. For what God has done through Jesus happened on the basis of his faith and petition, and of its nature could happen in no other way. Thus, however decisive this event may be for the world and its salvation, the world cannot partake in it except on the basis of the faith and petition of those that live in it. And it follows that their faith and petition cannot be addressed to Jesus – not in the sense, at least, that it is he who fulfils their petition and makes possible what faith believes. We can see that Jesus himself did not take it in this sense from the fact that he speaks neither of faith directed towards himself, nor of petitions addressed to him.[3] We also saw that the God to whom, in Jesus's understanding, this petition and faith are addressed is not the God of a ready-made concept of God.[4] Rather, God shows himself as him who he is only to someone who, in the petition and faith which is concerned more than anything else with 'all things', commits himself to the point at which 'all things' become possible and are given to him. To him, God shows himself as him who gives to him who asks, and makes 'all things' possible to the believer. What kind of God it is to whom Jesus addresses himself in his petition and faith, because he can appeal in his preaching of the coming kingdom of God to him and to him alone, can be experienced by one who commits himself in his own petition and faith to the point at which 'all things' are at stake. Now if there is a relationship of dependence between this petition and faith and that of Jesus, then it must be sought in what we have just described as the condition for God's revealing himself to this petition and faith as him who he is. This condition is that one should commit oneself in petition and faith to the point at which 'all things' are at stake.

When and how this happens can perhaps be most clearly described by referring to what we saw earlier to be a characteristic of this petition and faith. That is, that the 'all things' with which it is concerned affect not only salvation but damnation.[5] In other words, Jesus's sayings, 'Ask, and it will be given you' and 'All things are possible to faith', only apply to petition and faith when someone dares to abandon himself to the ultimate depths of his lost condition in the sight of God, of which he is as certain in this faith as of the fact that his salvation is possible only by participating in God's life-giving power. The knowledge of the hopelessly lost condition to which man is subject without this participation, the admission of it and abandonment of oneself to it, are not the same in the case of Jesus as they are for other men, although he shares the same lost condition in the sight of God. The situation is the same as in the case of destiny which, as we saw, is always the same, but varies according to the stroke of fate in which each individual encounters it. So, too, the knowledge of his lost condition which someone gains in his petition and faith, which corresponds to his certain knowledge of his salvation, understood by his petition and faith as a participation in the power of God, differs according to whether it is only the salvation or lost condition of an individual, or, as in the case of Jesus, those of the whole world. Similarly, the 'all things' which are at issue in both cases are not the same. If I am concerned with salvation and damnation only in so far as they are my own, I can only commit myself in my petition and faith to the point where they, my own salvation and damnation, are the 'all things' which are at issue. But in his perception of the idolatrous way in which the world exists as such, Jesus recognized the lost condition of the present world. Thus his petition and faith are concerned not merely with his own salvation and damnation but – together of course with these – with the salvation and damnation of the whole world and all who live in it. And therefore he must inevitably commit himself far more deeply in his petition and faith – to the point where the salvation and damnation of the whole world are the 'all things' that are at issue.

Suppose, however, that someone commits himself, in his petition and faith, even to the point where it is only his own salvation which is at issue. He will likewise become aware of his lost condition only in so far as this is possible by contrast to the personal salvation which he seeks in his petition and faith. But this experience will make it possible for him to realize that his own lost condition – which, of course, was recognized by Jesus as being that of the whole world – is part of the reason why the concealment in which God's action in Jesus took place is much more profound than that in which his own destiny has come about in the vicissitudes of fate he has undergone. And he will be able to see that the 'all things' with which Jesus is concerned in his petition and prayer demanded of Jesus a commitment incomparably deeper than he himself can achieve. It will be possible for him to understand that in this way – to use a phrase from the Epistle to the Hebrews – Jesus is both the pioneer and also the perfecter of this petition of faith (12.2). For they were not perfected until Jesus's own petition and faith had led him into the very depths of knowledge of his lost condition and salvation, to the point where they are the 'all things' with which this petition and faith are concerned, the lost condition and the salvation of the whole world.

In this perfection, the petition and faith to which Jesus calls are dependent upon his own petition and faith. But this dependence in those to whom his preaching applies cannot mean that it is Jesus who fulfils the petition and makes possible what faith believes. If it is understood in this sense, then Jesus is put in the place of God, and the best that could be said of God would be that he, God, endowed Jesus with an ability to save which exceeded all human capabilities. This would make God's own actions and salvation superfluous for then it would not be God who saved, but Jesus, through this special ability. But it would be strange that Jesus never said to those who he healed that their faith *in him* had healed them. Instead, he made only such statements as 'Your faith has helped you', or 'Be it done for you as you have believed' (Matt. 8.13; 9.22, 29; 15.28, etc.).

We are not of the opinion that the encounter with Jesus is of no significance for the faith of which he speaks here. But the question is, what kind of encounter is this, and what takes place in it? The faith of which Jesus speaks in absolute terms, as he does of the petition which accompanies it, is always such that what is believed is made possible by God and by him alone. Thus, what takes place in the encounter with Jesus in which faith is involved is what we have just described. The faith of those who turn to Jesus for help comes under the influence of his own faith, and thereby undergoes the perfecting through which the 'all things' in which they believe and for which they ask become solely what God makes possible and gives them. And we saw that what happened to Jesus on the basis of the petition and faith he exercised in the fate that came upon him and the destiny he encountered therein, was the act of God alone. So, likewise, the petition and faith which are perfected and receive their true meaning through his petition and faith, cannot be faith in Jesus in the sense that what is experienced in it is done by him. Rather, just because it becomes what it is through Jesus's own faith that God alone makes 'all things' possible to faith, it is faith in God, and in what God did in and through Jesus, by fulfilling his petition and making possible what he believed.

We said at the beginning of this chapter that the preaching of

Jesus would be robbed of its meaning if we took away from it the certainty that the salvation it preached was directly present in it. The same is true of the certainty that this salvation is not that of any individual person who is shown how to achieve it, but the salvation of the whole world. The true significance of the saying of Jesus, 'He who is not with me is against me, and he who does not gather with me scatters' (Matt. 12.30) can be understood only when it is seen from this point of view. The same is true of the saying: 'You are the salt of the earth; but if salt has lost its taste, how shall its saltiness be restored? It is no longer good for anything except to be thrown out and trodden under foot by men' (Matt. 5.13). This note of a final and ultimate decision, so characteristic of Jesus's preaching, is so compelling and unrelenting because the kingdom he preaches is not one which will be present in some future time, but is coming now, in this very hour. His preaching has this compelling note equally because it proclaims the salvation of the whole world. And the powerful but remarkably calm certainty with which Jesus proclaims it to the whole world can be understood only when we perceive that this note is also present in the Beatitudes. But the assumption in all this is that it is God, and God alone, from whom Jesus awaits this salvation – not only in the sense that God brings it about through something from which it results, but in the sense that he himself, in the presence of his deity, is the world's salvation.

In the chapter above on 'Jesus's World as an Individual'[7] we discussed the question where Jesus received the authority not only to preach salvation to the whole world in his message of the coming kingdom of God and the coming to an end of the present world, but also to assert that in this preaching it was already present. We also asked whether the claim he made at the same time, a claim he could not authenticate before any authority in the present world, was one of blasphemous arrogance. For the only possible understanding of this claim is in fact that Jesus was asserting himself to be capable of what lies solely in the power of God. We replied that God's will was experienced by him in his perception of the idolatrous way in which the present world exists as such, and that what he did to fulfil it was not planned by himself, so that he did not take it upon himself to carry it out on his own authority. For he did no more and no less than fulfil the demand of obedience to the will of God, which applied to him as to anyone else. We also considered what took place in Jesus's obedience to God's will. He accepted the experience of his perception of the idolatrous way in which the present world exists as such as the one stroke of fate which determined his whole life. He submitted to the destiny he encountered in this stroke of fate, a destiny which was that of a responsibility laid upon him for the whole world. Finally, this stroke of fate and destiny drew forth from him the petition and faith in which 'all things' are at issue. Thus in this petition and faith he attained to the certainty which is only possible in this way, that it is God who gives and God who makes possible what faith believes; that it is God himself, therefore, who was acting in him, and who by doing so through this stroke of fate and destiny, was acting through him upon the whole world. At this point in our study, our principal purpose is to make this last point clear.

The decisive question we must ask here is what is meant by the world, in which God acted through the stroke of fate and destiny which came to Jesus. In discussing the preaching of Jesus, we saw at once that with it the history of the world as such ceased to have an unambiguous meaning. For one important point signified by the crisis which this preaching brought about is that, since then, man has been faced with the decision either to be responsible to the world, as he unquestionably was before this, or to be responsible to God and ready to serve him, as the preaching of Jesus now demands. It is impossible to do both; one must choose one or the other. For if, in his responsibility to the world, man has a duty to the religious veneration of the world and its eternal and unchanging ordinance, on which its existence as the world is based, then the responsibility to God which Jesus's preaching demands of him is impossible. Similarly, in this responsibility to God, responsibility to the world and the religious veneration of the world are brought irrevocably to an end. For 'no one who puts his hand to the plough and looks back is fit for the kingdom of God' (Luke 9.62). But this 'looking back' does not refer simply to the world, as though man ought to have nothing more to do with it. We must emphasize this against the conventional understanding of Jesus's preaching. It refers rather to man's responsibility *to* the world, which makes his responsibility to God impossible. But the latter is by the same token intimately linked with man's responsibility for the world –

that is, for its ceasing to be the object of religious veneration.

With this responsibility for the world, which necessarily follows from man's responsibility to God, the reality of the world underwent a very profound and far-reaching change in the way it is present to man. It took on that distinctive character which we can perhaps best describe as 'natural', in the sense in which we use the expression when we speak of something 'quite natural', or coming about 'in a natural way'. We have already briefly discussed this,[8] and gave as an example of this change what happened to the sabbath through Jesus's statement that the sabbath was made for man and not man for the sabbath. A holy day, specially venerated because of the commandments laid down in the ordinance of the world to which it belonged, thereby became an 'ordinary' day. We might have chosen the tribute money as another example. Jesus drew attention to the image of Caesar on it, and the inscription, and so took away from it the sacred character which in the view of his opponents meant that it belonged to God and therefore should not be given to Caesar. But by pointing to the coin, and with his saying 'Render to Caesar the things that are Caesar's and to God the things that are God's,' he made it an 'ordinary' coin.

Associated with the 'natural' character of the reality of the world, when man becomes responsible for it and it ceases to be the object of religious veneration, is something else of importance for this responsibility and the way it is exercised. The religious veneration of the world means above all that the ordinance and commandments in force in it must be most scrupulously observed. For in them the world, as it is understood here, derives from itself its eternal and unchanging condition, and by submitting to this ordinance and obediently fulfilling its commandments, participates in this unchanging condition and its eternity. When the religious veneration of the world goes, so do this ordinance and its commandments. If they go, man is henceforth independent of the world in which he lives and decisions about what he has to do in the world are taken in responsibility for it, and not to it. And since what he has to do in the world has always something to do with the way it exists and continues as the world – that is, lest it relapse into chaos – this responsibility for the world affects its continued existence as such.

Assuming that man perseveres in his responsibility for the

world, in the responsibility to God in which that for the world originates, the enduring sustenance of the world is clearly something essentially different from that which we described in relation to the religious veneration of the world. This enduring existence of the world was considered as an unchanging and rational structure, maintained in being by the ordinance which prevails in this world and therefore as the object of religious veneration. But the continued existence of the world for which man is responsible in what he does, and of which he has to be conscious in the decisions he makes about what to do, cannot possibly be of the same kind. We have occasionally pointed to the difference by referring to the latter as the enduring historical existence of the world, in reference to the fact that it is subject to historical change.

The enduring existence of the world is historical in the sense that the way in which it exists and continues as the world – which is what is at issue here – affects the world in so far as its reality has taken on a 'natural' character; the consequence, as we saw, of its no longer being religiously venerated. But it thereby ceased to be a self-contained entity, such as it was as long as its unchanging condition was maintained by the ordinance which prevailed within it and which together with it was religiously venerated. Once it is no longer self-contained, however, the world itself is subject to the same change as everything that happens in it. Thus, the enduring existence of the world for which man is responsible in what he does, in the decisions he makes about his actions, no longer forms the unchanging and rational structure which was found in the world that is religiously venerated, and which provided a meaning, defined by the piety prevailing in it, to all the change that took place within it. Of course, even the case of the enduring existence which man has to care for, by what he does, still represents a structured order of changing events. But these events no longer take place within a world which itself remains unchangeable; the existence and continuance of a world which also changes is involved in them. For only where there is some kind of rational structure in these events can the chaos which constantly threatens man's world be excluded. But what has to be done must be done by man; and it is he who must make the necessary decisions.

We have described man, then, as taking a responsibility for

the enduring existence of the world, and the reality of the world as having taken on a 'natural' character. But the world here is not the world in the sense we have set out above, in which God acts on the world through Jesus. For if this action on the part of God takes place in the stroke of fate and the destiny which came to Jesus, it can only affect the world as it is manifest in man's encounter, in the vicissitudes of his fate, with the destiny prepared for him. By contrast with the present, enduring world, we called the world seen as the location of this encounter the world of each individual person. As we tried to show, Jesus became aware of this world in his perception of the idolatrous way in which the present world exists as such. For as a self-contained entity it was shut off from God, and barred the way to God for those who lived in it and upon it. In this perception he experienced the stroke of fate which determined his whole life and in this stroke of fate he encountered the destiny which is distinguished as peculiar to him by the fact that in it responsibility for the way the world exists was laid upon him. It was his responsibility that it should not seek its salvation, like this present world in which he lived, in the fulfilment of commandments and ordinances, but in God, and in him alone.

The clearest explanation of what it means to say that the salvation of the world is to be found in God, and in him alone, is given by Jesus in a number of sayings to which we have already referred: those concerning the new patch on the old garment, and the new wine in the old wineskins which ruin both garment and skins (Mark 2.21ff.), or that of the sound tree which produces good fruit and the bad tree which produces evil fruit (Matt. 7.17ff.), and, finally, that of the body which is wholly light or dark, depending on whether the eye is sound or not (Matt. 6.22f.). All these sayings signify that one can only attain to salvation by means of the whole, and never by manipulating the parts. For they are only what they are by virtue of the whole to which they belong. When something is not right, the whole of which it is part is altered. An old garment, no longer usable, can only be replaced by a new one. The attempt to repair it by means of a patch of new cloth makes it even more unusable. Similarly, new wine requires new wineskins. When a tree produces bad fruit, nothing can be done with the fruit that can turn it into a sound tree. A new tree, which is a sound one and therefore bears good fruit, must be planted in its place. And anyone who sees only bad in everything he looks at must receive a new sight before he can see good. When these sayings are applied to the salvation of man and his world, about which they are parables, they imply that any attempt to bring about the salvation of the world by dealing with individual sources of trouble in it is senseless. Such an attempt would be one made by instructions and guidance aimed only at various individual situations in the world. In order to be of any use at all, they would have to be concerned with partial matters, and as such could have no relevance to the whole. An unsaved world can only be saved by a change in the way in which it is the world. Only when this is changed can everything that belongs to it be saved.

Even more pointed are the few sayings in which Jesus explicitly mentions some of the evil circumstances he knew existed in the world, together with instructions for overcoming them. These instructions are 'the law and the prophets'. But it is not sufficient to understand these in the same way as the religious authorities of the present world (Matt. 5.20). For the salvation of this world to be brought about, no iota or dot of the law and prophets might remain unfulfilled (Matt. 5.18). For example, the law stated: 'You shall not kill; and whoever kills shall be liable to judgment.' But what this commandment requires would be fulfilled only if there were never the slightest trace of anger or contempt between brothers, for such deserves not merely judgment but hell-fire. Consequently, every conflict whatsoever had to be settled, at least when one was bringing one's gift to the altar to serve God. These commandments forbade adultery, but a person could only be free from this temptation if his heart was so completely free of all impure desire that he was ready to cut off and throw away any limb, even his hand or eye, which threatened to lead him to succumb. Even though it was necessary to swear oaths in the world, every oath, not merely a false oath, and regardless by what it was sworn, was an offence against God's honour. What was required instead was the most candid truthfulness, for which 'yes' meant nothing but 'yes', and 'no' meant nothing but 'no'. Finally, even if the saying 'An eye for an eye and a tooth for a tooth' was meant to place a limit on the recompense of evil, it served in fact only to increase the evil in the world. The only thing that was any use was not to resist evil (Matt. 5.17-42).

If these sayings of Jesus were understood as instructions for reducing or removing the evil they refer to, in order thereby to bring about the salvation of the world and of man, this would be just as senseless as telling the bad tree, which, as Jesus said, bears bad fruit because it is bad, to turn itself into a good tree in order to bring forth good fruit. It would be like trying to get grapes to grow from thorns or figs from thistles (Matt. 7.16). The same is true of men: 'The good man out of the good treasure of his heart produces good, and the evil man out of his evil treasure produces evil' (Luke 6.45).

The same is true of the world in which God acted by the mission and testing of Jesus, and which we called the world of each individual man, by contrast with the present world, which is always a general one, whether it is religiously venerated, as in Jewish piety, or the world as it always exists historically. For it is only in the world of each individual that man meets his destiny in the encounter in which the decision is made concerning the salvation or damnation of the world. It is with this salvation that Jesus is concerned in all his teaching. This is the reason why his preaching lacks any instructions for decisions about what man has to do in the world. Thus the reason is not that the world as it exists historically, in which man, who is responsible for it, has to act in every case according to his own decisions, was a matter of indifference to Jesus. Far less was it that for the sake of his salvation man had to withdraw completely from the world and everything in it that laid claim to him. At an early stage, and very often in later years, Jesus's words were understood in the latter sense, mostly as calling for some form of asceticism. In fact the sayings which speak to the world in a negative way refer to the world in so far as it is the object of religious veneration. Their purpose is, therefore, to call men away from this world, and away from the religious veneration of it. And therefore Jesus's call for repentance or a 'change of mind' is not one appeal amongst many in his preaching but is the primary and essential one. The lack of specific instructions shows most emphatically the nature of Jesus's concern for the salvation of the world and of the responsibility he felt for it. His responsibility is concerned not with the manifold aspects of what man has to do in the world, but above all with the way the world exists as such. He is concerned with whether it remains, like the world venerated by religion, enclosed in itself and therefore shut off from God in the passionate and inevitable intensity of the facts prevailing within it, or whether it is open to God and to the appreciation of his free rule within it, which is subject to no law and in which alone man can encounter the destiny prepared for him and gain the life destined for him by God.

The responsibility of Jesus for the world, therefore, corresponds most closely to his rule over the world. Just as the former is not concerned with the many and various things man has to do in the world, so Jesus's rule over the world is not directed towards these either. Like his responsibility for the world, it is concerned with the world as a whole. If this rule is sought by looking in Jesus's preaching for instructions that reflect it, it becomes impossible to recognize it where he actually exercises it. Thus Jesus's rule over the world, which is inextricably linked with the responsibility for it laid upon him in his apprehension of the idolatrous way in which it exists as such (for if one is responsible for anything, one is lord over it), is not exercised by him as a law-giver, by means of such instructions. Nevertheless, many of his sayings have constantly been taken in this sense, even though this interpretation of them can be made only at the cost of a disastrous misunderstanding of his whole preaching.

Before we discuss in detail how Jesus's rule over the world concerns the world as a whole and brings it salvation, and how it is God who acts in the world thereby, we ought to consider another question. If the reality of the world in which we live today has taken on the character of the 'natural', can Jesus's rule of the world still have any significance for us? For since this change in the reality of the world has, as must be admitted, established itself at every level, and the religious veneration of the world has become virtually impossible, the attack on this religious veneration, which underlies the whole of Jesus's preaching, seems to have lost all significance for us.

It is the purpose of this work to show that christology must proceed strictly from the true historical man, Jesus. Consequently, in speaking of the world with the salvation or damnation of which his historical life was concerned, we have to discuss it in terms of the particular world in which he lived, that of late Judaism and its distinctive piety. We were principally concerned with this world and his relation to it. We had to begin with Jesus's perception of the idolatrous way in which the world existed as such, when it was the object of religious veneration under the influence of the piety of late Judaism. Everything else we said about his relation to it, and therefore about his rule over it, assumed his passionate rejection of any religious veneration of it. The world of late Judaism, however, which for Jesus was the only world he knew – and therefore simply the world, without qualification – is for us today only one of many different worlds that have existed in the course of history. It may be of antiquarian interest, but it is in no sense a world in which, so to speak, we can still live.

If this is so, we are forced to ask whether the rule of Jesus over the world, brought about by his perception of the idolatrous way it existed as such and the responsibility for it which this laid on him, can have any significance at all for us and our relationship to the world in which we live today. It is no longer the world venerated by religion, out of which Jesus called those who, like him, lived in it. For our world, in which we live, and are, therefore, responsible for it and its condition, has become the 'natural' world[9] – as a result of this very responsibility we have taken on. Because its reality has this quality, it is impossible to accord to it the religious veneration against which Jesus's rule over the world was directed. Instead of this, man has become responsible in every respect for what takes place in this world, in so far as it has undergone this change, and also for what has come about as a result. He is, therefore, also responsible for what he has to do in it, and for the guidance he needs to exercise his responsibility for it.

In accordance with what we said above[10] about the two kinds of history, we can summarize the matter as follows: The world, and its historical condition at any time, for which man is responsible in the way described, is the world which we encounter as the object of modern historical scholarship and the idea of history which underlies it. When we tried to make clear the distinction between the two forms of history, the kind which came into being with Jesus and that which is the object of modern historical scholarship, we recognized that the distinction is particularly apparent in the different significance given to the idea of the whole of the world. Both are impossible without this concept. But the difference is that modern historical scholarship cannot avoid posing the question of the whole of history and of the whole of the world; yet it cannot answer it. But in history in the first sense, the important thing is that in it a decision is made about this whole, and whether it is lost or gained.

The reason why modern historical thought cannot avoid thinking of history, and the world which is the subject of this history, as a whole, is that otherwise the history with which it deals would crumble into fragments and would lose its true significance, that of the coherent structure of events in the world. On the other hand, neither the historian nor the exponent of the philosophy of history can grasp this whole by the methods he uses. If they try to answer the question which this concept poses – and the temptation to do so is all the greater in that the historicity of the events they study, and have to study, makes this question inevitable – they inevitably abandon history as they are bound to conceive of it in order to study it, and pass from historical thought to a philosophical world view. This happens when it is believed possible, by fulfilling one of the basic principles which have been discovered in the attempt to exercise responsibility for the state of the world in its present historical existence, not only to understand the world as a whole, but also to bring about its salvation. But all that this achieves is a remarkably modified repetition of the religious veneration of the world in pre-Christian times, by which men believed they had the whole of the world, and therefore their own salvation, under their own control. The preaching of Jesus brought about the change in this attitude of man to the world.

We spoke of a modification of this religious veneration. It is not simply the same as that against which Jesus's preaching was directed. This it cannot be, because through Jesus's preaching – not solely, but not least through his preaching – the reality of the world has undergone a transformation from the divine into the 'natural'. The assumption behind what one must perhaps call a righteous religious veneration of the world has disappeared. It is no longer possible to believe in the unchangeability of the world and its ordinance, to which man could submit himself with the aid of a piety in accordance with this world, believing that he could thereby ensure his participation in its eternal permanence. Nevertheless, we can speak here of a veneration of the world which is religious, or, if it is felt more appropriate, similar in nature to religion. For the result of it is that the world becomes, as in the pre-Christian period, the point of all-embracing reality, in which alone man believes he can find the meaning of his life. This is the decisive issue. Now, however, it is man himself who has to provide this meaning, by seeking to bring about the salvation of the world through his own actions, based upon his responsibility for the world.

As we have seen, then, Jesus's rule over the world is not directed towards the details of what man has to do in it, and he does not exercise his rule by giving man appropriate instructions. Rather, it is aimed at the way in which the world exists as such, and seeks to make it no longer a world venerated by religion and therefore an enclosed world, existing by and in itself, but instead a world open to God's free actions in it, which is not bound by the law of any world. The intention of this rule, therefore, whenever any significant modification of the religious veneration of the world takes place, will be to prevent it. Thus there is no basis for the idea that the rule of Jesus, exercised by him in responsibility for the world with the aim of preventing its religious veneration, is of no further significance for us who live in a much changed world. In spite of the change it is as valid now as it was in the world in which he lived.

But the responsibility of Jesus for the world, and his rule over it in accordance with his responsibility, have a significance which goes beyond their opposition to the religious veneration of the world. For his perception of the idolatrous way in which the present world exists as such, which as we have seen is the origin of his responsibility for the world, also includes the experience of responsibility to God. Indeed, it is only possible if it brings with it a realization of the disastrous confusion of God and the world, and the exchanging of responsibility to God for responsibility to the world. If this happens, responsibility *to* the world is changed from responsibility to God into responsibility *for* the world. There are two reasons for this. First, because men never exist without the world and, secondly, because responsibility to God as Jesus understands it would be impossible without responsibility for the world. For, as we have seen, to be responsible to God means to give oneself in response to God. And therefore this response is possible only for someone who is independent in the sense of one who possesses an enduring existence as himself. This he can have only as one who is responsible to God for the world. And, only in this double responsibility can he give himself to God in response to the word by which God calls him.

Since Jesus's responsibility for the world is such that in it he is responsible to God, it is clear that his rule over the world can be understood in its full significance only when it is realized what it implies for this rule to be in accordance not only with his responsibility for the world, but also with his responsibility before God, the former being, in so far as it is characteristic of Jesus, inextricably linked with the latter. We can only say that Jesus was speaking of the rule which is in accordance with this double responsibility when he said:

> You know that those who are supposed to rule over the Gentiles lord it over them, and their great men exercise authority over them. But it shall not be so among you; but whoever would be great among you must be your servant, and whoever would be first among you must be slave of all (Mark 10.42ff.).

Thus the basis of the rule to which Jesus is referring lies in responsibility for those over whom it is exercised, and since this responsibility is also responsibility to God, it can never lead to one who rules in accordance with it setting himself above those he rules like 'those who are supposed to rule over the Gentiles'. Even if Jesus spoke these words to the disciples when 'a dispute arose amongst them which of them was to be regarded as the greatest', as is suggested by the context in which it occurs in Luke (Luke 22.24), and he had this in mind, yet there can be no doubt, in view of the emphasis placed on these words in the context of his preaching, that they applied not only to the disciples but to himself as well. In any case, as we have often noted of Jesus's sayings, their deepest significance only appears when they are applied to him as one who, more than anyone, became by his preaching and what it imposes upon him the slave of all in the fullest sense, and as such the first of all. And just as no one is the servant of all, as he is, so can no one be the first of all as he is. We have already said, when we quoted this saying elsewhere in another context, that to be the slave of all, when applied to him, does not only mean that he bore the evil which lies upon him as upon all others who live in the present world, under the influence of the sentence of doom which prevails within it. For him it also means that, as a result of his becoming the neighbour of other men by his perception of the idolatrous way in which the present world exists as such, what we may call his private evil included the evil of the whole world, and therefore that of the men with whom he lived in it. Thus what he had to bear was the fate of all who live in this world brought about by trusting in this world and in the ordinance that preserves it in being; and it was this fate that was prepared for him as his own.

We believe from our understanding of Jesus's teaching that it is wholly in accordance with his own thinking to say that because, as the last of all, he is the first of all, and because in this profound concealment of God's action in him, which is the meaning of his being a slave, he exercises rule over the world, then, in this rule of his, the salvation of the world and of man is realized as it can be found only in God. This concealment of the action of God in him is the same as that of which he warned when he concluded his reply to the Baptist's question whether he was 'he who was coming', with these disturbing words: 'Blessed is he who takes no offence at me' (Matt. 11.6). We can now see that these words are disturbing because they state that in the most profound and all-embracing sense imaginable, that of the destiny prepared for him by God, which is to share the fate incurred by other men, he became the servant of all these, and it was he alone who was to exercise God's rule over the world. But this can be true only if it is God's rule, and no one else's, and is therefore the salvation of the world. And so Jesus can be the first by being last only because it is God himself who has revealed himself to him, the last of all, as the 'first of all', of whom Jesus said that in his sight the last shall be first.

If as the last and slave of all, Jesus exercises this rule over the world, and if in it God, whom Jesus proclaimed as giving to him who asks, letting him who seeks find and opening to him who knocks (Matt. 7.7f.), and to whom alone Jesus appealed, as such a petitioner, for the authentication of his preaching, is unambiguously acting through Jesus's rule in him, and through him in the world and in man for their salvation, I hardly think it necessary to state especially that this rule is not one in the exercise of which there is any use for any kind of commandment or instruction. For if the action of God, which alone makes this rule what it is, took place in the decisive stroke of fate that came upon Jesus and the destiny he encountered in it – and it is this which is meant when we speak of him as the servant whom God lets rule over the world in his name and in his power – then over and above anything else that can be said of it, this rule affects the world, in so far as it is there that man encounters the destiny prepared for him by God in the vicissitudes of his fate. But as we have seen, this is the world which we called the world of each man as an individual.

If anything resembling an instruction can be found here at all, only one is possible. This is the instruction that is meant to be followed in taking the decision with which man is faced by the destiny he encounters. It is that man should subject himself to this destiny prepared for him by God. But how does he bear this instruction, and what does he hear in it, if he really hears it? This call with which, when it comes to man and he lets himself encounter it, destiny calls him to a decision inevitably bound up with it and characteristic of it, is the very same by which man is called by God's word to be responsible to him. We have already said much about this responsibility, and about what happens in it when man is able to answer it in the only way possible if he is to vindicate himself before it. We can now go on to say that as long as what is meant to be heard in man's encounter with his destiny is taken as an instruction, that is, as a commandment, what is meant here is being missed. For what is being stated here is what may be called the boldest saying in Jesus's preaching.

This is the affirmation of the forgiveness of sins. It is to be sought not only where Jesus explicitly says: 'Your sins are forgiven', as in the story of the healing of the paralytic (Mark 2.5) or that of the woman who was a great sinner (Luke 7.48). In the story of the Pharisee and the tax collector we read: 'This man went down to his house justified' (Luke 18.14). It is the tacit assumption in Jesus's fellowship with 'tax collectors and sinners', who were excluded from the present world of late Jewish piety. For him to call them, or, as we prefer to translate, invite them into the kingdom of God which he preached, implies the forgiveness of their sins. It shows, moreover, that in this forgiveness life is given, life which is given by God to man and can be lived through God alone. This is also the sense of what is said to the Prodigal Son in Jesus's parable when he confesses: 'Father, I have sinned against heaven and before you; I am no longer worthy to be called your son.' His father says: 'My son was dead and is alive again; he was lost and is found' (Luke 15.11–24).

This affirmation of the forgiveness of sins is, one may assert, present in some way in almost everything Jesus said. We can see how bold an affirmation it was from the reaction of the authorities of the world maintained in being as the present world by the piety of late Judaism. They were 'questioning in their hearts. Why does this man speak thus? It is blasphemy! Who can forgive sins but God alone?' (Mark 2.6f.). They did not know that what Jesus said has nothing to do, and could not have anything to do, with the world and the piety in which they lived and which alone they knew. Nor did they know anything of the sin which Jesus was forgiving. For this was not the sin of which people become guilty in that world, and in the sight of its piety, in hundreds of ways. 'It was calculated during the third century AD that there were 613 regulations.'[11] The only sin which Jesus forgave was that of unbelief, in which man rejects the call of the destiny prepared for him by God, and does not submit to it. Just as the knowledge of this sin is possible only in the world which is that of each man as an individual, in which his destiny faces him with the decision characteristic of it, so also it can only be forgiven there. But this is the world in which Jesus has authority. And if we are correct in what we have said about the significance of the forgiveness of sins in Jesus's preaching, that it is present, if only tacitly, in almost all he both says and does, we can then go on to say that forgiveness is the way in which he rules over the world.

We can sum up what we have said about Jesus's rule over the world as follows. It is not a rule which replaces, or seeks to replace, the rule of God. Wherever and in whatever form the idea of this rule appears in Jesus's preaching, it is perfectly clear that it is thought of in one way alone. Jesus was endeavouring to lead those on whose behalf he accepted this rule as the slave of all to God's own rule, as that in which and through which everything had happened which has happened in and through himself, Jesus. We have seen this both in our study of faith *in* him, and in considering his rule over the world on the basis of his preaching. It is true of the way he exercises his rule over the world in respect of the way it exists as such, by making it impossible for it to be the object of religious veneration, and so making impossible the idolatrous way it existed as the world in the piety of late Judaism. It is also true of his making accessible the world in which man encounters the destiny prepared for him and can hear the word of God, receiving from it the life God gives him to live, if he is able to give himself in response to this word. Jesus was able to do all this by submitting himself, in responsibility to God, to the destiny incurred by his brethren as that prepared for himself.

In understanding the responsibility of which we speak, what takes place in it should not be seen as affecting only the actions of the person taking on the responsibility, as though this were the primary and decisive factor. It affects above all his existence, because it is only with his very existence that he can respond appropriately to the word which calls him to responsibility. It needs constant watchfulness to maintain this understanding, for our thinking, and not least our theology, has long been the victim of a tendency to treat everything in moral terms. But it makes it possible to see in its true light something we have frequently referred to, but can only now discuss in its full christological significance. What is said of Jesus can become christological, and speak of Jesus as the Christ, only when, as in the New Testament, it is able to present what happened in the world through the life and fate of Jesus as carried out by God. It must show it, moreover, not merely as having happened on one single occasion – which would be true of Jesus if he were regarded only within the framework of the historical study carried out by the methods of the modern concept of history – but instead happened once for all. This is meaningful only if it is possible to say that what took place in and through Jesus took place in the history of what happens between God and man. And it is only this which makes it meaningful to speak of what was seen from Jesus's preaching to be the central point of his personal history: that by taking place between him and God, it also took place between him and the world, the world being here the whole world.

It is necessary to return here to our discussion of the way it is possible to speak of faith *in* Jesus.[12] We concluded that the asking and believing in which 'all things' were at stake, and in which according to Jesus's own words God reveals himself as him who gives and who makes possible to faith what it believes, were not the same for Jesus as for others. The difference is not only that, as we have said,[13] the 'all things' to which others gain access, and with which they are concerned in their petition and faith, is only their own personal salvation, while for Jesus – included in his own salvation – it is that of the world. This difference also provides the only way of recognizing what makes his rule what it is, a rule exercised over the world in the name, and therefore in the power, of God for the salvation of the world. In order to grasp this difference, we must recall that, as we have seen,[14] the nature of this petition and faith is that it is concerned not merely with salvation, but also with damnation. In fact, it is the petition and faith we are discussing here only when in it the ultimate depths of this damnation are recognized. But this depth of damnation, and the inevitability with which it lies upon man, is grasped only when it is understood as the damnation of the whole world. And only when it is recognized that Jesus's petition and faith are concerned with this damnation does it become clear what the difference is between his petition and faith and that of others. It is this difference, too, which makes it possible to speak of faith *in* Jesus, in the sense that, as we have said,[15] it was possible for the petition and faith of others to be carried down by Jesus into the very depths of the knowledge of damnation and there of the power of salvation which corresponds to this damnation, these ultimate depths being attainable only by Jesus's own petition and faith.

It is in these depths that the history of Jesus took place, between him and God, and at one and the same time between Jesus and the world. If this is so – and we believe that we have shown with the aid of Jesus's preaching that it is indeed so – then we can also say that it was God himself who, in the history that took place between him and Jesus, did and intended what took place in the history between Jesus and the world, and in what took place during and through this history. We can also go on to say that the world we are speaking of here, both in the history between God and Jesus and the history between Jesus and itself, is that with which God is concerned. That is, it was not only the world which formed the present world at the time of Jesus under the domination of the piety of late Judaism. That was, of course, the world through which Jesus, recognizing the idolatrous way in which it exists as such, perceived the world in a completely different mode of existence, in complete contradiction to the way the present world exists. He saw it as that which we have called the world of each man as an individual. This, then, is the world with which God was concerned in the history of Jesus.

In order to make clear what we have in mind when we speak of the world of each man as an individual as that with which God was concerned in the history of Jesus, we must mention again how this differs from the general world, the universe. We have sometimes called this general world the present world as it exists historically, at any time. By this we meant that it is the world as it appears in history, in so far as history takes place between man and the world. What takes place in this world, and so provides the content of its history, consists above all in the juridical, governmental and social order which man has constantly to work out anew and recreate in the face of the constant change in all the circumstances of this world. It also includes everything which he has to bring into being in an unending labour of creation to keep his relationship to this world a living one and to make it habitable for himself. And it is in this world that he undergoes what we have called the vicissitudes of fate. The world of each man as an individual is distinct from this world, in that in it, and in the vicissitudes of fate he experiences in it, man encounters his destiny.

In this destiny, and in the decision which unavoidably accompanies it once he has encountered it and accepted the encounter, the issue is not any particular matter, great or small, about which a decision has to be made in the present world as it exists historically. As we have constantly asserted, the issue in the decision which man's destiny demands of him is rather that of his existence as a whole: its salvation or its damnation. For here he must put this existence at stake and decide whether to submit to his destiny – and so gain the life destined for him in it by God – or reject it – and so he will lose this life.[16] In this – if I may so term it – fateful decision, which he can make only as the whole man which he becomes in it to his salvation or his damnation, he also experiences the world as the whole which it is as his own individual world; we repeat, to his salvation or his damnation. What man experiences here does not belong to the world with which modern historical scholarship is concerned, nor can it be grasped by the methods used there. Rather, it belongs to the history which began with what happened through Jesus.

If, then, the world of each man as an individual, the world in which alone he experiences what we have just described, is that with which God was concerned in the life and history of Jesus, two things follow. The first we have already mentioned: that it is God who acts on the world, through Jesus, by manifesting it as the world of Jesus as an individual. We mentioned this in particular when we were trying to show from Jesus's preaching that the one concern which preoccupied his whole life was that of the right relationship between the world and God. That is, that its salvation should be God and him alone. This is the reason why the purpose of almost all his words is to help men's faith to be truly placed in God and not in the world. For only when this is so can the world participate in the salvation that comes from God and from him alone. It was of particular importance here that in this concern he was not diverted into preaching a *doctrine* concerning the right relationship between God and the world, and therefore concerning correct faith in God, in such a way that this became the whole content of his preaching. His preaching can only be properly understood when it is seen that its proper and total 'content' is his history as he experienced it in the events which we described as his being a neighbour to the world, or as his unity with it. This history, we must add, is that which he experienced as taking place between God and himself.

Once we realize the full significance of this duality in the history of Jesus, that it took place between him and the world and between God and him, and remember that it took place in the world which is the world of each man as an individual, it is possible to speak of the second matter. This is the world with which God was concerned in the history of Jesus. If the first point is that it is in this history that God has acted through Jesus on this world, the second is that in the purpose of God, which he intends with regard to the world in the history lived by Jesus, and in which he turns towards it as he who is, his purpose also includes Jesus as the one who in obedience to his will and therefore in his, God's power, became one with the world, and the servant of all for the world's salvation.

Thus we can now say that the history of Jesus, the basis of which is that in it God exercises his purpose for the world and in this history acts on the world in accordance with his purpose, did not merely take place once, when Jesus lived upon earth, so that it is now past, and lives on only as a memory. Instead, it takes place once for all, and therefore is constantly renewed, when a person experiences, in the petition and faith he exercises for the sake of his salvation, that he is carried down by the petition and faith of Jesus, and so by the preaching he uttered, into the profoundest perception of damnation, which Jesus took on himself when God made him neighbour to the world. There God reveals himself to him as him who gives to him who asks and makes possible what the believer believes. But this is the salvation of man and the world, which is God, and cannot be other than he.

NOTES

1. Cf. above, p. 229.
2. Cf. above, pp. 184f.
3. Cf. above, p. 240.
4. Cf. above, p. 237.
5. Cf. above, p. 242.
6. Cf. above, p. 241.
7. Cf. above, pp. 193ff.
8. Cf. above, pp. 167f.
9. Cf. above, pp. 167f. and 263.
10. Cf. above, pp. 157ff.
11. Bultmann, *Das Urchristentum im Rahmen der Antike*, p. 70; tr. *Primitive Christianity in its Contemporary Setting*, p. 66.
12. Cf. above, p. 260.
13. Cf. above, p. 259.
14. Cf. above, p. 242.
15. Cf. above, p. 259.
16. Cf. above, pp. 185f.

19

POSTSCRIPT

THE SUBTITLE of this book is meant to show that it is not intended to put forward a comprehensive christology, which would be possible only within a complete dogmatic theology, nor to provide what might be called the 'outlines' of christology. It is concerned rather with basic questions, and how at least they should be posed, before it is possible at the present day to construct an honest christology. In the present intellectual situation it is mainly concerned with questions which arise from a fact already pointed out by Ernst Troeltsch in 1898, but which have never found an adequate answer. This is the fact that historical thinking (in the passage to which we refer Troeltsch actually speaks of 'historical method', which is, however, only an application of historical thinking, from which its justification and limits are both derived), once its place in theology has been accorded, works like a ferment 'which transforms everything and finally shatters the whole previous pattern of theological method'.[1] Since it is the historical human being, Jesus of Nazareth, by whom Christian faith stands or falls, it is obvious that the transformation of theological method which has been brought about by historical thinking has nowhere had so profound an effect as in christology.

Thus in this book we have set out to answer the questions which arise for theology as a result of this change. It is, moreover, impossible to circumvent the problem of historical thinking and its significance for theology, and since it affects christology more even than the rest of theology, the problems to which it gives rise cannot be treated as incidental. They must be dealt with on their own account. But this is evidently impossible except by taking into account what christology is concerned with. It is essential in dealing with them to be quite rigorous in working them out in relation to the whole theme of christology, seeking in them their significance for the understanding of this whole matter. As we saw at the beginning,[2] this whole theme is unity of God and man in Jesus of Nazareth. This was brought to utterance by the church of the early centuries through lengthy labours, taken up anew on many occasions, and the resultant christology held sway for over a thousand years in the western church. But it must be admitted that it remained wholly untouched by the historical thought that was developed only in the modern age. This cannot be ignored, and must necessarily be applied to christology. One is then faced, whether one likes it or not, with the question of how far the solutions worked out in the christology of the early church of the problems presented by the unity of God and man in Jesus of Nazareth are still possible and binding on us. If no clear answer is given to this question, it is inevitable that these solutions will be taken up into the new christological thinking we have to work out for ourselves, will cause confusion, and will give rise to internal contradictions in it, making the christology it proposes necessarily unacceptable to faith.

We have already seen, and found expressed most emphatically in Luther's passionate assertion of the significance of the humanity of Jesus for the knowledge of God, how great the difference is between the christology of the early church and one worked out in historical terms. The former supposed it possible to know 'God in his majesty'; Luther was convinced that this was something which one should not even attempt. A historical christology requires that one should abandon human and metaphysical rules for the knowledge of God and 'leave God alone', as far as seeking him in this way is concerned,[3] and instead concern oneself with the humanity of Christ.[4] Strangely enough, it has been supposed that Luther's thinking 'can only be brought to its conclusion, if one approaches the humanity of Christ without taking for granted a belief in his divinity'.[5] But this is a twofold misunderstanding. First of all, it suggests that when Luther speaks of the humanity of Christ, as he does in numerous utterances, he was not thinking of a human being, a belief in whose divinity was taken for granted. Not only were the 'consequences' which would result from such a view of the humanity of Jesus 'totally remote from Luther in his historical situation', but there is not the slightest evidence in his thinking for any such idea. Secondly, it ignores what he is rejecting by pointing towards the humanity of Jesus, although he mentions this often and clearly enough in the same context. What he is trying to prevent, as he explains for example in a letter to Spalatin, is that in ignoring the humanity of Christ, one should stray into unrestrained speculation about the deity. Then the soul would no longer be able to endure before the greatness of the power, the majesty and the wisdom of God. He, Luther, and many others had often plagued themselves in the most elementary and dangerous manner with this endeavour. Consequently, he repeats, and warns time and again, 'whoever will think of God and speculate about him in a way that promotes his salvation must set behind him everything except the humanity of Christ'.[6] The humanity of Christ, towards which Luther is concerned to direct the attention, is far from being one whose divinity is not taken for granted. Rather, he is thinking of a knowledge of God unobtainable elsewhere than in this humanity, when one 'comes to and grasps in faith, how the Son of God was revealed in flesh'. This is in complete contradiction to a knowledge which dawns upon one in seeking for the majesty of God, and by which one is crushed to the ground.[7] Thus, he says, one should not do 'as the philosophers and worldly-wise do, and try to begin at the top, and so they become fools; one must begin at the bottom, and reach the top after'.[8]

Of course this does not mean that with his recognition of the supreme significance which the humanity of Christ has for a knowledge of God of the kind he regards as the only true and saving knowledge, Luther was explicitly attacking the christology which was first formulated in Nicaea and Chalcedon in the closest connection with the doctrine of the Trinity, and was made authoritative for the whole church. But there are certain utterances in which he reduces the doctrine of the Trinity to that of the one God and the three persons, and the divinity of Christ, while he asserts of the latter that it is revealed only in the humanity of Christ and ought therefore to be sought there alone. As far as the unity of humanity and divinity in the person of Christ is concerned it is characteristic of Luther's thinking on the matter that he says of Christ that he himself accords everything to the Father as author; whatever he does or says, he always refers to the authorship of the Father: 'As he commands, I do; what I hear from him, I say.' He always attributes his divinity to the Father. This is an art finer than we can understand. I like it a lot; it is not as clear to speak of the Father and the persons. [I understand this statement to mean that if one speaks like dogmatic theology of the Father and the persons of the triune deity, it is not so clear as when Christ himself speaks here of his unity with the Father.] Thus Christ's rule is this, that whatever he does or teaches he attributes to God as the author. Thus, when I look upon his words, his blood, his tears, I see through him himself, and in him himself, into the will of the Father.

To understand fully what Luther is saying here, it is necessary to bear in mind that his intention is to express at the same time the full content of Christian faith as he understands it. For as he goes on to say in the same passage, 'Christ attributes all he does and says to the Father, and this makes God's name no longer terrible to us, but comforting.' And he asserts at the same time that this is

> a new kind of doctrine, unknown to the world; but it is the best that the devout can hear. Whoever hears it, hears in it the authority of the Father. They are interwoven . . . it must not be skipped over with superficial attention, as if God were to be found elsewhere. . . . While you are groping around, you miss both the Father and the Son. This is the way to speak of the true divinity.[9]

Thus while Luther does not explicitly oppose the traditional christology of the church, it is difficult, in considering his ideas of the full significance of Christ's humanity for the sole true knowledge of God, to overlook the fact that, to put it mildly, he does not merely set out in a completely different direction, but in some places does not understand the humanity and divinity of Christ in the same way. Of course, both Luther and the theologians of the early church were concerned with the unity of God and man in the one person of Jesus Christ. One can even say of the similarity in their doctrines that both consider this unity within the framework of the doctrine of the Trinity. But it is here, in the understanding of this unity, that the difference begins. The theology of the early church works it out in relation to the immanent Trinity, the Trinity as it exists in itself. Luther understands it in the sense of the Trinity of the economy, the Trinity as it is revealed. In the first instance, the divinity of Christ is understood as that of the second person of the triune God, and consequently it is the divinity understood in this sense alone which provides the basis for the understanding of the unity of divinity and humanity.

Since this divinity or, as one might put it, this divine person, possesses its nature, as the second person of the triune God, in relation to the two other persons, the Father and the Holy Spirit, and therefore has its place in the activity of God within the Trinity, in which he is directed towards himself, it is scarcely possible for the humanity of Christ, which belongs to the revelation, the movement in which God turns towards the world, to be understood as anything other than more or less an instrument of which God makes use in turning to the world, and not in such a way as to avoid its losing any of its integrity. Thus it is easy to understand why in an essay entitled 'Chalcedon – End or Beginning'[10] Karl Rahner speaks of an 'inadequacy' of the christological formula which was the outcome of Chalcedon. It is admittedly an 'inadequacy' which the formula 'maintains, and does not remove'. But because with regard to this inadequacy it is 'not merely an end, but a beginning', he believes that he can return to it, which is of course something different from simply repeating it.

This 'inadequacy' exactly describes what we have been discussing. For, as Rahner asks,

> How can christological dogma as a whole be formulated in such a way that either as its starting point, or with increasing clarity as it proceeds, the Lord appears as the Messianic Mediator, and therefore as the true man who in free human obedience to God stands on our side, is the Mediator, and directs his action towards God, and cannot be thought of *merely* as the action of God and as a nature conceived of purely as an instrument, ontologically and morally passive with respect to the Logos.[11]

In order to understand more precisely what Rahner is referring to when he speaks of the Mediator as 'true man' let us quote the following passage from the same essay:

> We must constantly remind ourselves that human existence is not an absolute and self-contained entity, cut off and existing in total isolation, which is joined together by a miracle from outside to something else, in this case (i.e. christology) with the Logos. Rather, human existence is a reality which proceeds here from a complete openness to above, to its highest, albeit 'unmerited' *perfection*, to the highest reality of human existence, when in it the Logos itself becomes existent in the world. . . . The more one thinks of this humanity not merely as something attributed to God, but understands it as the presence of God himself in the world, and thereby (not 'nevertheless') realizes that it possesses genuine and independent freedom towards God, the more the enduring mystery of faith becomes comprehensible and also becomes a statement of our own existence.[12]

We have said that Luther works out his account of the unity of humanity and divinity in the one person of Jesus Christ not, as in the theology of the early church, from the immanent Trinity, as it is in itself, but from the Trinity as revealed. And in his view, as we saw, no one should know of any God apart from this man and should therefore 'let alone' God and his majesty,[13] when it comes to the question of one's relationship with him. If this is so, it follows quite unambiguously that Luther proposes not to understand the humanity of Christ from his divinity, but to understand his divinity from his humanity. This is not meant in the sense of an arbitrary choice between two otherwise acceptable methods. Rather, it is in accordance with Luther's view of how God means to reveal himself.

> Thus it is of no use for you to call upon God like the Jews and the Turks. . . . The divine nature is too high and incomprehensible for us. Thus for our sakes he has come down into the nature which is best known to us as our own. It is there he acts for us, it is there he wishes to be found, and nowhere else; whoever calls him here is soon heard; here is the throne of grace, from which none who comes to it is shut out![14]

Thus the way in which we approach God must be in accordance

with the way in which he approaches us. But if 'God himself has lowered himself in order to be comprehensible to us, it would be the most godless wantonness for man to follow the inclinations of his own mind and look for another way'.[15] This is why Luther will not know any God 'other than in this humanity. For if you stray from this person, who was born of Mary, and look elsewhere, the Devil is leading you. . . . The fullness (of the godhead) dwells in Christ, the other speculations are about the majesty of God and they terrify us'.[16] And thus the humanity of Christ is the way God deals with us.

According to Luther, this humanity is above all to be recognized in the cross. And therefore 'to know Christ means to know the cross and perceive God beneath the crucified flesh. For this is what God wants. This is God's will; and more, it is God himself'. When Luther says this, he has in mind the very central content of faith, as is shown by the statements that follow:

> This is what God says here [i.e. through the humanity of Christ]: Do not be afraid and do not think that you are lost when your courage is small because whatever you suffer is against your expectations. But be wise, know the Lord, understand his will; turn your gaze away from what is of naught, for the Lord is wonderful in his saints. Something different is happening, something far different from what appears. We see that he kills, but in reality he is making alive; he smites, but in reality he is making whole; he strikes down, but in reality this is when he is glorifying; he brings down into hell, but in reality he is bringing out – and one could go on. What is more marvellous than this will of God? He lives on high, but looks down graciously on the lowly; he makes men foolish, for them to become wise; he makes them weak, in order to make them mighty.[17]

This is God, as he lets himself be known in the humanity of Jesus.

Luther, then, understood christology by starting resolutely with the humanity of Jesus, and no longer understood the central theme of christology, the unity of divinity and humanity in the person of Jesus Christ, by deriving the divinity of Christ from the second person of the triune God, but by understanding it as the basis of his humanity. We are not of the view that the christology, the basic issues of which we have tried to set out in this book, is exactly the same as Luther's. We have seen that a consequence of his view was that the doctrine of the Trinity, which both in the form of the immanent Trinity-in-itself, and of the economic Trinity, was of such predominant importance for the christology of the early church that it provided the only possible basis for it, fell into the background to such an extent in Luther that only the second form was of significance as the basis for christology. Furthermore, by deriving his understanding of Christ's divinity from his humanity, Luther thinks of both in the way we have seen in the passages quoted above. He says of Christ that he understood his own unity with the Father in such a way that 'whatever he says and does, he always refers to the authorship of the Father, and says "What he commands, I do; what I hear from him, I say"'. Luther adds that this is the way 'to speak of the true divinity'. One may conclude from this that Luther's statements in the homilies of 1522 on Hebrews 1.1–14, where he speaks of the divinity of Christ in a way peculiar to himself,[18] must be understood in the same sense. Here he comments on the statement of Hebrews that the Son is 'the very stamp (or image) of (the Father's) nature'.

> If an image is made of a man, the image is not an image of human essence or nature; for it is not man, but stone or wood, an image of stone or wooden nature made like a man. But if I could take human nature like a potter takes clay, and make an image of it, which would both be an image of the man and also would wholly contain in itself human essence or nature, behold, this would be an essential image, an image of human nature. There is no such image in any creature; for all images so made are of a different nature from that of which they are an image. But in this case the Son is an image of the Father's nature in such a way that the Father's nature is the image itself, which is not merely like and similar to the Father, but wholly contains in itself his whole essence and nature. . . . Now when I say of the image of a man, this is a stone or wooden image, so I say, Christ is an image made of God, that is, just as surely as this image is wood, so this image is God.

To understand how Luther tries to understand the unity of divinity and humanity in Christ with the aid of this simile of the image, which is the image of God, which is Christ, is 'of the same nature as that of which it is an image', we must note two things. Firstly the 'image' of which Luther speaks is not understood by Luther as a 'copy', the meaning of which would go no further than that of being 'like or similar' to what it reproduced. But Luther explicitly states that more than this is true of this 'image'. We can perhaps express what he is saying with the word 'formed' – as it were, Christ is something 'formed' of God. Only of such a thing would it be possible to assert what Luther says of it, that it is 'also the essence itself of that of which it is the image'. This, of course, is only so when it is formed of this image. The second point is this. What is 'the Father's nature', 'out of which this image is made' in such a way that 'it contains in itself his whole essence and nature'? Luther spoke of this nature in the words we have quoted from his exposition of Psalm 4, where he says: 'the Lord is wonderful in his saints', not least in him who is his Holy One in the highest sense, Christ the Crucified. For it is in him that he is making alive when he kills.[19]

This, then, is the Father's nature, of which Christ is the 'image' and 'is given his nature wholly by God and of God'. And because Christ is the 'image' of God in this way, Luther can make of him the astonishing statement that apart from him 'there is no God'. For just as Christ is the 'image' of God, God's nature as Father is itself this 'image'. Elsewhere an image is never of the nature as that of which it is the image, but 'here the image is also the nature itself, of which it is the image, and needs no other image than its nature'. Luther concludes his argument:

> Here faith is necessary and not a lot of acute speculation; the words are clear and strong enough (i.e. that Christ is an image of the Father's nature, and in what way he is). If there is any- one to whom these words do not affirm the divinity of Christ, then no one can.

Thus Luther does not think at all that in the christology which he believes should be based on the humanity of Christ, faith in his divinity cannot be taken for granted. For his chief concern is to assert that a true faith, either in God or in the divinity of Christ, can be gained from this humanity alone. This is why with Christ 'the deeper we can go into his nature and flesh, the more comforting it is for us'.[20]

Once we have understood aright, as Luther meant it, his doctrine of the humanity of Jesus, and the fact that the true and saving knowledge of God is found only in 'clinging' to it, and that in it alone the unity of the humanity and divinity of Christ can be known, it can be said that he comes remarkably close to a historical understanding of the person of Jesus such as we have tried to set out in this book. This is to say that in considering the essential issue of what happened in and through Jesus – that as the true man which he is, he is one with God – he did not make use of the metaphysical concepts of two natures, the divine and the human, but that he thought of what it was most important for him to express as a historical event. For example, he says that 'Christ is not called Christ because he has a divine and a human nature, but because of the office and work which he took on, but not because he took on flesh and blood'.[21] And therefore for Luther 'to believe in Christ' is

> not to believe that Christ is a person who is God and man, for that is of no help to anybody; but that this person is Christ; that is, that for our sakes he came from God and into the world, and then left the world and went to the Father. This is to say that it is Christ who for us became man and died, rose and ascended to heaven. Because of this work he is called Jesus Christ, and to believe this of him, that it is true, is to be and abide in his name ... what Christ, that glorious person, was to die for us and now has done, was God's pleasure from eternity. ... [22]

In this way Luther can sum up the whole series of events which bears the name of Christ, referring to Paul in Philippians 2.8, as follows: He did everything 'to be obedient to the Father'. And he adds that in these words Paul

> opens heaven and allows us to feel how what Christ, that glorious person, was to die for us and now has done, was God's pleasure from eternity. ... It is this, I hold, which is to come to the Father through Christ. ... O, how many preachers of the faith are there who think they know everything, and have

neither smelt nor tasted this matter? How soon do they become masters, who have never been pupils! They do not taste it, and so they cannot give it, and remain useless babblers.[23]

But it is characteristic of Luther's theological thinking that he speaks in this historical, non-metaphysical way of the humanity of Jesus particularly when he is explicitly concerned with faith in Jesus Christ. We must recall that Luther had an understanding of faith which was completely different from the traditional one, and which forms the beginning and end of his whole theology. The direction he took in it was his own, and it led him far beyond the paths trodden by traditional theology. This is true above all when he speaks of faith as the only thing by which man is able to be justified before God. But it is also true when he speaks of faith in the sense that it is faith alone which gives man a part in what happened in and through Jesus for his salvation. The best known of Luther's statements on this subject – though they are still scarcely understood in their full significance – are those in which he distinguishes between a faith which knows only of the *res gestae*, or, as Luther puts it elsewhere, the *solum factum* of what happened through Christ, and faith which comprehends the *usus* of the *res ipsa Christi*. The *usus* of Christ is that for which he died. A faith which believes only 'that this history is true, as it sounds ... does not help, because all sinners, even the damned, believe that'. Such a faith, Luther goes on,

> is not taught in the scripture and God's word; it is a work of nature without grace. But the right faith, rich in grace, required by the word and work of God, is that you believe firmly that Christ was born for you, and that his birth happened for you, for your good. For the gospel teaches that Christ was born for our sakes and did and suffered everything for our sakes.[24]

And therefore Luther says that Christ as he is believed in in the faith which is only 'a work of nature without grace', 'is not in his work and in his power'.[25] His work and power, or, as Luther himself calls it, his *usus* or his *res ipsa*, is what he has done as the man who he is, and by the power of that humanity. And thus the Christ who is believed in in this faith must first be believed. For it is only such a faith which has a part in that for which Christ was born.

As far as the difference is concerned between Luther's christology and that of which we have tried to pose the basic issues in this book, it lies in the fact that we have asked what the significance is of posing the decisive question of christology, that of the unity of God and man in the person of Jesus of Nazareth, not as before with the help of the concept of the two natures, but in historical terms. For as we have seen, it is characteristic of historical thought that once it gains entry into theology it works like a ferment in it, 'transforming everything and finally shattering the whole previous pattern of theological method'. And its main effect on christology is that the person of Jesus must itself be thought of in historical terms in a way which is simply impossible within the previous theological method.

We have already said that with his doctrine of the humanity, and of the way in which not only is the true knowledge of God to be found in clinging to it, but also the divinity of Jesus can be recognized there alone, Luther comes remarkably close to the historical understanding of the person of Jesus. But, on the whole, it does so only when it is concerned with the faith in which alone it is possible to participate in what happened in and through Jesus. And we must also bear the following point in mind. However firmly Luther distinguishes this faith from that which he says is 'a work of nature without grace', and which even the sinners and the damned have, and indeed which he thinks even the devil has, he never thinks of abandoning that faith and what is believed in it. He cannot, for this faith is, as it were, a picture of the world which was an automatic assumption held by virtually everyone at Luther's time, including Luther himself. One might say that it is the view of the world presented in the Bible, and in accordance with it people believed the history of the world as it was found there. Without this world view and without the automatic way in which Luther, like all others at his time, held it to be true, it would have been impossible for him to argue out his theology at all. For only someone who regards as true the whole range of what the Bible says, and who was therefore able to appeal to the Bible for what he taught, could be regarded as belonging to the church. And likewise only someone for whom this was possible could properly expect his assertions to be taken seriously by others. Moreover, because the Bible was 'God's testimony of himself',[26] Luther believed that one should 'prize a single tittle and letter' in it 'more highly than the whole world, and . . . fear and tremble before it as before God himself'.[27] For 'no jot or tittle of the scriptures was written in vain'.[28]

In addition to the universal truth of the Bible, it was also taken for granted that it had to be interpreted correctly, that is, in a way appropriate to it. For in order to believe in it and follow it, one had to understand what it said. This is the point at which Luther, in his theological thinking, began increasingly to depart from the traditional theology. This resulted from his realization that the true key to the understanding of the scripture is Christ, and Christ alone: 'Take Christ from the Scriptures – and what will you find in them?'[29] In him

> the Lord shows us the proper method of interpreting Moses and all the prophets. He teaches us that Moses points and refers to Christ in all his stories and illustrations. His purpose is to show that Christ is the point at the centre of a circle, with all eyes inside the circle focused on him. Whoever turns his eyes on them finds his proper place in the circle of which Christ is the centre. All the stories of Holy Writ, if viewed aright, point to Christ.[30]

This is what Luther has in mind when he says that the scripture itself is 'the most certain, easiest and most obvious interpreter of itself'.[31] As the scripture interprets itself, it is unambiguously clear that the Christ 'to whom it points as a whole', is Christ who alone justifies. And because Luther has realized in this way that the 'article of justification', that is, of faith in Christ who alone justifies, is 'the master, prince, lord, leader and judge of every kind of doctrine, which upholds and governs the whole of church teaching and gives us a clear conscience before God',[32] he is also certain that it is not an arbitrary choice to understand the *iustificatio sola fide Christi*, justification by faith in Christ alone, as the article which must underlie the interpretation of everything the scripture says. It is the scripture itself which requires this interpretation of it. And thus, as Luther himself affirms, 'in my heart there rules this one doctrine. . . . From it, through it, and to it all my theological thought flows and returns, day and night'.³³

It is obvious that there is a not inconsiderable tension here. We have, on the one hand, this unquestioning faith in every word written in the Bible, which was for Luther not the 'true faith, rich in grace, demanded by the word and work of God', but 'a work of nature without grace', which therefore 'is of no help' before God, and yet without which, according to the view of his time, which Luther shared, no one can be a Christian. On the other hand, there is Luther's teaching that only the article of justification through faith in Christ alone permits a right understanding of the scripture, by turning it from a dead letter to the living word of God. This tension is to be found throughout Luther's work. Once it has been perceived, it can be seen in almost everything he said. Nor is it present solely in respect of this 'article'. It is the tension between the two worlds, between which it was his lot to live – the Middle Ages, drawing to their close at his time, and the modern age which in his lifetime was just beginning.

It is not too much to say that as one who was living between these two conflicting worlds, and without being clearly aware of it, he was destined to bring the Middle Ages to an end and to provide the starting-point for what the modern age became.³⁴ The question often discussed, whether Luther belonged to the Middle Ages or the modern age, can only be answered by saying that he belonged to both. And therefore the tension that runs through all his work, is between the medieval man, which he was and the modern man, which he was also. He is a medieval man in that although his whole world view was called into question, he remained throughout his life a believer in the world presented by the Bible in its usual medieval interpretation, a world filled like that of pre-christian times with demons and spirits, not the least of which was the Devil. But, at the same time, he was a modern man, in so far as he was concerned to utter in all its purity the faith he had learnt from the Bible, not without severe inner struggles.

It was the Bible then, which brought about this tension, so characteristic of his intellectual nature and the pattern of his thought. This explains why there constantly occurred in his work a mixture between what the Bible says in one or other of the modes of interpretation which are in conflict here. This happened not only in the almost superhuman quantity of written and oral statements we possess from him (I am thinking in the latter case of the sermons, almost all recorded for us in notes taken by others). It also pervaded his thinking itself. Of course, this happened particularly when Luther's attention was not particularly concentrated on the new ideas he was proclaiming, which he could do only by a polemic as unequivocal as possible against the traditional understanding of the Bible and what it says.

He was fully aware of the novelty of these ideas, and found himself drawn into a profound and all-embracing opposition to the received theology of his time. This can be seen perhaps most clearly in the Schmalkald Articles, which he drew up at the request of the Elector, in the context of the conciliar politics of the 1530s. At the end of the first section, which in four paragraphs deals with the articles concerning the divine majesty (1–3 on the Trinity, 4 on the incarnation of the Son), we read that 'these are in no dispute or quarrel, since both sides (i.e. Protestants and Papists) confess the same'. Luther had first written at this point 'believe and confess'; but then he deleted 'believe'. That it was not merely a correction of style which led him to delete this word and leave only 'confess' as common to both can clearly be seen from the fact that we read immediately afterwards in the 'First and Principal Article'; 'That Jesus Christ our Lord and God died for our sins and rose for our justification'; and the comment is:

> Now since this must be believed and cannot be attained or understood otherwise by any work, law, or merit, it is clear and certain that such faith alone makes us righteous. . . . One cannot yield or concede anything of this Article. Let heaven and earth fall, and all that does not remain . . . everything stands by this article, which we teach and live against the Pope, the Devil and the world.[35]

Thus by summarily denying that the Papists have faith, Luther is also denying that they have a part in what he admits they confess, but which, because it is without faith, is of no use to them.

We have already noticed that the tension in Luther's mind

between the two worlds in conflict, that of the Middle Ages drawing to their close, and that of the modern world in its earliest stages, led to the presence in his exposition of the Bible of much that contains scarcely any trace of the understanding of the Bible which is brought by 'the true faith, rich in grace, demanded by the word and work of God'. Such ideas are similar to the point of confusion to the understanding of the Bible which is in accordance with the other kind of faith, of which Luther says that it is only 'a work of nature without grace', and can therefore only comprehend the *res gestae* or *solum factum* – what in modern terms we would call the historic facts – recounted in the dead letter of the Bible. Faith of this kind can find anything in the Bible, beyond the bare facts, only when it is driven by the Devil to understand what the Bible says as metaphysical statements about the majesty of God. Luther says that when it is a matter of justification, or of how God is to be found as he who justifies on the basis of faith, one should 'let God alone and cling to the humanity of Christ and nothing else'.[36] For faith of this kind such statements are bound to be completely incomprehensible or even blasphemous.

But if the tension of which we have spoken is not simply a contradiction that cannot be resolved, and must be accepted as such for better or for worse, we must insist that we cannot be content, in understanding Luther's expositions of scripture, with what they would signify in accordance with an automatic belief in the letter of the Bible. For Luther does not allow such a belief to be right belief in scripture. Luther, on countless occasions, made clear what it was his intention to say, and it was this alone which made possible his breach with the Pope and his followers, with all its consequences. If we are to understand this, we must at least make the attempt to understand these parts of his exposition of the scripture in accordance with what elsewhere he stated perfectly clearly concerning justifying faith and the understanding of the Bible which such faith alone can bring. This is so even when at first impression (ignoring the fact that must be emphasized, that Luther can expound the Bible, and often these same passages elsewhere, in a masterly fashion) they really contain nothing more than this automatic belief in scripture would see in them.

. . .

This is the reason, then, for the tension which occurs in Luther's statements, and which shows that he was a man of the end of the Middle Ages, as well as of the beginning of the modern world. As the former, it was impossible for him not to expound the Bible in the sense which follows from the faith with which it was believed in as a matter of course by everybody, almost without exception, at the time at which he lived. In terms of this belief in the Bible it was possible for him to use its statements in arguing against his opponents. But as a man of the modern age which was just beginning, and such it was his lot to be, he expounds the Bible in accordance with the faith which cannot be held in the manner of a 'world view' and laid down once for all, but which each individual must venture to believe for the sake of the justification which it alone can bring. As we said, it is the same Bible which he believes in with 'faith' of the first kind, yet which teaches him this other faith. And for this very same reason, it is one of the main objects of his theology to distinguish these two kinds of faith from each other.

We have seen that when Luther is concerned to express this faith in as pure a form as possible, he speaks in his characteristic way of the humanity of Jesus as that which alone makes possible the faith that can justify. We mentioned that with his doctrine of the humanity of Jesus and its significance for the true knowledge of God, he comes remarkably close to the historical understanding of the purpose of Jesus and the christology which is our task at the present day. We can now say that it is the tension in Luther's understanding of the Bible which, in spite of the repeated successful steps he took towards overcoming the metaphysical structure of traditional theology, restrained him from making a final breakthrough to a historical understanding. It was easier for this to happen, in that at Luther's time there could be no question of the introduction of historical thought into the realm of theology and its problems. It was not even possible to make use of the term 'historical' for a phenomenon such as that of justifying faith, as Luther understood it, although there can be little doubt of its historical nature in the sense we have put forward. Thus the fact that it was historical remained only a latent awareness, and it was relatively easy for it to be held at the same time as ideas which were clearly unhistorical, without any contradiction being felt. This is sometimes the case with

Luther's interpretation of the Bible, and is the reason why in such cases, with the best will in the world, we find his interpretation incomprehensible. For we are no longer like Luther men of the Middle Ages, and therefore we notice the contradictions. But we must say of Luther that although the modern age began with him, he was still a medieval man, and could not do anything but share an unquestioning faith in the Bible and its contents. He was consequently able to accept the tension between this unquestioning belief of his age, and the justifying faith that every individual has to venture and gain for himself alone, without its becoming an intolerable contradiction for him. But it is impossible for us to become medieval men, and whether we are willing to appreciate it or not, we are still – thanks, of course, in part to Luther – modern men. Our thinking and our whole existence has thereby become completely historicized, and we can recognize and acknowledge only what is historical as a reality which concerns us as men. Such a contradiction, then, would make faith incredible to us. The consequence of this is that if we are not able to think of Jesus in resolutely historical terms, he and everything a christology can say of him loses all reality for us. It is evident from all we have tried to make clear in the present work that the historical understanding which alone is capable of restoring the reality of Jesus, which has already been lost to an alarming degree both within and outside the church, cannot be of such a kind as modern historical scholarship is constantly trying to produce. It must be an understanding gained solely from the historical thinking that has its origin in Jesus's own preaching.

NOTES

1. Troeltsch, 'Über historische und dogmatische Methode in der Theologie', *Gesammelte Schriften*, Vol. 2, Tübingen, 1913, p. 730.
2. Cf. above, p. 1.
3. *Weimar Ausgabe* (the Weimar Edition of Luther's works, Weimar 1883–, cited throughout as WA), 40 I, 77.
4. WA 57 H, 99.
5. J. Gottschick, 'Luthers Theologie', in *Zeitschrift für Theologie und Kirche*, 1914, Erg. Heft 1, 28.
6. 12.3.1519; WA Briefe 1, 328f.

7. WA 39 II, 255.
8. WA 10 I.2, 297.
9. WA 40 II, 254ff.
10. In Vol. 3 of *Chalkedon Heute*, the great work on the Council of Chalcedon 'in history and at the present day', published for the jubilee of the Council, Würzburg, 1951ff.
11. Op. cit., p. 14.
12. Op. cit., pp. 34f.
13. WA 40 I, 77.
14. WA 10 I.1, 356.
15. WA 57 H, 99.
16. WA 20, 605.
17. WA 5, 108.
18. WA 10 I.1, 155ff.
19. WA 5, 108.
20. WA 10 I.1, 67.
21. WA 16, 217.
22. WA 17 I, 255.
23. WA 17 II, 244.
24. WA 10 I.1, 71.
25. WA 26, 65.
26. WA 50, 282; tr. Robert R. Heitner, in *Luther's Works*, eds. Pelikan and Lehman, Concordia Publishing House and Fortress Press, Philadelphia, 1955–, Vol. 34, p. 227.
27. WA 26, 450; tr. Robert H. Fisher, *Luther's Works*, Vol. 37, p. 308.
28. WA 5, 184.
29. WA 18, 606; tr. J. I. Packer and O. R. Johnston, *Martin Luther on the Bondage of the Will*, James Clarke and Co., London, 1957, p. 71.
30. WA 47, 66; tr. Martin H. Bertram, *Luther's Works*, Vol. 22, p. 339.
31. WA 7, 97.
32. WA 39 I, 203.
33. WA 40 I, 33; tr. Jaroslav Pelikan, *Luther's Works*, Vol. 27, p. 145.
34. Cf. my book *Der Mensch zwischen Gott und Welt*, 2nd ed., Stuttgart 1956, pp. 277ff.
35. WA 50, 198ff.
36. WA 40 I, 77.

INDEX OF SUBJECTS

Christology (concept and task), 1, 44ff., 65, 194, 202, 276, 281ff., 288ff.
Cross and resurrection, 73ff., 83, 87, 89f., 93

Damnation: *see* Salvation/damnation
Decision, 29, 33f., 63f., 93, 110, 118, 143, 166, 171f., 183ff., 193, 196, 237f., 261, 274, 278
Destiny: *see* Fate

Eschatology, 13ff., 52, 101ff., 117
  eschatological character of Jesus's preaching, *see under* Jesus
Exchanging of the creator for the creature, 58f., 67, 74f., 83, 85, 100, 105

Faith, 15, 39ff., 61, 71f., 81ff., 102, 115f., 147, 160, 166, 181, 214ff., 237ff., 248f., 291
  faith of Jesus, faith in Jesus, *see under* Jesus
  see also Petition and Faith
Fate
  personal destiny of individual, 185ff., 190f., 196, 236ff., 241, 245f., 250, 256, 265, 278
  of world and mankind, 57, 60, 67, 71, 74ff., 83, 87ff., 93, 118, 211, 273ff.
  vicissitudes (strokes) of fate, 185, 246, 256, 265, 274, 278
  fate of Jesus; decisive stroke of fate in life of Jesus: *see under* Jesus
Forgiveness of sins, 275f.
Futility, 74, 76f., 83, 85f., 93

God
  who calls into existence the things that do not exist, 59, 70, 75, 77, 83f., 87, 90, 93
  concealment of God's actions, 248, 251f., 273
  kingdom of God, 101ff., 114f., 120ff., 125, 132f., 136ff., 144, 151f., 172f., 178, 193ff., 197, 232f., 247f.
  righteousness and truth of God, 199f., 204ff.
  God's free rule over the world, 29, 138, 153ff., 173, 183, 220
  will of God, 77, 90, 146ff., 154, 164, 166f., 180f.

Historical thought, its urge to express history as a unity, 169ff., 270
History
  totality of (universal history), 169ff., 177, 187ff., 191, 270
  two kinds of, 7, Ch. 13, pp. 156–176, 279
  the modern concept of critical historical scholarship, 7, 12, 156f., 168ff., 174, 177, 179, 187ff., 196, 269f., 279
  history which began with the preaching of Jesus, 140, 155ff., 159, 161f., 168, 171ff., 177, 179, 220, 269, 279
  the suprahistorical, 140, 161
Hypocrisy, 104f., 110, 118, 121, 127, 210

Independence
  of man with respect to the world,

Index of Subjects

Independence (contd.)
  130f., 168, 175f., 186, 195
  of man with respect to God, 130f., 168f., 175f., 187
Instructions, guidance, for human action in the world, 108, 113f., 164ff., 173, 188, 211, 220, 221, 226, 244, 250, 266ff., 271, 274

Jesus
  his faith, 40, 45ff., 61, 87, 90, 161, 240ff.
  faith in Jesus, 240, 254ff.
  fate (personal destiny) of Jesus, 60, 67, 87, 93, 118, 152, 196, 203, 209, 211, 244, 246, 250ff., 262, 265, 273f.
  fate, decisive stroke of in life of Jesus, 246f., 250ff., 262, 265, 274
  historicity of his existence, 51, 98, 143f., 152, 155, 160f., 221, 268f., 278
  his obedience, 61, 71ff., 76f., 87f., 90, 95, 203ff., 210, 261f.
  his concrete individual personality, 9, 19, 24, 30f., 49f., 54, 65, 196
  his preaching, 95ff.
  eschatological nature of his preaching, 108, 110, 116ff., 125
  his petition and faith, 244ff., 250, 252f., 257ff., 262
  his responsibility, 60, 68f., 72, 74ff., 87f., 90, 117f., 138ff., 145, 151f., 157, 161, 196, 208f., 217ff., 268f., 271
  his rule over the world, 55, 59f., 63f., 80f., 90, 96, 100, 118, 254ff.
  the world of Jesus as an individual, 193ff.
Judgment, 102f., 110, 115, 136, 208f., 216, 223ff.

Kerygma, 11, 14, 17f., 46, 66ff., 87, 95, 97, 194

Law, 98, 105ff., 109, 126, 153f., 165f., 194
Life
  the meaning of life, 185f., 188f., 191
  gaining and losing life, 111, 114f., 137, 146f., 205, 215ff., 238

Obedience, 15, 83ff., 200
  obedience of Jesus: *see under* Jesus

Perversion, 67, 75, 86, 199, 206
Petition and faith, 237ff., 243, 252, 257ff., 280
  petition and faith of Jesus: *see under* Jesus
Piety (cultic and legal), 87, 99, 102ff., 109, 111, 118, 121ff., 126ff., 133, 138f., 142, 144f., 193ff., 198ff., 210, 220

Religion (cultic and legal), religious devotion, practice and worship: *see* Piety
Repentance, 111, 118, 144, 145, 152f.
Responsibility, 68, 83, 85, 87, 99, 117f., 143, 145, 154f., 158f., 162ff., 174ff., 186f., 189f., 192, 194, 214f., 219ff., 237f., 262ff., 268, 274
  responsibility of Jesus: *see under* Jesus

Salvation/damnation, 52, 61ff., 85, 98, 115ff., 132, 141, 151, 168, 173, 176, 179f., 189ff., 192, 196, 207, 211f., 223f., 233, 242, 247, 254ff., 258ff., 266, 273, 278f., 280
Satan, 57, 126, 139, 228
Sentence of doom, 60, 63, 67f., 74ff., 83, 85f., 95, 100, 103, 118, 146, 151, 199f., 202, 205ff., 211, 213, 217f., 222, 224, 226, 244f., 250, 273
Signs, 72, 119, 138, 144, 151ff., 197, 231f., 247f.

Index of Subjects

Sin, 68, 74, 86, 88f., 91, 99, 123f., 128ff., 220, 274f.
see also Forgiveness of sins

World
the present world as venerated in religion, 74ff., 99, 104f., 118, 121, 124, 133, 135, 140f., 144f., 146ff., 152, 157, 174, 182ff., 196ff., 202, 227, 231, 236, 245f., 246, 250f., 263ff., 267ff., 270, 273, 275, 278
the world as it exists historically, 143f., 156f., 159, 166f., 171ff., 175f., 182ff., 250f., 264, 267, 269
the two ways in which the world exists as such, 141ff., 145, 153ff., 157, 162, 164, 170ff., 183f., 197f., 202, 219ff., 228, 244, 251, 262ff., 268, 271, 276, 278
the natural reality of the world, 167f., 263ff., 268f., 270
the world of each individual man, 177ff., 195ff., 236, 251, 265, 267, 274f., 278f.
change (transformation) of the world, 58ff., 65ff., 69f., 100, 110, 115f., 152, 174f., 223f.

INDEX OF AUTHORS

Althaus, Paul, 13f., 17ff., 23, 31f., 50f., 72, 80ff., 91f.
Augustine, 2

Bartsch, H. W., 11
Bauer, Walter, 134, 229
Bornkamm, Günther, 24, 29ff., 50
Bousset, Wilhelm, 9
Bultmann, Rudolf, 9ff., 23f., 27, 31, 35ff., 50f., 53f., 124, 127, 133, 136, 203, 218, 275

Comte, 190
Conzelmann, H., 39, 98
Cyril, 1f.

Diem, Hermann, 14
Dilthey, Wilhelm, 156ff., 161, 170

Ebeling, Gerhard, 34, 38ff., 44, 47, 240
Elert, Werner, 2f.
Ellwein, Eduard, 50

Fuchs, Ernst, 32ff.

Gadamer, H. G., 170
Gogarten, Friedrich
  Der Mensch zwischen Gott und Welt, 295
  Die Wirklichkeit des Glaubens, 19
  Entmythologisierung und Schrift (Demythologizing and History), 83

Verhängnis und Hoffnung der Neuzeit, 101, 167, 195
Gottschalk, J., 282

Hilary of Poitiers, 2

Jaspers, Karl, 170, 191

Kähler, Martin, 17
Käsemann, Ernst, 11, 24ff., 46f., 49f., 101
Krüger, Gerhard, 156f.

Löwith, Karl, 157, 189f.
Luther, Martin, 1ff., 44, 282ff.

Marx, Karl, 157

Proudhon, 189

Rahner, Karl, 285f.
Reimarus, 8
Robinson, James M., 17, 23

Schniewind, Julius, 234
Schweitzer, Albert, 8f.

Troeltsch, Ernst, 158, 281, 292

Vico, Giambattista, 157

Wittram, Reinhard, 157f., 160, 171, 188
Weiss, Johannes, 9
Wrede, William 8

INDEX OF SCRIPTURE REFERENCES

Deuteronomy
6.16   203

I Chronicles
29.11   199

Psalms
65.6f.   139
91.11f.   203

Isaiah
1.11ff.   199
35.4ff.   229

Jeremiah
23.24   200

Matthew
3.2   223
3.7ff.   222
3.11   228
3.12   231
3.13   222
4.17   223, 254
5.3   125
5.13   261
5.17ff.   266ff.
5.21ff.   106f.
5.22   54
5.23ff.   180
5.29f.   111
5.36   213
5.45   135
6.1   122, 235
6.1ff.   107
6.10   235
6.13   228
6.19ff.   227
6.22f.   212, 265
6.24   120, 193
6.25ff.   246
6.27   213
7.7f.   114, 236, 273
7.8   248
7.11   226
7.13f.   227
7.16   267
7.17ff.   265
7.18   212
7.21   257
8.5ff.   237
8.13   260
8.20   256
9.3   201
9.13   123, 129
9.22   237, 248, 260
9.29   260
9.36   150, 152, 230
10.27   233
10.29   179
10.34   198
11.1f.   229
11.2f.   134
11.5   223
11.6   273
11.7ff.   223
11.19   123, 231
11.28   134
12.29   126
12.30   119, 261
12.39   144, 231
12.43ff.   126
13.11   248
13.34   248
13.34f.   102
13.44   102
15.11   103
15.14   227

Matthew (contd.)

15.22ff.	237
15.28	237, 260
16.1ff.	119
16.4	144, 226
17.20	238
18.3	178
18.6	239
19.30	131
20.1ff.	134
20.16	233
20.28	60
21.31	114, 124
23	224
23.5	122
23.5ff.	105
23.13	122, 144, 227
23.15	122
23.17	227
23.23	105, 123
23.25ff.	104
23.26	227
23.29ff.	121
24.30	54
25.31ff.	149, 179
26.53	202
28.18	54

Mark

1.4	222
1.22	54, 133
1.35ff.	119
1.44	119
2.5	274
2.6f.	275
2.15f.	123
2.17	231
2.18f.	224
2.21ff.	212, 265
2.27	103, 164, 167
3.1ff.	123
3.4	168
4.9	232
4.16ff.	254
4.30ff.	232
4.34	248
7.1ff.	122, 144
7.6	111
7.9ff.	123
7.15	164
8.32f.	203
8.35	183
8.36f.	246
9.23	239
9.24	242
9.42	240
10.14	114
10.17ff.	256f.
10.18	139, 207
10.27	238
10.31	124, 142
10.35ff.	202, 257
10.37	147
10.42ff.	272
10.43f.	203, 218
11.22	239f.
12.13ff.	174
12.30f.	111
12.41ff.	85
13.44ff.	215

Luke

3.10ff.	226
4.1ff.	228
4.5ff.	228
4.16ff.	223
4.21	243
6.20ff.	114
6.27ff.	112
6.32ff.	112, 181
6.35	113, 180
6.40	256
6.43	106
6.43ff.	267
7.34	197
7.48	274
9.57ff.	256
9.62	102, 262
10.18	139
10.18f.	119
10.19	126, 228
10.23	225
10.23f.	119, 254
10.25	209
10.25ff.	149
11.20	223

Index of Scripture References

11.21	228	3.22	195
12.13f.	108	3.25	69, 73
12.49	198	3.25f.	59
13.4	124, 207	3.28	83
14.16ff.	223, 235	4.1ff.	83
14.25ff.	256	4.3	83
14.28ff.	228, 257	4.4f.	83
15	225	4.5	59
15.2	130	4.9ff.	83
15.7	129	4.11	83
15.11ff.	275	4.17	59, 70, 75, 77
16.1ff.	172	5.15	91
17.1f.	240	5.18	77
17.10	136, 207	5.19	61, 69
17.12ff.	249	8.3	69, 88, 91
17.20f.	234	8.5	66
17.33	111	8.20	58, 67
18.9ff.	215, 242	8.20f.	103
18.10ff.	131	8.21	70
18.14	274	8.29	91
19.1ff.	131, 204	8.32	69
22.24	272	9.4	106
22.53	228	10.4	194
24.26f.	53	12.2	99

John

1.1ff.	55		
1.29	68		
3.17	69		
4.34	71		
5.19	70		
5.24	36		
5.30	70		
8.28	70		
9.1f.	124		
12.49	70		
14.10	70		

I Corinthians

1.30	195
3.19	58
5.10	66
7.20	66
7.24	67
7.29ff.	236
7.33	66
8.3	68, 86
8.6	55
13.12	115
15.3	68
15.24f.	77

Romans

1.3	55
1.3f.	1
1.18	67, 74, 99
1.19ff.	86
1.20	58, 67
1.21	58
1.21ff.	59
1.25	67, 74, 75
1.28	58, 86, 105

II Corinthians

2.15f.	36
4.4	58
4.16	58
5.16	13
5.17	57
5.18	73, 91
5.18ff.	36
5.21	55, 59, 68, 77

Galatians

1.4	69
2.20	69, 89
3.10	99
3.13	53, 55, 59, 68, 75, 77
3.23	99
4.1ff.	163
4.4	55, 60, 68f.
4.5	59
4.9	86
5.24	89

Ephesians

1.19ff.	77f.
2.1ff.	57
2.12ff.	56
3.9	55
4.21ff.	89
4.22	93
5.2	69

Philippians

2.5ff.	90
2.7f.	55, 61
2.8	290
2.9f.	55, 59
3.12	63

Colossians

1.12f.	61
1.15ff.	55f.
1.18	77
2.15	56
3.1	63
3.1ff.	62

I Peter

1.3	90
2.24	68
3.18	68

II Peter

3.10ff.	101

I John

5.19	99

Hebrews

1.1ff.	288
1.3	55, 70
5.4ff.	61
9.14	69
11.1	215
12.2	259

KJW

DATE DUE			
NOV 23 '81			
GAYLORD			PRINTED IN U.S.A.